Excellence and Leadership
in a Democracy

Excellence and Leadership in a Democracy

Edited by

STEPHEN R. GRAUBARD

and GERALD HOLTON

 1962

COLUMBIA UNIVERSITY PRESS

New York and London

This group of essays originated in the
American Academy of Arts and Sciences
and some of them were first published in
the fall 1961 issue of its journal *Dædalus*.

Contents

CONTENTS

Acknowledgment

IT WOULD BE difficult to exaggerate the importance of the topic treated in this book. In virtually every aspect of public and private life the question of excellence and leadership is central. The Edgar Stern Family Fund is to be thanked for the support which it gave to the American Academy of Arts and Sciences for this project. This included joint sponsorship with Wesleyan University of a conference at which the authors discussed early drafts of their papers. This work is only one of the most recent evidences of the Edgar Stern Family Fund's continuing concern with the problem of excellence.

S. R. G.
G. H.

Excellence and Leadership
in a Democracy

HENRI PEYRE

Excellence and Leadership

Has Western Europe Any Lessons for Us?

THERE ARE AT LEAST three subjects (and probably a dozen more)
on which no wise man should ever attempt to write: love, genius,
and leadership. Of the three, the last is the most mysterious and the
most unpredictably and capriciously feminine. No amount of training, no sedulous nurturing by the family or the social group, no long
line of ancestry piously dedicated to the eventual flowering of a
leader, not even the stern flexing of intellectual muscles or the cultivation of character through cricket, baseball, warfare, or flogging
has ever proved a sure means of developing leaders. Few teachers
have with any degree of certainty been able to predict which of
their pupils would some day march ahead of the common herd and
mold events. Fewer still among the school or college friends of future leaders have perceived, or acknowledged, the germs of that in-
definable quality in them. Many who graduated very young and
were laden with the richest promises from Harvard, Oxford, or the
Ecole Polytechnique have turned out at forty-five to have left their
future behind them. Others, like Winston Churchill's successor at
the head of the Conservative party, happened not to be served by
their health or by circumstances and missed an opportunity which
seemed to be theirs for the asking.

History, which affords us a comfortable insight into the mistakes
of others, may explain actions long after the event, but the decisions
through which some men become leaders while others are crushed
in defeat cannot in most cases be anticipated. Léon Blum, one of the
most intelligent observers of events and an actor gifted with keen
foresight in some of them, remarked in a volume of memoirs on the

1

Dreyfus affair, published a year before he took over power in France in 1936:

> The aligning of individuals with one or another of the two camps surprised me no less than the very emergence of those camps. I was young, and experience had not yet taught me one thing: that the most fallacious of all the operations of the mind is to calculate in advance a man's or a woman's reaction to a really unforeseen ordeal. We are almost regularly mistaken when we claim to solve such a calculation through applying psychological data already acquired, thus prolonging the logic of the known character of past life. Any ordeal is new and every ordeal finds a man who is also new.

In no country have as many volumes on the subject of leadership appeared as in the United States. The reading of most of them is a dismal, when it is not a ludicrous, experience. They dissert at length on the necessity for candidates for leadership to make friends, to coordinate, to get things done, to lead "the strenuous life" once dear to Theodore Roosevelt, to learn how to conduct conferences. The last item must be a source of considerable embarrassment to many men of affairs: for they are laboriously advised to decorate their conference rooms with "irenic green," also favored by insane asylums. to promote "togetherness" through calling every one by his first name; to devise well-planned recesses, during which background music should be played softly; not to hang modern abstract art on the walls, for it makes uneasy "those who don't know what the garish splotches mean." Data are then gathered to prove that, among other attributes, leaders enjoy a taller stature than ordinary mortals. Bishops average 70.6 inches, but preachers in small towns only 68.8; university presidents rise to a 70.8 inch average, presidents of small colleges have to be content with 69.6; sales managers average 70.1 inches, salesmen a mere 69.1. Shades of Napoleon, of John Keats, of Stalin, who never reached the height of even a sub-salesman or of a dean of a very insignificant college!

The perusal of a few such volumes should be enough to convince anyone who is not a worshiper of statistical data and of factual surveys that leaders are indeed mystery men, born in paradise or in some devil's pit, but that they never must have become leaders through the study of books on management or of treatises on the making of higher executives. The process by which excellence is reached, or aimed at, in countries of Western Europe and through which leaders ("principi," "Führers," "élites," "chefs" in the countries where the word "leaders" is without an equivalent and the word "leadership" as untranslatable as that of "commonwealth") are prepared, cannot be described methodically and accurately. Schools for leaders have at some time or other been attempted, from the Order of the Templars and the Turkish janissaries to the German Ordensburg seminar under Nazism, the Communist party in Russia, and the short-lived *écoles de cadres* in Vichy France. It would be an insult to American democracy to hold them up as examples. Leadership can but be a broad ideal proposed by the culture of a country, instilled into the young through the schools, but also through the family, the intellectual atmosphere, the literature, the history, the ethical teaching of that country. Will power, sensitivity to the moods of an age, clear thinking rather than profound thinking, the ability to experience the emotions of a group and to voice their aspirations, joined with control over those emotions in oneself, a sense of the dramatic and even the pliability of a *commediante*, such as Bonaparte evinced at will, are among the ingredients of the power to lead men: they are not easily absorbed through education, not even through imitation.

But conditions can perhaps be created under which potentialities for leadership would not be stifled and might even develop faster or ripen more fully. And although leadership and excellence are far from synonymous, we may take it for granted that few would quarrel with the need to stress quality versus sheer numbers, and excellence rather than adjustment to life and its mediocrity, in education today. It is highly questionable whether European countries have produced more or greater leaders than America has over the last sixty years, relative to the population. Even in diplomacy and foreign policy (fields in which many Americans seem to be afflicted with a complex of inferiority over their achievement and like to moan over their fumbling), the record of Britain and France between the two world wars, that of Germany before and under Nazism, that of Litvinov, Molotov, Stalin himself, and their present successors is in no way more enviable than that of the United States. Statesmen, generals, admirals, business organizers and executives, during World War II and since, have in this country led with as much (or more) foresight and decision as those of any other land. Educators and scientists have rated second to none. A European-born professor in America may deplore the smaller role granted here to intellectuals and the emphasis on a democratic process which at times seems to fear "élites" and to balk at eliciting leadership from the masses. Bold would he be, untruthful probably, and tactless to

3

boot, if he advocated any wholesale import of Western European methods of aiming at excellence in a very different environment.

But this country has now long been mature enough to know that learning from the past is what distinguishes the civilized man from the animal or from the uncivilized; that many of the boldest moves in art and literature have, in our own century, come from a redis- covery of a phase of the past (Egyptian art, Romanesque sculpture, medieval philosophy, Greek tragedy). America's capacity for diges- tion, moreover, is such that it can devour what tempts her in other cultures and easily assimilate it. Rome, France, Germany, Russia, Japan once proceeded thus at the height of their vitality. A survey of several realms in which progress in fostering excellence could be achieved in America, owing to the example of other democracies, may be not without some utility. Those realms are education, the sciences, letters and the arts, and the place of the intellectual in so- ciety, insofar as it may be assumed that leadership is a virtue which highly developed intellectuals may possess more than other groups of citizens.

Education in Greece and Rome, then in the countries of Western Europe, differed from education in America in that it never was aimed at the vast mass of the people, indiscriminately; it never had to mold into a nation with one language and one civic ideal, into a conformity of tastes, of behaviors (and of buying habits) a motley crowd of peoples who had broken off ties with their native land and had come, to a large extent, from the less cultured segments of the populations of eastern and southern Europe, of Ireland, of Scotland, or of Germany. For a long time in the nineteenth century and the first decades of the twentieth, the goal of education at the secondary level was to prepare leaders for the professions—the church, the army and navy, diplomacy, administration. Scholarships have al- ways made it relatively easy—even in Britain, where access to Eton and Harrow, Oxford and Cambridge, was through a strait gate—for the children of poorer families to receive a solid general and tech- nical culture. Still, secondary education in a *lycée*, a *gymnasium*, a private or a grammar school in England was sharply separated from primary education. Those who came from the affluent classes of so- ciety enjoyed an advantage over the boys from poorer homes; it was due to conversation with their parents, to reading facilities at a time when public libraries for children were unheard of, to ampler lei- sure, and a cultural tradition in their family. Nine tenths or probably ninety-five percent of those who made a name as scientists, statesmen, or intellectuals were from the gentry or the middle class.

The number of positions to be filled by the youth thus trained, in engineering, in administration, in diplomacy, in the liberal professions, failed in our century to increase proportionately to the ever growing mass of young men—lately, also, of young women—eager to occupy such positions. A feature of our age is the reluctance of men with even a mere smattering of education to be content with the trades by which goods are actually produced, metals extracted, the earth tilled, or the cattle raised. Marketing, salesmanship, insurance, transportation of the goods produced by the unhappy people who know no better, and promotional work of every kind hold more attraction for any man who has gone to school. Such a man bolsters his ego through signing papers brought in an "in" basket and gravely shifting them to the "out" one. The result has meant an intense competition to enter the tertiary sector of any economy and a stress on degrees, diplomas, hurdles at every stage. Every young Frenchman, Italian, or German from the middle class and every one who covets entry into the middle class has therefore to undergo competitive examinations at every stage, from the age of eleven to eighteen or twenty. The grades given by teachers would, if translated into an American scale, range from ten or fifteen to seventy-five or eighty. Barely forty percent of pupils reach the average of fifty (out of a maximum of a hundred). Nearly sixty percent of the pupils at the end of their secondary studies fail in the final examinations which open up the gates of the universities. The whole of secondary education, in France especially (and the Russian system was organized along the lines of the Napoleonic university), but also in Britain where scholarships to Oxford, Cambridge, or Liverpool are in keen demand, is geared to university education and to stiff competitive examinations on a fixed syllabus. The results are not altogether felicitous. A majority of French children study mathematics, theoretical physics, thermodynamics, history, Greek, and Latin according to programs, imposed by the Ministry, and for a very few, for admission to the Ecole Polytechnique, the Ecole Nationale d'Administration, or the Ecole Normale Supérieure. One alone out of five or ten candidates to these bastions of the intellectual elite forces entry into them. Those who fail fall back upon less glamorous professions: often they wander into business. But a sad wastage of potential talent occurs, for the line which separates the candidate who reaches the thirtieth rank, where thirty only are admitted for the whole country,

5

from the thirty-first is necessarily a very tenuous one. At the present day, the countries of Western Europe have awakened to the need of training, not just three thousand engineers for a country of forty-five million people, all men versed in the arcana of theory and with a highly trained intellect—but fifteen thousand. The tyranny which the prestigious French *Grandes Ecoles* exerted over the country has had to be relaxed, and their demanding requirements have been waived in new, rivaling institutions, designed to stress empirical rather than abstract knowledge.

The very severe competition for the positions of leadership to be won by the graduates of those celebrated *Ecoles* spreads to all levels of education. Little time is spent or lost on sports and games. The waste which according to many American educators prevails in the last year of high school in this country is avoided: the years with which secondary education ends, at the ages of sixteen to eighteen, in continental Western Europe, are on the contrary the most arduous and the most severely competitive. Philosophy, as the crowning discipline completing the earlier study of languages and of history, or mathematics and the physical sciences for the scientifically minded students, occupy the last year. In every one of the three terms into which the academic year is divided, "compositions," more solemn and more feared than "tests" are in our system, take place in every subject. Emulation is in no way supposed to be contrary to equalitarian democracy; students are ranked as first, second, third ... twentieth, and little sympathy is poured on the last ones for having tried their meager best and failed. Such a system is exacting, but bracing mentally. The ranking at examinations is done without any regard to the identity of the candidate: his name is not revealed to the examiner, who should never be the same teacher who taught him in class. In Oxford and Cambridge, in Stanford or Yale, some leniency may be evinced by boards of admission, if not by professors, to sons of the nobility or of the rich or to those of influential alumni, on the theory that since they will belong to the ruling class anyway, because of birth or money, and may have funds to dispose of, they might just as well be exposed to some education. More democratic equality prevails in the continental nations. Education at the advanced level is the only key which can open the locked treasures of influential positions: it is already professional. It could not deserve the strictures of R. M. Hutchins, who condemned the conception of a university as "a waiting room in which a student must consume his time in harmless triviality until he can go to work." Far from being looked down on as undemocratic or as a breeder of complexes, the will to excel is taken for granted and the desire to do so is instilled into every child: he naturally aims at belonging to the "elite"—an elite which is cultural rather than social.

Along with universal competition at all levels, accepted as a matter of course in old countries, where there are far fewer positions for white-collar workers and for executives than there are able candidates to fill them, the abhorrence of specialization characterizes Western European education. Scientists, humanists, philosophers, doctors, army leaders, men of affairs, in France in particular, but also in Italy, Austria, and Germany, have repeated that "general culture" is essential to any one who will be called upon to lead, to initiate ideas, to envisage a problem as a whole, and to devise imaginative solutions for it. Scientists like Claude Bernard, Pasteur, Henri Poincaré, Einstein, or Freud were not only widely read persons but also men whose solid humanistic culture had never slowed down in their later scientific pursuit. It is commonly contended that the ability to range over the past stimulates boldness to grapple with the future and that a scientist, a manager, or an industrialist can only gain as a leader if he is aware of the motives which have always moved men. Henri Bergson, in one of the earliest addresses he gave, condemned specialization as a form of laziness, more fit for the animal which does one thing to perfection, but one only, than for men.* Julian Huxley would agree; in *New Bottles for New Wine*, he reassesses the myth of progress and declares that "specialization—in other words one-sided adaptation to a particular mode of life—eventually leads to an evolutionary dead end." A general like Lyautey, who displayed rare talents of organization and had begun his career with a revolutionary article on "the social role of the officer," reflected assiduously on leadership and trained a number of leaders in Morocco. According to him, the need and the function of anyone who would command was "the technique of general ideas." The conviction is sacrosanct with most continental European educators. Any leader must eschew imitation, revolt against narrow-mindedness, prove adaptable to new situations, and be able to generalize from his experience. Such men exist in more empirically minded countries, like the Anglo-Saxon. But it may be confessed that a circumscribed outlook, a sense of bewilderment when deprived of their usual and reassuring environment, a parochialism or a timidity,

* For references and titles of works alluded to in the text, see the bibliography.

whenever the conversation turns on ideas or on general political or philosophical problems, too often mark most American men when in contact with their European counterparts. The influence which American leaders today should wield in world affairs has been sadly impaired thereby.

The defect goes back to the schools, and it is not easy to remedy, even today, when American schools have incurred severer blame than they had for a whole century. Diversity is the rule in American education when compared to that of Europe: there is no ministry of education, no common standard, no way to persuade some fifty thousand school boards that they should raise their sights, make their syllabi harder and less immediately (and deceptively) practical, pay their teachers more generously, and recruit better ones. The fear of federal authority imposing itself on the states and of politics (with its accompaniment of lobbying, favoritism, venality) is so ingrained in America that a reversal of the trend is not likely to occur. Yet we may well have reached a stage today when a rapid mutation has become indispensable. A much larger share of national investments should go to the improvement of the schools, or else the chance to have more leaders, more scientists, more statesmen emerge from American democracy may well not be seized. If the prejudices against the tyranny of the central government over states' rights is too strong, the universities, both private and state, will have to assert themselves: the general desire to go to college is such, the desire to enter a graduate or a professional school later is also such that universities and colleges for the first time in history can impose higher, national standards on American education. Less premature specialization and narrowing down, a wider perspective of history, more intellectual independence, and a greater propensity to envisage one's subject in its relation with other fields would probably contribute effectively to solving the predicament in which America finds herself today. Today, four or five continents are clamoring not only for experts skilled in practical know-how, but also for teachers, lawyers, diplomats, men of affairs also endowed with "think how" and able to adapt the lessons of American success to very different cultures and to proud and sensitive peoples. The number available of such men is far from adequate. With our college population of three or four million, we have failed to train enough potential leaders.

If the examples of ancient Greece and of three or four Western nations in Europe today can be conjured up, their lesson, as we may presume to interpret it, is as follows:

First, we have underestimated the role of the teaching profession, probably the most important as well as the most difficult in any country. With the school age prolonged until fourteen or sixteen, only those teachers who have some intellectual power, mental curiosity, and some breadth can fire boys and girls with the impulse to go on studying. It will be a revolution in the mores of this country when teachers are paid as much as lawyers, doctors, and businessmen, when scientists are as respected as millionaires and become the Florida or Georgia weekend guests of Presidents: but such a revolution cannot long be postponed. It is positively paradoxical and well-nigh absurd to see a businessman surrounded with awe in his community, admired as a civic and church leader, courted by ever hungry college presidents, because he has discovered a new cosmetic, a new pharmaceutical pill, skillfully advertised a new girdle, or built a new electrical appliance, while teachers, preachers, and scholars are discreetly scorned and politicians treated with even less discreet contempt as men necessarily ready to be bought and perhaps not even loyal enough to stay bought.

The revolution in the minds of Americans will have to start from very high up—in Washington, Hollywood, Wall Street. Universities should provide the example. Their presidents go about clamoring for better schools, a more generous recognition of the intellectual, more respect for the humanities and for an ideal of a good life as preferable to an affluent one. But none of them has yet dared add a few educators, an eminent scientist or a poet, some representatives from his faculty to the businessmen, financiers, and lawyers who, almost exclusively, sit on his corporation or board of trustees. As a result, those trustees, timid in all that pertains to education and to science, exercise no leadership over the faculty and are lamentably devoid of constructive views on education. They are considered by the faculty as potential money-raisers or as convertible donors (to be converted from potential to actual ones by a persuasive president), seldom as inspirers or leaders. Those who teach and those who do not are thus kept separate as if they belonged to different social strata or different planets. Historians of French culture are wont to stress the advantages in prestige which accrued to literature in France when the Academy was founded, with archbishops, ambassadors, princes, and dukes sitting at the same table, defining words for the same dictionary, side by side with dramatists, poets, and grammarians. A similar intellectual and social gain would be effected if scholars and educators could explain their points of view to

9

trustees of their institutions and learn from those men of affairs what the world expects from education.

Second, a consideration, even a cursory one, of the training which appears in Western Europe to produce excellence oftener than in America would soon, in our opinion, lead to denouncing the lack of an ideal for the child to aim at. Many a leaf here could have been stolen and pondered from the works of ancient Greece. But, even when classical studies were more widespread than they are today, we had failed to derive or to apply lessons from Greek education. Distinguished scholars, among whom Werner Jaeger is pre-eminent, have pointed to *paideia* as the key to "the unique educational genius which is the secret of the undying influence of Greece on all subsequent ages." The Greeks, for the first time in history, conceived civilization as the deliberate pursuit of an ideal and proclaimed that education meant, as Werner Jaeger puts it, "deliberately molding human character in accordance with an ideal." In that ideal, *arété* or virtue in a broad sense was primary, while utility was relegated to the background. The man who drew near to that goal of *arété* was legitimately proud of the ideal he was pursuing. In the *Iliad* (VI, 208, and XI, 784), first Glaucos in addressing Diomedes, then the aged Nestor in discoursing on Achilles, repeat the admonition, "Always be the best and keep well ahead of the others."

Such an educational ideal was transmitted to the Italians of the Renaissance, to the French ideal of the *honnête homme*, to the British concept of the gentleman. The faith which these three nations have in their educational ideal (and which the French, more than the others, have turned into an actual cult, not devoid of arrogance toward the less fortunate beings whose culture is not French) leads them to this day to establish schools wherever they go: French imperialism has always been more cultural than economic. Except for a number of missionary colleges they have founded in the Near East or in Africa, chiefly for the natives of those lands, Americans have not usually carried their educational ideal with them when living abroad. In no realm probably are they afflicted with such doubts amounting to a genuine complex of inferiority as where their educational institutions, especially at the secondary level, are concerned. The culprit there is equalitarianism. The French, to be sure, have long ago made a fetish of equality; but, after proclaiming that all men are born free and insisting with Rousseau on a political and social system which corrects natural inequality through equality before the law, the French have never doubted that intellectual gifts were unequally spread and that efforts had to be most unequal on the part of some men as compared to others. Equality should not result in the disregard of quality. An American who has an important position on *Time* magazine has written most discerningly on what he terms *The Waist-High Culture* (1959), Thomas Griffith, himself an alumnus of a Western state university and no snobbish admirer of Europe, very sensibly remarked (pp. 180-81):

> The legal fiction of universal equality is a denial of the truth of an inequality of merit; but worse, it is also a repudiation of the value of unequal effort, and we may wonder how many American school children have demanded less than the best of themselves for fear of the unpopularity that goes with wanting to excel. . . . Of all the wastes in American society, not the cutting down of forests but the stunting of intellectual growth is our most costly squandering of resources.

Two other lessons might well be learned anew from the examples imparted to us by the people whose thinking centered around training the leaders of society, the Greeks: first the relative disregard of technique and the stress upon self-expression and communication with others, then the high value set upon maturity and manhood as opposed to childhood. We live today in a technological civilization, and no modern man in his senses can advocate a purely literary education which would ignore science and the Baconian necessity to understand nature, and thus to obey it, in order to command it. But technology has also broken up our lives and our world into shreds while appearing to simplify them. The same author quoted above, Thomas Griffith, warns us after assessing the "waist-high culture" of his country: "Technology and comfort add nothing to our characters, and may increase our problems while weakening our ability to confront them."

Most men build only parts of a machine or of an object; very few ever construct a whole or create inventively. The corrective to such a technological civilization lies in fostering a keener zest for literature and the arts, which to the Greeks embodied the expression of all higher culture. The absurd prejudice that those who do should not be overly concerned with expressing themselves, and that distinction in writing and speaking implies an inability to do, should be eradicated. There are, after all, only two ways of governing man: one is through violence and tyranny, and it brooks no discussion, scorns persuasion; the other is through speeches (fireside chats, radio talks, television debates, parliamentary discourses, United Na-

11

tions jousts of eloquence). The word *logos* appositely designated both speech and reason with the Greeks. To them, the cultured man was one who could express himself and persuade others. The Sophists, the greatest of Hellenic educators, in spite of the poor reputation with which Plato has afflicted them, asserted it, and Thucydides, who was not remote from them, lent to Pericles the famous pronouncement (II, 60): "The man who can think and does not know how to express what he thinks is at the level of him who cannot think."

The nonchalance with which those who should lead us today treat the English language in the country of Jefferson and of Lincoln, their affectation of familiar, if not vulgar, speech, and their disregard for grammar and for simplicity and terseness or their preference (alas, sincere) for slipshod and barbaric jargon have become one of the chief impediments to their potential influence on the masses. Woodrow Wilson, quoted by Ordway Tead in his volume on *Leadership,* rightly laid stress on the power to exhort, "to creep into the confidence of those you would lead," as a prerequisite to political leadership. The power of the spoken word has, if anything, grown in the last two or three decades. Our leaders in business, politics, diplomacy, and education are nevertheless least fitted for what they will have to perform almost daily: expressing themselves forcefully so as to teach, convince, and enlighten others. Oral examinations should be given in our schools from the age of twelve up.

We pride ourselves on having discovered the child and, since Rousseau and Wordsworth, then with Freud and our psychoanalysts, we have been fond of repeating that the child is father of the man and that much of what men and women are, or of what they fail to become, is to be traced back to their childhood or to their infancy, or to the crucial months which preceded the traumatism of their birth, when they basked in the maternal security to which they will hark back ever after. Enormous gains have thereby been achieved by child psychology. Education has endeavored to adapt itself exactly to the capacities of the child at every stage of his progress. Every adolescent has been treated as a network of problems, and his neuroses or his whims have been surrounded with awe. The teacher of teen-agers enters the classroom as he would a psychiatric hospital; the parents, fearful of asserting their own influence on these youngsters in their critical stage of metamorphosis, secretly to make themselves alike to their progeny, whose complexity and scorn for the elders baffle them, raise their hands in despair and pray that the adolescent may "go steady" and thus find "stability" with a friend of the opposite sex, since he fails to discover it in the home. The whole shift of interest from the man to the boy has brought us a fascinating crop of novels and plays written by, for, or about adolescents.

Meanwhile, the therapy of sublimation and the ideal of transcending that adolescent phase are being ignored. Through treating every child and every teen-ager as a potentially unbalanced person, through evincing a ridiculous punctilious respect for every manifestation of his personality and every mumbling of his self-expression (before there is much to be expressed), through our fear of stifling a potential Mozart or a Rimbaud in our schoolboys, we have failed to assist the child to develop into a man, to strive to become a leader. It is high time the trend should be reversed. There again, the Greeks and the Romans (it may be less invidious to invoke them than the French or the Russians) did differently, and perhaps no less well. *Paideia*, with them, consisted in the training of the man, in the preparation for *humanitas* and in the molding of a *vir*. Childhood and adolescence were only a momentary stage, to be transcended—not ends in themselves. Education, as Nietzsche also wished it to be, was a liberation from all that hampers the unhappy individual who is not yet a grown up. A system which produced Pericles, Demosthenes, Plato, Euripides, Phidias, and Euclid or, in another place and age, Hamilton, Jefferson, Washington, Franklin, and Marshall cannot have rested upon altogether wrong psychological assumptions.*

The present state of scientific leadership or of literary creativity obviously cannot be surveyed in the compass of a single essay. Our remarks must needs be limited to whatever profit the examples of other Western countries may afford us and what mistakes they may help us not repeat in our turn. Here again, neither in science nor in the arts and letters is excellence, or eminence, less often reached in the United States than in other democracies. The wave of breast-

---

* Henry Steele Commager is among several thoughtful Americans who today voice their objections to the "social law" of the prolongation of infancy first formulated by an American, John Fiske. "Americans," he notes, "have perhaps carried the practice to excess. A rich nation can doubtless afford financially the prolongation of childhood and youth well into the twenties, but a sensible people will not permit the growing waste of years and of talents involved in our current educational practices."

beating and of chauvinistic spite which followed Russia's recent scientific feats was ill-considered. While the scientific spirit is one of free inquiry which sooner or later calls everything into question, it is also true that when scientists have been prevented from speculating on the absolutes of philosophy or of politics, usually because the political regime under which they lived (Richelieu, Louis XIV, Napoleon, Communism) frowned upon such inquiries, they were thereby enabled to devote more attention to their purely scientific disquisitions. It would be a fallacy to believe that Fascism, Nazism, Stalinism, or Chinese Communism, because they are tyrannical regimes, are necessarily deprived of great scientists—or of great writers. Moreover, any revolution suddenly brings wholly new layers of people to literacy, to culture, to self-consciousness; it pushes those new elites to the summit from which the former privileged groups have been dethroned, and thus taps new sources for leadership (political, military, administrative, intellectual), as France did between 1789 and 1800 or even 1815. America hardly stands in need of a revolution to spur its conquest of space.

But she might well do with a number of relatively minor reforms, the effect of which could be far-reaching. One would be the general adoption of the metric system. Another would be to elicit more scientific vocations through the teaching of scientific courses in the last years of high school and in the first two years of college by truly competent and inspiring teachers. As things stand, hardly any American student in the large universities ever enters into contact with a scientist of repute until he reaches graduate school: and many wander toward law, or business, or the compiling of statistics for insurance groups or for accountants, for lack of an incitement toward scientific research with which a gifted teacher would have provided them. A third measure might consist in de-emphasizing the mania for collaboration which has become characteristic of American science: too many papers are signed by three or four authors and show all the defects of multiple authorship. The young may gain some prestige from having their names bracketed with that of an elder statesman with whom it is to their interest to agree; the older scientists may unwillingly appropriate the ideas of the younger men or, worse still, may entrust their assistants with all the drudgery of firsthand experimenting and thus lose contact with essentials, and gradually emigrate into an administrator's office. But the history of science, even in the century of Becquerel, Planck, Einstein, Fleming, Morgan, and Pavlov should remind us of the way in which most of the epoch-making discoveries were made: through "the lone musings of genius," by solitary men who did not necessarily submit to the way of life of businessmen, working at regular hours in an office or a laboratory, surrounded by assistants and secretaries and dictating machines: their capacity to dream, to disregard organized order and a conventionally neat and sterilized desk, to listen to the whims of fantasy and to the knockings of chance at a well-prepared mind was more beneficial to them than the fear of audacity which cramps men working in gentle compromise and in the affected cordiality of "togetherness." Cooperation is obviously necessary where the complexity of science has become infinite and the mass of accumulated knowledge is doubled every fifteen years: no scientist can be an island any longer. But he can still retain some individual personality in the presentation of results reached in a collective undertaking, and set nonspecialists afire, or a-dreaming, with the poetry of science.

Warnings of far-seeing scientists in Britain (Sir Lindor Brown) and in America (Egon Orowan among others) have pointed to another reason, linked with that passion for working together, which has kept science in those countries from bold pioneering: the fascination with organization on a grand scale. An American professor of mechanical engineering like Egon Orowan, conceding that many of the fundamental steps forward in science have been taken by Europeans or by Americans who had been trained in part in Europe, wonders whether "the strict Roman organization of life can be adopted without losing the Greek fertility in new ideas." It may be excessively complimentary to the Russians or to the Germans to compare them with the Greeks, while to be assimilated to Rome has in our age become curiously derogatory: Corneille, Rousseau, and Danton thought otherwise. But the harrowing question in our civilization is: "Have not American universities been less successful than others in escaping the suffocating grip of the social assembly line?" (Orowan). In the past, it was not uncommon for a Claude Bernard or a Chevreul to continue working fruitfully in his laboratory long past middle age. Nowadays, as the same author observes,

An unusually able scientist is on the scrap heap sometimes at the age of 30 or 40: he becomes director of research of a large unit, or head of a large department, a dean, or an important committee man oscillating between his home town and Washington, D. C. . . . Not that he ceases to be useful; but he is doing work which many others could do equally well

15

or better, and he has to abandon work, usually more important in the long run, in which there is no substitute for him.

The implicit model which business life proposes to, and insidiously imposes upon, scientists, social scientists, and humanists alike lies at the source of that evil. In business, the goal is to be an executive, that is, a person who tells others to do the work and whose importance is measured by the number of people under him, if not by the number of telephones on his desk. If Pasteur or Einstein had likewise been lured in mid-career to an executive job or to a position with one of the large foundations, if Beethoven after his First Symphony had been appointed Director of Musical Creation at an Academy of Music (the suggestion is Egon Orowan's), if Toulouse-Lautrec had been made visiting artist and critic at some American art school, the world would be much the poorer by it. Our affluent society, and perhaps our whole system of free enterprise in intellectual life, even the generous tax deductions which permit the proliferation of foundations (often of four perfunctory or semi-lunatic ones for one of great usefulness) constitute a danger to the emergence, and even more to the persistence, of leadership in intellectual life in America. Great names are utilized to go and wheedle funds out of foundation officials when, as in some other countries, they might be left alone as honored members of an Academy while state officials took over the work of raising or distributing funds. While in countries with a more centralized organization young researchers and professors are assigned positions by the government, and the mature scientist or the artistic creator or even the great professor of literature may enjoy the privilege of seldom answering his mail and of refusing to attend committees, an incalculable amount of time is devoured in America by the writing of letters of recommendation. The placement of his graduates is the elder professor's heaviest burden. The same young man will commonly apply for five different grants every year; and the master who numbers one hundred such former students among his followers would betray their democratic claims on him if he refused to write five hundred letters. No wonder if at forty-five an American scientist or an American humanist feels all creativity in him dried up and mournfully allows himself to become an organization man, invested with a semblance of power, since he assists in the distribution of funds and of promotions made possible by the wealth of others, but painfully aware of his own abdication. In no other country is it taken for granted so placidly that after forty-five or fifty a writer or a scientist has little left to contribute and had better consent to the role of a "lost leader."

Any attempt to speculate on the relative creativity or the relative degree of excellence displayed by writers, painters, musicians, critics, and scholars in America and in Western Europe would require a volume in itself. The present writer has already expressed himself on the subject elsewhere. Suffice it to say that sheer creativity is certainly no less remarkable today in this country than in Britain, France, or Germany. If formal excellence is often lacking or less sedulously pursued than in other cultures, if the inner life of fictional or dramatic characters is less persistently explored, and if the portrayal of passion is seldom mature, those three glaring weaknesses of American letters are compensated for by greater vitality, more epic audacity, and a less egocentric cult of literature and of its practitioners by authors and public alike. The serious gap from which American culture suffers most is the inability of critics to create a public of connoisseurs around the writers, which alone might, through the understanding and prestige which that public would provide, offset the attraction of money and of Hollywood royalties.* The critics themselves and the professors in the many realms covered by the vague denomination of "humanities" are often mortified by their awareness of not wielding the influence which in Tsarist Russia and in the liberal countries of Western Europe was, or is, that of their corresponding numbers. Those who think, who are at least as numerous and as outstanding as any in Europe, suffer from not influencing those who act.

To be sure, the gulf between theory and practice is ever vast and deep. Professors of political thought are not necessarily successful as politicians, or even as counselors of statesmen. Theoretical economists can err strangely in their contradictory prognostications, and their frequent lack of contact with either politicians or business life reduces their voices to so many unheeded cries in a wilderness. Men of action do not object to inviting thinkers and academic scholars in order to have it explained why they act as they do; then they continue doing it with either a strengthened good conscience or with a bad one painlessly silenced. Great financiers and effective secretaries of the Treasury in this country or in Europe, great statesmen such as

---

* The reader whom the subject may interest is referred to my *Writers and Their Critics: A Study of Misunderstanding* (Ithaca, Cornell University Press, 1954).

Clemenceau, Churchill, or Roosevelt were often men whose political philosophy, if ever expressed consistently, would have appeared childish to professors of law and Ph.D.'s in government and economics. Their thought was contradictory, often improvised at the prompting of circumstances: but they were able to size up events, to divine trends, to interpret the aspirations of the masses, and to guide them.

Intellectuals are not by necessity incapable of action: Disraeli, Lenin, De Gaulle, Salazar were after all intellectuals, and so once were Pericles and Caesar. Woodrow Wilson, himself a trained intellect and a stern moralist, wrote in his youth a very revealing essay which he read (he was then thirty-four) as a commencement address in Knoxville, Tennessee, in 1890, and again at Oberlin, in 1895. He, like many others who have helped make history, had in himself the dual personality of a man of thought and of a man of action. He soon perceived the weakness of intellectuals: they do not stand as close to the mass as those who act. They cherish proportion, restraint, academic greyness, niceties of character; they tell others what they should do, but they do not "creep into their confidence" in order to persuade them. He added:

> Leadership, for the statesman, is interpretation. He must read the common thought; he must test and calculate very circumspectly the preparation of the nation for the next move in the progress of politics. . . . No man thinking thoughts born out of time can succeed in leading his generation, and successful leadership is a product of sympathy, not of antagonism [pp. 42 and 53].

Even earlier, while he taught at Bryn Mawr in 1885, he had yearned for a statesman's career and written to his fiancée to that effect, confiding to her: "I love the stir of the world." He proclaimed in his inaugural address at Princeton in 1902: "We are not put into this world to sit still and know; we are put into it to act." Few statesmen indeed have achieved as much as Wilson did in domestic reform and imaginative mapping of the future during his first presidency. His countrymen may well be proud of having had in this century the one intellectual who also could act with foresight and, until the ill-fated last years when the art of compromise deserted him, could translate independent meditation and loftiness of purpose into deeds.

The lessons of continental Europe in this domain are not altogether admirable, and the clamor of many continental Europeans who look down on Americans as beings deprived of *Weltanschauung* and as incapable of formulating their attitudes philosophically need not impress us overmuch. The elites have long been stratified in Europe, and they have tended to close their ranks against those who do not share their educational or financial privileges. They are often tainted with snobbery, unmindful of the warning of one of the French intellectuals, André Suarès, that "the first condition for belonging to the élite is not to call oneself one of the élite." They are frightened by vulgarity and forget that vitality often must go with some lack of polished veneer. In literature and the arts, the self-styled elites affect always to choose a vanguard position, to cherish what is esoteric and obscure and therefore closed to less subtle minds than theirs. In politics, a tone of intellectual arrogance is wont to keep them apart from the masses or leads them to an excess of quibbling and a trend towards refined sophistry, from which even men of high mental stature like Mendès-France or Raymond Aron are not altogether immune.

It is no wonder that many an Anglo-Saxon thinker should recently have been wary of the seduction of continental European intellectuals for an America which, since 1933, has gained an influx of uprooted intellectuals, all adept at wielding philosophical concepts and often at wrapping their thoughts in barbaric English, but with little or no audience in this country outside a few reviews and university halls. Bertrand Russell scornfully defined the intellectual as "a person who pretends to have more intellect than he has," and an American President, angered by the foreignness of the very notion, mocked the intellectual as "a man who takes more words than is necessary to say more than he knows" (quoted in Eric Goldman, *The Crucial Decade*, 1956). A former college president who has always thought independently and acted fearlessly, Harold Taylor, more reasonably indicted systematic anti-intellectualism, but rejected the extreme respect granted by some Europeans to their intellectuals; for this country refuses to accept "a class of political or social leaders whose function it is to think for the rest." More recently still, the most intellectual of American playwrights, Arthur Miller, in a thoughtful interview given to Henry Brandon (*Harper's Magazine*, November, 1960), stressed the dissimilarities between himself and Beckett, Sartre, and other French representatives of the *théâtre d'idées.*

Our culture resists knowing what it is doing. . . . In France, to a much greater degree, the people are aware that, if they don't know what they're doing . . . somebody knows what they're doing, and that this is a legitimate kind of work, so to speak. . . . Abroad, there are more people who have learned to tip their hats to the idea of an intellectual. . . . Here no writer would regard himself, as in Russia and France, as spokesman for the national spirit or something of the kind. . . . In a word, we are not so much persecuted as ignored. But everybody else is ignored, too.

The record of European intellectuals in public affairs or in their pronouncements during years of crisis is certainly not a uniformly admirable one: many are those who took a long time to discern the perils of Pan-Germanism, like Thomas Mann, or of Nazism, like Heidegger and scores of philosophers, scientists, and writers. Goebbels after all was an intellectual, and so was Gentile, and so were Henri de Man, and a number of French artists and writers who, flattered by the tribute of the enemy occupying their country, collaborated with him in wartime. There have been many intellectuals, like Ruskin and D'Annunzio, to sing paeans to war as a regeneration and to espouse rabid nationalism, and there are still a number of them who have successively sided with Trotsky, Lenin, and Khrushchev. Power and self-assertiveness can exercise a curious fascination on the feminine side of those creators who must apparently have something of a woman in them to be complete. Even Goethe did not escape the magnetism of Napoleon trampling his country under his horse's hoofs. "Some of the biggest swine in human history have been great intellects. Some of the weakest spots in Western free society are due to excessive preoccupation with intellect, with analysis," as another of the finest minds among our college presidents, Harry Gideonse, warned us. The failures of our sister countries in Europe may prove to us to be just as instructive as their success when that success is unquestionable. Too few of the Western European intellectuals in our century seem to entertain a dauntless faith in the future or to be willing to translate words and thoughts into deeds in order to bring about that future.

Faith, and a warm if at times naïve passion for fraternity, on the contrary, mark American culture as it is lived. These qualities are more than ever to be valued today. Behind much of the criticism (occasionally raucous and even rancorous) of this country voiced elsewhere in the world, there lurks a disappointed admiration for it and an inadequate comprehension of its goals, because they are all too seldom defined in broad, universal, and dynamic terms. The paramount issue in this country today is, in our eyes, to restore links between those who think and those who act, to turn more potential leaders away from the world of business, where they all too often become lost in routine, toward ideas and the problems of today, which are educational far more than economic, ideological even more than military. There will soon be four or five millions of young people attending American colleges: are they made to think independently about what they read and hear? Are they spurred to develop into leaders through an adequate realization of the challenges facing them?

Our faith in the effects of reason, or of more rationality, on mankind has been shattered: reasonableness has hardly made a dent on the emotional forces within us. Our faith in the effects of material comfort has likewise undergone deadly blows. Man is not evil merely because he suffers from inadequate housing, hygiene, or diet, contented or "good" because he is prosperous, well fed, and rich. Would that life were indeed that simple! Old-fashioned optimism is dead and gone, once and for all. We must put an end to colonialism, but that will nevertheless create a thousand more difficulties than existed before. We may reach an agreement on atomic warfare, but it will not constitute the end to our fears of world destruction. We may devise another agreement on Berlin or on Middle-Eastern oil, but any agreement merges well-nigh insoluble problems into new or bigger ones; it does not solve them for good. Peace is not the absence of wars or the result of treaties. It is a continued and dynamic creation, far more challenging than war, and it should be proposed to the youth by our leaders as the paramount goal of the second half of the twentieth century.

It is sad to watch the leaders of the country who are now entrusted with guiding the free world, and also that part of it which we do not consider as free, to higher destinies, fritter their energies away in secondary matters and negative thinking. The panicky fear of Communism obsesses them; they are trapped by Russia into fighting for half-reluctant allies on the least favorable of terrains and into jeopardizing their moral superiority through an insensate fear of subversiveness. Meanwhile, their intellectual leaders allow the good men coming out of college to squander their ardent young minds on frivolities: the latter rush into business, work strenuously to find out what the public might want, and secretly knows it needs not. But who takes the trouble to awaken aspirations in a country where soon half of the adult population might be made up of college graduates? The genuine leaders would be those who might propose: an alternative to armament expense as a cure for any prospect of a recession;

other goals than an even higher dose of publicity to persuade citizens to purchase what will only clutter up their homes and dull their minds; and, what they do not even think of wishing, spacious thinking—not a hypnotized acceptance of the doings of other powers in the East. The author whom we have quoted above and who is more familiar with American business life than most academics can be, Thomas Griffith, concludes his volume with words which may be endorsed:

> If a great effort must continually be made to provide against Russian assault, our real expenditure of imagination must be in lighting the chaos inside us, and recovering a clarity of purpose. Only in this way will we regain health as a nation, or hope to inspire others to admire us. The only competition that should matter to us as a nation is not with Communism, but with that best we ourselves might be.

BIBLIOGRAPHY

1. Amidon, Beulah (editor), *Democracy's Challenge to Education.* New York: Farrar and Rinehart, 1960.

2. Anthony, R., "Le Rôle des hommes de pensée dans le politique et le social," *Revue Internationale de Sociologie,* 1929, 37: 41-47 (refutation of Julien Benda's *The Treason of the Intellectuals*).

3. Aron, Raymond, *L'Homme contre les Tyrans.* Paris: Gallimard, 1946.

4. Babbitt, Irving, *Democracy and Leadership.* Boston-New York: Houghton Mifflin, 1924.

5. Bergson, Henri, *La Spécialité.* Angers, 1882 (quoted in Algot Ruhe and Nancy Paul, *Henri Bergson: Account of His Life and Philosophy;* London: Macmillan, 1914).

6. Bouglé, Célestin, *Humanisme, Sociologie, Philosophie.* Paris: Hermann, 1938.

7. Bogardus, Emory S., *Leaders and Leadership.* New York: Appleton-Century-Crofts, 1934.

8. Brown, Sir Lindor, *The Perils of Leadership in Science.* The David Russell Memorial Lecture. London, 1960.

9. Caillois, Roger, *La Communion des Forts, Etudes de Sociologie Contemporaine.* Mexico City: Quetzal, 1943.

10. Commager, Henry Steele, "Why Do We Lack Statesmen?" *The New York Times Magazine* Section, January 17, 1960.

11. Dautry, Raoul, *Métier d'Homme.* Paris: Plon, 1937.

Has Western Europe Any Lessons for Us?

12. Domenach, Jean-Marie, "Définitions," in *La Démocratie est une idée neuve* (*Esprit,* Septembre 1959, no. 9, pp. 198-219).

13. Dugas, L., "La Pensée et l'action," *Revue de Métaphysique et de Morale,* 1928, 35: 435-438 (discussion of Benda's *The Treason of the Intellectuals*).

14. Fayol, Henri, *Administration industrielle et générale. Prévoyance, organisation, commandement.* Paris: Dunod, 1920 (translated as *Industrial and General Administration,* London: Pitman, 1930).

15. Ferry, Giles, *Une Expérience de Formation des Chefs.* Paris: Editions du Seuil, 1945.

16. Gardner, John, *Excellence: Can We Be Equal and Excellent Too?* New York: Harper & Brothers, 1960.

17. Gideonse, Harry D., *On the Educational Statesmanship of a Free Society,* New York: The Woodrow Wilson Foundation, 1959. Pamphlet no. 5.

18. Girard, Paul, *L'Education athénienne au Ve et au IVe siècle.* Paris: Hachette, 1891 (2nd edn.).

19. Goldman, Eric, *The Crucial Decade, 1945-1955.* New York: Knopf, 1956.

20. Grasberger, L., *Erziehung und Unterricht im klassichen Altertum.* Würzburg: Die Stahel'sche Buch-und Kunst-Handlung, 1864-1881.

21. Griffith, Thomas, *The Waist-High Culture.* New York: Harper & Brothers, 1959.

22. Hall, Sir Noel Frederick, *The Making of Higher Executives: The Modern Challenge.* New York: New York University, School of Commerce Publications, 1958.

23. Heidsieck, Patrick, *Rayonnement de Lyautey.* Paris: Gallimard, 1941 (Lyautey's essay, "Le Rôle social de l'officier," 1891, is ch. 3).

24. Huxley, Julian, *New Bottles for Old Wine.* London: Chatto & Windus; New York: Harper & Brothers, 1957 (see "A Redefinition of Progress," pp. 18-40).

25. Jaeger, Werner, *Paideia: The Ideals of Greek Culture.* New York: Oxford University Press, 1939-1944.

26. Jennings, Eugene, *An Anatomy of Leadership.* New York: Harper & Brothers, 1960.

27. Keyserling, Hermann Alex von, *Menschen als Sinnbilder.* Darmstadt: Otto Reichl Verlag, 1926 (see "Schopenhauer als Verbilder," "Spengler der Tatsachenmensch," "Kant der Sinneserfasser," and "Jesus der Magier").

28. Lasswell, Harold D., and others, *The Comparative Study of Elites.* Hoover Institute Studies B, no. 1. Stanford: Stanford University Press, 1952.

29. Madariaga, Salvador de, *Anarchy or Hierarchy*. London: George Allen & Unwin, 1937.

30. Marrou, Henri, *A History of Education in Antiquity*. New York: Sheed and Ward, 1956.

31. Maurois, André, *Dialogues sur le Commandement*. Paris: B. Grasset, 1924.

32. Metcalf, Henry C. (editor), *Business Leadership*. New York: Isaac Pitman & Sons, 1930.

33. Miller, Arthur, "The State of the Theatre in America," a conversation with Henry Brandon, *Harper's Magazine*, November, 1960, pp. 63-70.

34. Orowan, Egon, "Our Universities and Scientific Creativity," *Bulletin of the Atomic Scientists*, 1959, *15*: 236-239.

35. Paschal, Elizabeth, *Encouraging the Excellent. Special Programs for Gifted and Talented Students*. New York: Fund for the Advancement of Education, 1960.

36. Peyre, Henri, *Basic Education in French Secondary Schools*. Washington: Council for Basic Education, 1960 (pamphlet).

37. Roosevelt, Theodore, *The Strenuous Life*. New York: The Century Company, 1900.

38. Steffens, Lincoln, *Autobiography*. New York: Harcourt, Brace, 1931, 2 vols.; in vol. 2, p. 739, Steffens quotes a conversation with Woodrow Wilson in which the latter declared, "An executive is a man of action. An intellectual, such as you and I, is inexecutive. In an executive job, we are dangerous, unless we are aware of our limitations and take measures to stop our everlasting disposition to think, to listen, to—not act."

39. Taylor, Harold, "The Intellectual in Action," *Bulletin of the Atomic Scientists*, 1958, *14*: 368-373.

40. Tead, Ordway, *The Art of Leadership*. New York: Whittlesey House, McGraw-Hill, 1935.

41. Toulemonde, Jean, *Essai sur la Psychologie de l'autorité personnelle. Etude d'interpsychologie et de pédagogie*. Paris: Bloud & Gay, 1929.

42. Urwick, Lyndall, *Management of Tomorrow*. London: Nisbet & Company, 1933.

43. Valentine, Alan, *The Age of Conformity*. Chicago: Henry Regnery, 1954.

44. Ward, John W., "Individualism Today," *The Yale Review*, March, 1960, pp. 380-383.

45. Whitehead, Thomas North, *Leadership in a Free Society*. A study in human relations based on an analysis of present-day industrial civilization. Cambridge: Harvard University Press, 1936.

46. Wilson, Woodrow, *Leaders of Men*. Princeton: Princeton University Press, 1952 (address first given at the University of Tennessee on 17 June 1890).

HENRY STEELE COMMAGER

Leadership in Eighteenth-Century America and Today

WITH HIS CUSTOMARY INSIGHT Tocqueville observed back in the 1830's that leadership was more difficult in a democracy than elsewhere, and more difficult therefore in the New World than in the Old. In the Old World leadership was already given: it was attached to birth, rank, position; in the New World it had to be achieved by trial and error, and as there were no fixed standards the chances for error were limitless. In the Old World there was no problem at all of formal leadership: it was all arranged by birth and inheritance—the kings, the princes, the aristocracy; in the New World there was no such thing as formal leadership—it had to be won each time, and each time the rules of the contest might change.

Yet who can doubt that in the last quarter of the eighteenth century it was the New World—not democracy by our standards but certainly democracy by European—that provided the most impressive spectacle of leadership, rather than the nations of the Old World? Who can doubt, for example, that in the crisis of 1774-1783 the American colonies and states enjoyed far more competent leadership than the British Empire?

The situation is too familiar to rehearse. In the last quarter of the century the new United States—a nation with a white population of less than three million, without a single major city, and wholly lacking in those institutions of organized society or civilization so familiar in Europe—boasted a galaxy of leaders who were quite literally incomparable: Franklin, Washington, Jefferson, Hamilton, John Adams, Samuel Adams, John Jay, James Wilson, George Mason, Benjamin Rush, James Madison, and a dozen others scarcely less distinguished.

What explains this remarkable outpouring of political leadership, this fertility in the production of statesmen—a fertility unmatched

25

since that day? Was it a historical accident? Was it a peculiar response to the time or the place, or to a combination of the two? Or was it a product of conditions and attitudes that were cultivated and directed to calculated ends, and that can be if not recreated at least paralleled in our time?

There is of course an element of mystery, if not of fortuity, in the outbreak of genius at any time. How, after all, explain the flowering of the little Athens of Pericles and Sophocles and Phidias; the Florence of Michelangelo and Raphael and Machiavelli; the England of Hakluyt and Shakespeare and Francis Bacon; the Copenhagen of Hans Andersen and Thorwaldsen and Kierkegaard; the Vienna of Haydn and Mozart and Beethoven? We do not know with any certainty, yet clearly it would be absurd to ascribe these and comparable outbursts of genius, or of talent, to chance. There must be some principle that explains why the climate of fifth-century Athens was favorable to literature and philosophy, why the climate of fifteenth-century Florence encouraged art and architecture, why the climate of sixteenth-century England encouraged the discovery of new worlds of geography, science, and philosophy; why the climate of eighteenth-century Salzburg and Vienna grew musicians. And there must be some principle that explains why the little frontier colony of Virginia, with a white population less than that of present-day Syracuse or Dayton, without a single city or a major university or a proper school system or a press, produced in one generation Washington, Jefferson, Mason, Wythe, Madison, and Marshall. It is not enough to say that statesmanship was the specialty of Virginia as art was the specialty of Florence and music of Vienna. We want to know why.

The first consideration is elementary and practical. Eighteenth-century America offered extraordinarily few opportunities for the unfolding of talent. Almost the only opportunities it did offer were in the public arena. American society was pastoral and undifferentiated; American economy, rural and parochial; American life, singularly uninstitutionalized. In the Old World the young man of talent—certainly if he belonged to the upper classes—could take his choice, as it were, among the institutions which invited or even competed for his services; nor was he in fact limited to the institutions of his own country but could operate almost anywhere. The New World had few of these institutions, and those which did exist, in a kind of elementary fashion, offered few temptations; and while some colonials—Benjamin West and John Singleton Copley come to mind—could move to the mother country, the overwhelming majority could not. What Henry James later wrote of Hawthorne's America was far more true of and more pertinent to the America of Thomas Jefferson and John Adams. Like Hawthorne, they looked out upon a "negative spectacle"—how fortunate that they did not know this: [1]

> No State, in the European sense of the word, and indeed barely a national name. No sovereign, no court, no personal loyalty, no aristocracy, no church, no clergy, no army, no diplomatic service, no country houses, nor parsonages, nor thatched cottages, nor ivied ruins, no cathedrals, nor abbeys, nor little Norman churches; no great Universities, nor public schools . . . no literature, no novels, no museums, no pictures, no political society, no sporting class.

If these things were left out, said James, everything was left out. Yet the spectacle that greeted a Jefferson or an Adams was even more negative, even more barren, for one might add: no capital, no cities, no manufactures, no newspapers, no journals, no libraries, no professions (except, somewhat feebly, the law and the clergy), no Society. In England, or France, or the Empire, a young man of talent could go into the Church; there was no Church in America, with a capital C, and religion had lost much of its appeal. In the Old World the young man could enter the army or the navy; the new America had neither. He could become a scholar and attach himself to an ancient university, or a man of letters, or an academician. In America these and similar activities were avocations.

Not only did the New World offer few opportunities for the display of talent except in the public arena; it presented few temptations to distract talent from preoccupation with public concerns. There was no quick way to wealth and no likelihood of piling up great riches: nothing is more eloquent of the simplicity of American life than Washington's casting about to borrow a few hundred dollars to take him to the Inauguration, or Secretary of the Treasury Hamilton's requests for a loan of twenty dollars or so. There were no fields for military glory or adventure; the challenge to adventure was there, but with no promise of reward, and soldiers who had served their country well ended their days in penury, while officers who naïvely hoped to enjoy membership in the Society of the Cincinnati were regarded as models of depravity to be compared only with an Alcibiades or a Caligula. Society offered no distractions—indeed there was no Society in the Old World sense of the term, for that was a function of cities, of courts, of a class system. In the

Old World young men of talent might become courtiers or adventurers, but it is almost as difficult to imagine a Madame Du Barry,
a Lady Hamilton, or a Madame de Staël in eighteenth-century
America as a Chesterfield, a Struensee, or a Casanova. It is relevant
to recall Jefferson's warning[2] that young men who went abroad to
study would surely sink into debauchery, or John Adams' feeling of
outrage at the avuncular gallantries of the aged Benjamin Franklin;
it is relevant to note that Benjamin Thompson and Aaron Burr, who
were adventurers and gallants, found Europe more congenial to
their talents than America.

Such talent as there was, then, had no effective outlet except in
public channels. But how did it happen that there was so much talent? And how did it happen—it is a question Henry Adams never
ceased asking himself—that American society of the eighteenth century was prepared to encourage and use such talent as was available,
whereas the America of a century later was not.

Here, again, we do well to begin with a practical consideration.
Not only were the opportunities for leadership and for distinction
almost wholly in the public arena, but the opportunities in the public arena were numerous, urgent, and inviting. Has any one generation of less than a million adult men ever been called upon to do
more than the generation of Washington and Adams and Jefferson in
these creative years? They had to win independence; set up state
governments; write a constitution; win the transmontane West and
defend it against Indians and against formidable foreign powers;
create a nation and all those institutions, political and cultural, that
go into the making of a nation. There is nothing like war for bringing out courage; there is nothing like emergency for bringing out
ingenuity; there is nothing like challenge for bringing out character.
This is Arnold Toynbee's argument of challenge and response; it is
the moral put in simpler form by Lowell's once familiar poem, "The
Present Crisis":

New occasions teach new duties; time makes ancient good uncouth,
They must upward still, and onward, who would keep abreast of
Truth.

In the last quarter of the eighteenth century Americans were exposed to new occasions as well as to new duties. They found themselves not only required to perform heroic deeds, but challenged to
do so by the special circumstances of their being. No one can read
their public papers or their private correspondence (and how the

28

two are alike!) without realizing that these men saw themselves as characters in history, and that they were weighed down (or perhaps buoyed up) by a special sense of responsibility. A hundred quotations propose themselves, but the best is the most familiar: Washington's moving admonition to the states in his "Circular Letter" of June 1783:[3]

> This is the time of their political probation, this is the moment when the eyes of the whole World are turned upon them, this is the moment to establish or ruin their national Character forever. . . . For according to the system of Policy the States shall adopt at this moment, they will stand or fall, and by their confirmation or lapse, it is yet to be decided whether the Revolution must ultimately be considered as a blessing or a curse: a blessing or a curse, not to the present age alone, for with our fate will the destiny of unborn Millions be involved.

The Founding Fathers—even the term is not improper—were quite aware that the American people were the first to break away from a mother country, the first to set up as a nation, to try the experiment of self-government, to write constitutions, and to fashion a new colonial system. They thought of themselves not as actors on some provincial stage but as characters in the greatest drama of all history. Thus Jefferson's comment that "Americans undertook to make a communication of grandeur and freedom" to the peoples of the entire world. Thus Tom Paine's conclusion that "we have it in our power to begin the world over again. A situation similar to the present hath not happened since the days of Noah until now. The birthday of a new world is at hand."[4] Thus Ethan Allen's assurance that "it is in our power to make the world happy, to teach mankind the art of being so, to exhibit on the theatre of the universe, a character hitherto unknown . . . to have a new creation entrusted to our hands."

And now we come to the heart of the matter. What was it that impelled so many Americans, from the seacoast of Maine to the frontiers of Georgia, from tidewater Virginia to the backwoods of Pennsylvania, into service to the commonwealth? What was it that made that service on the whole so spontaneous and so harmonious, so that eighteenth-century America presents a spectacle of consensus and cooperation without parallel in modern history? What was it that seemed to give the same character, the same animus, the same style even, to almost every public man—an aristocratic soldier like Washington, a Puritan like John Adams, a Scots immigrant like James Wilson, a West Indian immigrant like Alexander Hamilton, a scholar-statesman like Jefferson and Madison, a scientist like Benjamin Rush, so that their philosophies, their conduct, and even their letters are almost indistinguishable from their public papers? We have greatly busied ourselves with identifying the authorship of the disputed numbers of the *Federalist Papers;* we have not sufficiently remarked how astonishing it is that there should be a dispute: imagine a dispute over the authorship of contributions to a volume by Eisenhower, Stevenson, and Truman!

When we study our history in a vacuum, or in isolation, as we so commonly do, we exaggerate differences and minimize similarities. Contrast the American Revolution with the English Revolution of the seventeenth century, or the French from 1789 to 1815, or the many revolutions in the states of Latin America: what emerges most sharply is the harmonious quality that pervades the American. We pivot history on the contest between Jefferson and Hamilton, but their similarities are more profound and pervasive than their differences. We have made much of the differences between Jefferson and John Adams, but the two men cherished the same philosophy of history and even of man, worked happily together on the Declaration of Independence and on state constitutions, and in their long and fascinating correspondence rarely wandered off common ground. How much alike, too, are the constitutions of the states and that of the United States; how similar their Bills of Rights; how almost monotonously familiar are the arguments over the ratification of the Federal Constitution in the various conventions, how superficial the criticisms, how insignificant the proposed amendments; how interchangeable the two factions or parties before and after ratification! Of this whole generation of statesmen and public figures, we can say that the things that divided them were inconsequential, and the things that united them were fundamental.

It is not merely that they were all children of the Enlightenment, consciously or unconsciously: so, for that matter, were Lord Shelburne and Diderot and Casanova. It is more to the point that they were all part of what we may call the American Enlightenment—an Enlightenment that differed strikingly from the French and English versions in that (unlike these) it found support in experience as well as in philosophy, vindicated itself by reference to environment and circumstances, as well as to imagination and logic. That, I suppose, is the underlying reason why John Adams was not really a misanthrope, despite his natural inclinations in that direction; why Washington was not really a Tory, despite his natural predisposition to be so; why Hamilton was such a failure as an aristocrat or an oligarch.

But there were other common denominators for the Americans of this generation besides the ideas of the Enlightenment and the realities of an environment, or a Providence, which "by all its dispensations proves that it delights in the happiness of man here and his greater happiness hereafter";[5] there were other common denominators that operated to encourage service to the commonwealth. There was, for example, the growing secularism, or deism, of society generally and of the upper classes (if we can use such a term for America) in particular. It is suggestive that whereas in the seventeenth century the best brains tended to go into the church, after Jonathan Edwards few first-rate minds were content with theological speculations, and the clergymen who are most familiar to us are remembered for other than contributions to theology: the politically minded Jonathan Mayhew, for example, or the brave John Peter Muhlenberg, or the egregious Manasseh Cutler, or the omniscient William Bentley. But it is not merely that men of talent no longer gravitated instinctively into the ministry; it is rather that deism supplanted piety and that virtue came to be judged by classical rather than Biblical standards. The passion that had earlier gone into the service of God was transferred into service to the commonwealth, and the expectation of personal immortality was transformed (is it possible to say sublimated?) into concern for historical immortality and for the welfare of posterity.

The confession of obligation to posterity can, of course, be merely a rhetorical flourish—doubtless it was in Jefferson's grandiose reference to "our descendants to the thousandth and thousandth generation." But no one who immerses himself in the writings of the men of that Revolutionary generation can doubt that it was genuine and pervasive. Remember Tom Paine's plea for independence: " 'Tis not the concern of a day, a year, or an age; *posterity* are virtually involved in the contest, and will be more or less affected to the end of time." Or John Adams' moving letter to his beloved Abigail when he had signed the Declaration, "Through all the gloom I can see the rays of ravishing light and glory. *Posterity* will triumph in that day's transaction, even although we should rue it, which I trust in God we shall not."[6] Benjamin Rush recalled that "I was animated constantly by a belief that I was acting for the benefit of the whole world, and of future ages, by assisting in the formation of new means of political order and general happiness."[7]

No one appealed more frequently to posterity than Washington; nowhere is that appeal more moving than in the Newburgh address:

"You will, by the dignity of your Conduct, afford occasion for Posterity to say, when speaking of the glorious example you have exhibited to Mankind, 'had this day been wanting the World had never seen the last stage of perfection to which human nature is capable of attaining.' "[8] Were the echoes of this in Churchill's mind when he spoke of "their finest hour"? And here is Washington's friend, Arthur St. Clair, accepting the governorship of the Northwest Territory in 1788: "I am truly sensible of the Importance of the Trust" and aware "how much depends on the due execution of it—to you Gentlemen over whom it is to be immediately exercised, to your Posterity! perhaps to the whole Community of America."[9] Or listen to George Mason's admonition to his children in his will: "If either their own inclinations or the necessity of the times should engage them in public affairs, I charge them . . . never to let the motives of private interest or of ambition induce them to betray nor the fear of danger or of death deter them from asserting the liberty of the country and endeavoring to transmit to their posterity those sacred rights in which they themselves were born."[10] Finally, here is Jefferson on the eve of death—and beyond mere rhetoric—to his friend James Madison, "It has been a great solace to me to believe that you are engaged in vindicating to posterity the course we have pursued, of preserving to them, in all their purity, the blessings of self-government which we had assisted in acquiring for them."[11]

A fourth common denominator of the minds of the late eighteenth-century Americans was education, formal and informal. It is customary now to disparage eighteenth-century education, to equate the colleges of that day with the better high schools of our own day, and to recall how few Americans were exposed to the advantages of formal education. Yet the products of the eighteenth-century educational machinery seemed to think more deeply (certainly in the political realm) and to write more clearly (in any realm) than the products of the far more elaborate educational systems of our own time. But again what is most interesting is that almost all the public men of that generation appear to have absorbed the same maxims of conduct, to have studied the same texts, to have subscribed to the same philosophical precepts. All of them knew Plutarch and Thucydides and Tacitus; all knew (at first hand or merely as the common sense of the matter) John Locke and Bolingbroke and Hume and Montesquieu. Almost every one of them might have said, with the Rev. Jonathan Mayhew, "Having been initiated in youth in the doctrines of civil liberty, as they are taught in such men as Plato, Demosthenes, Cicero, and other persons among the ancients, and such as Sidney and Milton, Locke and Hoadley among the moderns, I liked them; they seemed rational." [12] Almost everyone might have provided in his will, as Josiah Quincy did, that "I leave to my son, when he shall have reached the age of fifteen, the Works of Algernon Sidney, John Locke, Bacon, Gordon's *Tacitus* and *Cato's Letters*. May the spirit of Liberty rest upon him." [13] How familiar the *Maxims of Civil Conduct*, which the youthful Washington learned; how familiar the long excerpts that went into Jefferson's *Commonplace Book*, or that made up the substance of so much of John Adams' *Defence of the Constitutions*, and *Discourses on Davila*. Adams—as representative a figure as you can find in this generation—took for granted the duty of the academies to inculcate virtue and the love of liberty, and saw to it that the education which he arranged for his son did just that. Thus the youthful *Dissertation on the Canon and the Feudal Law* concluded with the appeal that "the colleges join their harmony in the same delightful concert. Let every declamation turn upon the beauty of liberty and virtue, and the deformity and turpitude and malignity of slavery and vice. Let the public disputations become researches into the grounds and nature and ends of government, and the means of preserving the good and demolishing the evil. Let the dialogues and all the exercises become the instruments of impressing on the tender mind . . . the ideas of Right and the sensations of freedom." [14]

It is unnecessary to elaborate on what is so familiar. What is important are the lessons that this generation drew from its study of the classics of Greek and Roman literature and of the literature of English liberty. It learned (the predisposition was there, of course) that the same rules of morality operated at all times, in all places, and in all societies; that the affairs of men were controlled by undeviating "laws of Nature and Nature's God," laws which neither God nor Nature could alter; and that there was, in the words of Washington, "an indissoluble union between virtue and happiness, between duty and advantage, between the genuine maxim of an honest and magnanimous policy and the solid rewards of public prosperity and felicity." And they learned that the first duty of the good citizen was service to the commonwealth. "Every man in a republic," said Benjamin Rush, "is public property. His time and talents, his youth, his manhood, his old age, nay more, life, all, belong to his country." And Elbridge Gerry (something of an expert on the matter of public service) observed that "it is the duty of every citizen though he may have but one day to live, to devote that day to the service of his country."[15]

This was what philosophy admonished; this was what history taught.

History—almost inseparable from literature and philosophy— is a fifth common denominator of the American mind, or character, in this generation, a fifth influence beckoning or persuading men into the public service.

Few aspects of American intellectual history are more astonishing—perhaps we should say puzzling—than the contrast between political and historical writing in the last quarter of the eighteenth century. For the generation that gave us, indisputably, the most eloquent and profound political treatises in our literature—the *Farmer's Letters,* the *Summary View,* the Declaration of Independence, the Virginia Bill of Rights, the Virginia Statute of Religious Freedom, the Constitution, the *Federalist Papers,* Washington's "Circular Letter," his Inaugural and Farewell Addresses come to mind—gave us not a single work of formal history that anyone but an expert can remember or that anyone, even an expert, can read except as an act of duty or of piety. Hutchinson's *Massachusetts Bay* is pedestrian; Gordon's *American Revolution* is plagiarized from the *Annual Register,* and so, too, much of Ramsay's sprightlier *American Revolution;* the Rev. Jeremy Belknap is interesting chiefly to antiquarians and local historians; Ebenezer Hazard was a collector; Noah Webster a dilettante; Mercy Warren lively but unreliable and amateurish; John Marshall's ponderous five volumes on Washington (much of it cribbed from other books) is universally unread. Only the grotesque Parson Weems wrote histories that survive, and everyone agrees that he was not a historian, that he really belongs in the Romantic era, and that his books are fiction anyway.

Yet no other American generation has been so deeply immersed in or preoccupied with history. Indeed, we might say with considerable justice that the Founding Fathers thought history too serious a business to be left to the historians. It was the concern of all, but especially of statesmen—the view that Winston Churchill has taken all his life. If we want to read the historical writing of this generation, then, we turn to the writings, public and private, of John Adams, Jefferson, Madison, Franklin, Hamilton, Washington, Rush, Wilson, and others. And the great historical treatises are not the formal histories, rather such books as the *Defence of the Constitu-tions,* or *Notes on Virginia,* or the *Federalist Papers,* or Wilson's *Lectures on the Constitution,* while commentary and interpretation of history run like a broad stream through the correspondence of most of the leading statesmen.

The evidence here is overwhelming: see, for example, the con-tinuous rain of references to the experience of the ancient world in the debates in the Federal Convention and the state ratifying conventions, and the preoccupation with ancient history—and some more modern—in the *Federalist Papers.* All John Adams' major writings were historical, and so was much of what John Dickinson, James Wilson, and Madison wrote as well.[16]

But the view of history entertained by the philosophers of the Enlightenment was very different from that which had been ac-cepted in the past, or which was to be embraced by the future. It completely repudiated the antiquarianism of the Annalists of the seventeenth century; it would have repudiated, just as convulsively, the narrative and romantic history of the nineteenth century and the scientific history of the nineteenth and twentieth centuries, which addresses itself to what actually happened.

Certainly what happened did not interest the historian-philoso-phers of the Enlightenment.[17] "Other historians relate facts to in-form us of facts," wrote Diderot to Voltaire. "You relate them to excite in our hearts an intense hatred of lying, ignorance, hypocrisy, superstition, tyranny."[18] The tribute to Voltaire was just: "Con-found details," that historian had said, and the reason was, clearly enough, that details tended to confound the historian. The same point of view is reflected in the statesmen of the New World when they turned their attention to history. "The sacred rights of man-kind are not to be rummaged for among old parchments or musty records," wrote the youthful Hamilton. "They are written as with a sunbeam in the whole volume of human nature by the hand of Divinity itself."[19]

Particular facts, then, were of no interest or importance; only general facts. Details were insignificant and trivial; only general truths commanded attention. When Lessing reviewed Voltaire's *Essay on Manners* (a characteristic eighteenth-century title), he observed that "to know man in particular . . . is to know fools and scoundrels. The case is quite different with the study of Man in general. Here he exhibits greatness and his divine origin."[20] That is what the American statesmen-philosophers were interested in, man in general. "When in the course of human events," Jefferson began his great Declaration, and it is a breathtaking phrase. It is "the laws of Nature and Nature's God" that entitle the American people to "assume among the powers of the earth an equal station." The truths that justify this claim to equality are "self-evident" and apply to "all men" and to "any form of Government."[21]

So American statesmen, when they turned to the past, drew with equal confidence on the histories of Athens and Sparta, of Carthage and Rome, of the Swiss cantons or the low countries, of Anglo-Saxon England or Stuart England; it was all one. They had in fact no sense of place, as they had no sense of time; they repeated with Samuel Johnson (whom they otherwise detested):

> Let observation with extensive view
> Survey mankind from China to Peru;
> Remark each anxious toil, each eager strife,
> And watch the busy scenes of crowded life
> —*Vanity of Human Wishes*

The laws of nature were everlastingly the same, and so, too, the laws of history, for the same laws that regulated the movement of the stars in the heavens regulated the movements of politics and economy on earth—the anxious toil, the eager strife, the busy scenes of crowded life.

And just as evolution was unsuspected in the natural order, so it was excluded from the historical. Progress, if it existed, was cyclical, or it was a happy parallel to the movement of the sun from the east to the west: it was as simple as that. The Enlightenment was not really interested in the past at all; in its sight a thousand years were as one, and if the thousand years did not yield a moral lesson, they were as nothing. The historians of the Enlightenment were like Diogenes; they went about the past with a lantern, looking for truth. They knew truth when they saw it, and brought it forth into the light, but they had no interest in what was not truth.

This is one reason they had so little interest in individuals, but only in the individual as a type, and they were always putting contemporaries into some historical niche. Washington was Cincinnatus, and Greene was Fabian, and Burr was Cataline, and Franklin was Solon, and so it went. It is no accident that the American Enlightenment did not produce a single biography of any value: Marshall's *Washington* was not really of any value, and Weems's *Washington* was not a product of the Enlightenment at all.

History, then, in the era of the Enlightenment, in America as in the Old World, addressed itself to great public questions, to broad general issues, to profound moral problems, and left the details to the pedants and the antiquarians. The historians of that day wrote on Man, not men; on the spirit of the laws rather than on specific laws; they gave lectures on the study of history, or commentaries on the Constitution, or provided a *Defence of the Constitutions,* or *Notes on Virginia.* When they submitted "facts to a candid world," they did so only as illustrations of a general principle, and it did not so much matter if the facts failed to illustrate the principle, for the principle was valid anyway.[22] The best of histories—the American in any event—were all designed to prove something: *Notes on Virginia* to prove the superiority of the American environment over the European; *Defence of the Constitutions* to prove the superiority of the Massachusetts Constitution to the kind of constitution celebrated by Turgot; the *Federalist Papers* to prove the adequacy of the new Federal Constitution; the *Rights of Man* to prove the necessity of revolution in Great Britain, and so forth. Thus, history was utilitarian, but only in a highly moral sense. It took the place of the Bible, and drove home truths which heretofore had depended for authority on the Scriptures.

But if human nature was always the same, and if history was regulated by the laws of nature, what hope was there that man and nature would be different in America? What reason was there to suppose that the New World could escape the fate of the Old? That was a hard nut to crack. In a sense, it was the secular version of the familiar conflict between predestination and free will. Was there any room for the exercise of free will in American history? What a question to ask, in this New World whose very existence was a monument to the exercise of free will, in this new nation which had come into existence through a mighty effort of free will! What a question to ask of a people who were not only prepared to new-make the world, but were actually engaged in doing so!

History was not inexorable, nor was Man's Fate. History, rightly read, presented a spectacle of virtue as of vice, of weal as of woe, of triumph as of failure. The outcome depended on what man did with nature and nature's laws. More specifically, it depended on three things: the natural environment, the political and social institutions, and the character of the men who served—or betrayed—the commonwealth.

Environment was important, far more important in the New

World than in the Old, where it had been tamed and brought under control. All Americans were by nature (as they still are) environmentalists, for in America environment triumphed over inheritance. It is the awareness of this that explains the almost convulsive reaction of so many Americans to the Raynal-Buffon theories of degeneracy in the New World. Those theories were not actually extreme, and Raynal at least apologized handsomely enough for his errors, but Jefferson and Franklin and others found them unforgivable.[23] For to attack nature in America was to destroy the promise of American life. The expectations of future glory so confidently entertained by Washington and Jefferson and Paine and their colleagues were based in considerable part on the American environment. Nor was that environment a simple matter; it operated in two distinct ways to assure both America's escape from the evils that had afflicted the Old World and the promise of future well-being: both can be read luminously in the public papers of Washington and Jefferson. First was the sheer physical bounty of the New World—soil, forests, water, sheer size—"land enough for . . . the thousandth and thousandth generation." Second was isolation from the Old World; as Jefferson put it, we were *"kindly* separated by Nature from the exterminating havoc of one quarter of the globe; too high-minded to endure the depredations of the others." The isolation was not only physical but social, political, and moral as well.

Here, then, was something really new in history: for the first time a numerous and virtuous people were vouchsafed an ideal environment and were freed from the tyrannies, the superstitions, the injustices, the vices, the miseries that had for centuries made a shambles of the history of the Old World. But a rich and spacious environment was not enough. It proved, to be sure, that "by all its dispensations Providence delighted in the happiness of man," but— if we may shift to Washington (and why not, as the Founding Fathers are philosophically interchangeable?)—"there is still an option left to the United States . . . it is in their choice and depends upon their conduct whether they will be respectable and prosperous, or contemptible and miserable as a Nation." In short, everything depended on what Americans did with their environment. Everything depended on the institutions they established, the constitutions they wrote, the laws they enacted. Everything depended on the health and the virtue of society. Everything depended on the integrity and devotion of its leaders. Here is where history, properly read, was really useful. For history was the great school of virtue.

As early as 1749 Benjamin Franklin drew up a series of Proposals relating to the Education of the Youth of Pennsylvania. History occupied a central position in that scheme of education. Among many other things it would: [24]

> . . . give occasion to expatiate on the Advantage of Civil Orders and Constitutions; how Men and their Properties are protected by joining in Societies and establishing Government; their Industry encouraged and rewarded; Arts invented, and Life made more comfortable. The Advantages of *Liberty,* Mischiefs of Licentiousness, Benefits arising from good Laws and from a due Execution of Justice, etc. Thus may the first principles of sound Politicks be fix'd in the Minds of Youth.

And Franklin added that in a proper system of education,

> The idea of what is true Merit should also be presented to Youth, explained and impressed on their Minds, as consisting in an Inclination joined with an Ability to serve Mankind, one's Country, Friends and Family.

Jefferson, too, thought that history occupied a central position in any scheme of education, because it taught the young the dangers of tyranny and the virtues of freedom. "History, by apprizing them of the past," he wrote, "will enable them to judge of the future; it will avail them of the experience of other times and other nations; it will qualify them as judges of the actions and designs of men; it will enable them to know ambition under every disguise it may assume; and knowing it, to defeat its views." [25]

This, after all, was but the common sense of the matter. Everyone agreed with Bolingbroke that history was philosophy teaching by example. Everyone read in Hume that, [26]

> History tends to strengthen the Sentiments of Virtue by the Variety of Views in which it exhibits the Conduct of divine Providence. . . . A regard to divine Providence heightens our Satisfaction in reading History, and tends to throw an agreeable Light upon the most gloomy and disgusting parts of it.

Though the Americans did not know him, they would have agreed with the fascinating Dr. Zimmermann of Berne and Hannover, who ransacked ancient history to discover "examples . . . that shine as patterns to posterity," and that [27] "awaken in every noble mind an irrefragable sense of the duties we owe to our country; and the preservation of the history of these examples is nothing more than the propagation of that national pride founded on real advantages," and who concluded that confidence and self-esteem, based on familiarity with the historical past, "gives us the power to exalt ourselves above the weakness of human nature, to exert our talents in praiseworthy enterprises, never to yield to the spirit of slavery, never to be slaves to vice, to obey the dictates of our conscience, to smile under misfortune, and to rely upon seeing better days."

The historical-philosopher with whom Americans were most familiar (after Bolingbroke, in any event) was the extraordinary Dr. Priestley, clergyman, scientist, statesman, and historian. All knew his *Lectures on History* (they had gone through many editions before Priestley came to the United States), lectures prefixed by an "Essay on a Course of Liberal Education for Civil Life" and addressed to that lively young Benjamin Vaughan whose later career was a monument to their value. Priestley's American friends could read in these lectures that history serves to amuse the imagination and interest the passions, that it improves the understanding, and that it tends to strengthen the sentiments of virtue.[28]

The chorus was harmonious; too, it was overwhelming; there were no discordant notes—none of any importance. History taught (that was its business) that man was master of his fate, that virtue could triumph over vice and reason over folly, and that the surest road to immortality was service to the commonwealth. The men whom history celebrated (it was the theme of the historians, the poets, the dramatists) were those who devoted their talents to their fellow men. That whole generations drew strength,[29]

. . . not merely from twice-told arguments—how fair and noble a thing it is to show courage in battle—but from the busy spectacle of our great city's life as we see it before us day by day, falling in love with her as we see her, and remembering that all this greatness she owes to men with the fighter's daring, the wise man's understanding of his duty, and the good man's self-discipline in its performance—to men who, if they failed in any ordeal, disdained to deprive the city of their services, but sacrificed their lives as the best offerings on her behalf.

And they knew, too, that "the whole earth is the sepulchre of famous men; and their story is graven not only on stone over the native earth, but lives on far away, without visible symbol, woven into the stuff of other men's lives."[29]

That was the immortality they sought, and it was the immortality they found; it is impossible to doubt the sincerity of their detestation of the adventurers or soldiers who solaced themselves with private rather than public gain, as it is impossible to doubt their own genuine desire for retirement to their farms or their studies.

These, then, were some of the circumstances, pressures, and considerations that help to explain the phenomenon of public leadership in eighteenth-century America. Talent was to be found everywhere, but in America it was directed, inevitably, into public channels. The zeal for service was to be found everywhere, but in America it could be satisfied on the public stage: who can believe that a Hamilton, a Gallatin, or a Wilson would have found scope for their talents in the countries of their birth? The philosophy of the Enlightenment flourished everywhere in the Western world, but in America it was given a chance to operate in the political and social as well as the moral and cultural realms, and that without the necessity of violence or revolution.

Eighteenth-century Americans assumed that history was philosophy teaching by example, and went far to prove it by modeling themselves on the examples they supposed—sometimes mistakenly —to be history. We no longer subscribe with any confidence to Bolingbroke's dictum, and even if we did we would be unable to agree on the selection or the interpretation of the examples. If we find history in general unusable in a direct or practical way, what of the experience of the Founding Fathers can we use in our search for leadership?

We know that all those who cry Lord, Lord, shall not enter into the Kingdom of Heaven, and we cannot take refuge in admonitions. Nor can we hope to lift ourselves by our moral bootstraps by an ostentatious search for values: our problem is not to define our values, but to realize them. Let us inquire rather what part of the eighteenth-century experience that provided our country with such distinguished leadership is or can be made relevant to our needs today.

First, we noted that in eighteenth-century America public careers were almost the only careers that were open to great talent. Today openings—indeed invitations—are innumerable, and talent finds more glittering rewards in private than in public enterprise. Can we do anything to tilt the balance back to public enterprise?

Certainly we can, if we will, do something to restore the balance in the purely material realm; in a society where prestige is associated with material status, that is not unimportant. We can and should pay salaries that do not impose too heavy a sacrifice upon those who enter public life. We can use the instrument of taxation to encourage education, literature, the arts and sciences, and to reduce

41

the financial rewards of private enterprise. We have not sufficiently explored these possibilities.

Second, we can and should protect our public servants from some of the more ostentatious penalties that are now associated with public enterprise; we might even give them the same protection and immunity that is enjoyed by those who are engaged in private business. Not only is public service poorly paid: it is exceedingly vulnerable. Horace Greeley observed during the campaign of 1872 that he did not know whether he was running for the Presidency or the penitentiary; a good many politicians, not Presidential candidates alone, must have felt that way during recent campaigns: the "twenty years of treason" campaign comes to mind. The civil servant, even with tenure, is at all times fair game: fair game for demagogues making political capital; for Congressional committees which allow themselves a degree of irresponsibility unparalleled in Britain or Canada; for security investigators whose work—witness the Service and Condon cases—is never done; for journalists who yield nothing to these investigators in their contempt for privacy and for decency. If we are to encourage able men to enter public life, we may have to curb the self-indulgence, vanity, and sadism which now operate to keep so many people out of it.

Third, can we do anything to encourage a livelier awareness of posterity and our responsibility to it? Perhaps the situation here is desperate; after all a people who were really concerned for posterity would not produce so much of it! Yet here too something might be done by deliberate policy. Remember Pericles' boast in the great Funeral Oration:

Ours is no work-a-day city only. No other provides so many recreations for the spirit—contests and sacrifices all the year round, and beauty in our public buildings to cheer the heart and delight the eyes day by day.

It is but natural, Pericles added, "that all of us shall work to spend ourselves in her service."

We can, if we will, emulate the Athenians who built so splendidly that their citizens "drew strength from the busy spectacle of our great city's life" and that posterity, too, could delight in its beauty and its glory. We can do this by the deliberate support of those monuments and memorials which are designed at once to remind us of our responsibility to posterity and to remind posterity of its obligation to us. Instead of turning the hearts of our great cities into scabrous parking lots—as Boston is doing even now—we can use public and private money to build parks, squares, fountains, galleries, libraries, theatres, operas—whatever will keep constantly before the eyes of the young of future generations a sense of the greatness of the city and of the spirit of those who built her. A society that wastes its affluence in self-indulgence cannot expect to excite in the young a passion to spend themselves in the service of the commonwealth.

Fourth, what role for education?

Eighteenth-century education with its emphasis on the classics and on history was designed to instill in the young an avid sense of duty and of civic virtue. The Fathers, we remember, were brought up on Plutarch and Cicero, and read Locke and Montesquieu and *Cato's Letters*. They saw history as a morality play whose acts unfolded in ceaseless progression, and themselves as cast in the roles of Solon or Aristides or Brutus or Cincinnatus. Often they consciously displayed the antique virtues which they associated with these Plutarchian characters.

It is an understatement that education and history no longer fulfill these traditional functions. Can they be persuaded to do so?

Certainly not in any calculated way; to "use" history to inculcate particular principles, even good ones, is a dangerous business. But at a time when the history of Greece and Rome and even of England have all but disappeared from the schools' curricula, and when history itself is giving way to civics, or current affairs, or "world problems," it is relevant to recall that the men who fought the Revolution and wrote the Constitutions and the Bills of Rights were brought up on the histories of Greece and Rome and England. At a time when narrative history has given way to "problems" and when the celebration of heroes is regarded as a vestigial remnant of Victorianism or a subtle attack upon the behavioral sciences, it is relevant to observe that, if we deny young people the wonder and excitement of historical narration and of heroes, we cannot expect them to respond passionately to the moral crises of our own time.

The eighteenth century, which vouchsafed us the most distinguished leadership that any nation has enjoyed in modern times, can, then, furnish us, if not with models and directives, at least with illustrations and guides. Our eighteenth-century experience suggests that leadership is not fortuitous, that both formal policies and informal attitudes influence its appearance and its character, and that considerations of material rewards, prestige, opportunity, philosophy, and education are all involved in the formulation of such policies and attitudes.

REFERENCES

1. Henry James, *Hawthorne* (1956 reprint), 34.

2. 8 Julian Boyd, ed., *The Papers of Thomas Jefferson,* 635.

3. 26 J. C. Fitzpatrick, ed., *Writings of George Washington,* 483.

4. *The Crisis,* no. 13.

5. Jefferson, First Inaugural Address.

6. 9 *Life and Works of John Adams,* 420.

7. *Memorial,* quoted in R. E. Delmage, "American Idea of Progress," 91 *Proceedings of the American Philosophical Society,* 314.

8. 26 *Writings of Washington,* 227.

9. 3 Clarence E. Carter, ed., *Territorial Papers,* 264.

10. 1 K. M. Rowland, *Life of George Mason,* 166.

11. 10 P. L. Ford, ed., *Writings* of Thomas Jefferson, 378.

12. William Tudor, *Life of James Otis,* 144.

13. Josiah Quincy, *Memoir of the Life of Josiah Quincy,* 289.

14. "Dissertation on Canon and Feudal Law," 3 *Works,* 448. When in 1785 Adams recommended his son John Quincy to Professor Waterhouse at Harvard College, he noted that while the boy was "awkward in speaking Latin," in "English and French poetry I know not where you would find anybody his superior, in Roman and English history, few persons of his age. He has translated Virgil's Aeneid, Suetonius, the whole of Sallust and Tacitus Agricola, his Germany and several books of his Annals, a great part of Horace, some of Ovid and some of Caesar's Commentaries . . . besides a number of Tully's Orations. . . . In Greek . . . he has studied morsels of Aristotle's Poetics, in Plutarch's Lives of Lucian's Dialogues . . . and lately he has gone through several books in Homer's Iliad." 9 *Works,* 530. An elaborate appreciation of the unifying role of the study of the classics on this generation is Douglass Adair, "Intellectual Origins of Jeffersonian Democracy," unpublished Ph.D. dissertation, Yale University, 1943.

15. Quoted in Saul K. Padover, *The World of the Founding Fathers,* 173.

16. Karl Lehmann's observation of Jefferson's historical-mindedness might apply equally to most of the Founding Fathers. "Patrick Henry seemed to speak like Homer, and Homer's language could not fail to be imbued with a

new and concrete vitality after listening to Henry, with that analogy in
mind. General Arnold's famous march to Quebec was a parallel to Xeno-
phon's retreat in Asia Minor as narrated in his *Anabasis.* John Adams, like
Themistocles in Athens, had been the constant advocate of the 'wooden
walls' of a navy. And the King of England would welcome American-
Tory-traitors as the Persian King had given refuge to the fugitive aristocracy of Greece. Burr was the Cataline of the American Republic." (*Thomas
Jefferson, Humanist,* 93.)

17. "What does it matter to me," wrote Madame du Châtelet to her friend
Voltaire, "to know that Egil succeeded Haquin in Sweden, and that Otto-
man was the son of Ortogrul? I have read with pleasure the history of the
Greeks and the Romans; they offered me certain great pictures which
attracted me. But I have never yet been able to finish any long history
of our modern nations . . . a host of minute events without connection or
sequence, a thousand battles which settled nothing . . . which overwhelms
the mind without illuminating it." It was the *cri de coeur* of that whole
generation.

18. Quoted in Carl Becker, *Heavenly City of the Eighteenth-Century Philosophers,* 91.

19. *The Farmer Refuted.*

20. Quoted in Ernst Cassirer, *The Philosophy of the Enlightenment* (Beacon
Press edn.), 216.

21. So John Adams concluded his *Defence of American Constitutions* with
the observation that "all nations from the beginning have been agitated
by the same passions. The principles developed here will go a long way
in explaining *every* phenomenon that occurs in history of government.
The vegetable and animal kingdoms, and those heavenly bodies whose
existence and movements we are as yet only permitted faintly to perceive,
do not appear to be governed by laws more uniform or certain than those
which regulate the moral and political world."

22. The comment of Helvetius on the factual evidence which Montesquieu
included to support some of his arguments in *The Spirit of the Laws,*
illuminates this attitude. "What the deuce does he want to teach us by
his treatise on feudal tenure," said Helvetius. "What new forms of legis-
lation can be derived from this chaos of barbarism that has been maintained by brute force, but must be swept away by reason? He should have
tried to derive some true maxims from the improved state of things that
is at hand." (Quoted in 2 J. W. Thompson, *History of Historical Writing,*
63.)

23. The literature on this subject is large, but it is sufficient to suggest here
Edwin T. Martin, *Thomas Jefferson, Scientist,* Daniel Boorstin, *The Lost
World of Thomas Jefferson,* and Gilbert Chinard, "Eighteenth Century
Theories on America as a Human Habitat," 91 *Proc. Am. Phil. Society,*
27 ff., and the references which they give.

24. 3 L. W. Labaree, ed., *Papers of Benjamin Franklin,* 412 ff.

25. "Notes on Virginia," Query 14.

26. *Lectures on History,* 75-76.

27. John G. Zimmermann, *Essay on National Pride* (London, 1797 edn.), 241 ff.

28. "History," said the omniscient Dr. Priestley, "by displaying the sentiments and conduct of truly great men, and those of a contrary character, tends to inspire us with a taste for solid glory and real greatness, and convinces us that it does not consist in what the generality of mankind are so eager in pursuit of. We can never again imagine, if we derive our instruction from history, that true greatness consists in *riches.* . . ." And he concluded, "We conceive more clearly what true greatness of mind is, at the same time that our hearts are more filled with admiration for it, by a simple narration of some incidents of history than by the most elaborate and philosophically exact description of it." *Lectures on History and General Policy* (Philadelphia, 1803 edn.), first lecture.

29. From Pericles' Funeral Oration. Jefferson had four copies of Thucydides' *History* in his library.

HELEN HILL MILLER

The Search for Purpose

Form and Purpose in the 1960's

MR. KENNEDY's personal popularity has for some months remained unprecedentedly high for a president in a time other than one of full war crisis. Yet the country is simultaneously experiencing a deep malaise. Why? Throughout the campaign preceding his election, Candidate Kennedy stressed the importance of getting the country moving again, and the country elected him. At his inaugural, President Kennedy said, "Let us begin," and the country was both willing and expectant. Yet over the ensuing months, while much happened, and while the Executive branch of the Federal government fairly buzzed with activity, there developed no clear sense of direction, no national confidence in being a people on its way. Instead, there was a vague but pervasive uneasiness at the absence of such confidence. Why?

Two components of this malaise may be taken as normal. In any two-party system, the out-party exists in order to subject the in-party to a scrutiny compounded of personal distaste, active advocacy of alternatives to the policies of those in power, and a mixture of hope and determination that the positions will be reversed the next time the country goes to the polls. Likewise, in any period when issues are as complex and dangers are as oppressive as at present, the responsible leaders of the official out-party will be pressed by unofficial out-parties, whose leaders, wishfully and irresponsibly, assure willing listeners that life can be simple again. Both these components of the present malaise are readily recognizable. But so is a third component, and this one is both unusual and unexpected. Uneasiness also exists among members of the in-party. It can be felt among a sizable number of those at the center of executive activity who now spend as long hours in government offices as they did in the field at the height of the 1960 campaign, and also among active, effective Democrats outside the Federal executive structure.

These Democrats, in strict contrast to the members of the out-party, find no comfort in the prospect of an alternative team: they do not know people who they believe could do the job better. If Nixon had won, they would have ascribed their uneasiness to a discriminating dissatisfaction with official personnel. Post for post, they could have named people who, if only they were in office, would surely exhibit the capacity to get the country moving forward. But their nominees are the very ones who now are in office, and, with scattered exceptions, the ones they would most like to see in office.

Practically all of today's administrators are experienced men. The last time the Democrats changed from being an out-party to becoming an in-party, Franklin D. Roosevelt had a much more limited choice of personnel. In putting the country under new management, he found few experienced managers. His administration was a curious mixture of rugged individualists, operators of party machines who came from the wrong side of the tracks and from back of the yards in the big cities and who had never had any truck with men of ideas, and men of ideas who came from ivory towers with no frontage on the market place. Most of them had to learn on the job. Roosevelt's capacity to get the country moving again was largely personal: to no small degree he carried a people made malleable by suffering and fear forward to new ideas by the timbre of an unforgettable voice.

In Mr. Kennedy's time, the choice of personnel is far broader. A Democratic president has the city machines always with him, but urban redevelopment has given a new look to what was once the wrong side of the tracks. Still more striking is the change in the relation of the universities and other sources of ideas to government. The United States has become a close-knit nation. The academics still deal with pure ideas, but they have been brought close to workaday realities by governmental and industrial contracts, by public and private consultancies, and by participation in government, local and state as well as national. Today, the man who is asked to come to Washington is very apt to have been there before, in one capacity or another. He is seasoned in the choreography of government operations. He knows who is who, and where the bodies of those who were are buried.

With such men as managers, the absence of an executive organization capable of producing a sure sense of national direction comes as a surprise. This administration is the product of the campaign technique that took Mr. Kennedy through the primaries, through the convention, through the election, and into office. It seems astounding that the structure that carried West Virginia should not be able to move other mountains. Again, why?

One explanation suggests that the trouble lies not in the people who are running the government, but rather in the greatly changed world, as yet unrealized by a local-minded affluent society, and in the domestic context in which today's public decisions must be made. This context is indeed a new one.

At the time of President Kennedy's inauguration, among the epithalamia with which the Western European press anticipated his political honeymoon, one mood-writer compared his taking office to the moment when the Sleeping Beauty is stirred by Prince Charming's kiss: he would rouse America from her immobilized enchantment of the mid-1950's. The fable chosen for this prophecy explains much. It originated in Europe, where the assumption about a princess come awake differs sharply from the American assumption. Europeans take it as axiomatic (and correspondingly undisturbing) that the prince finds the princess in a castle, a stout-walled structure surrounding a central keep, and that after they ride away on his charger they will live in a comparably stout-walled structure, also surrounding a central keep. Here is at least one reason why the country, no longer enchanted, is disenchanted. Americans do not like walled-in keeps; in their version of the Sleeping Beauty, the knight and his lady ride away into the sunset, westward, to a new frontier where no one will fence them in.

In recent months both country and administration have given evidence of a certain claustrophobia. European peoples, having lived for centuries within circumscribed spaces, know well that there are times when it can be accounted a political, economic, or diplomatic triumph if, by means of intense and intelligent activity, things are merely prevented from getting worse; and that even at the sound of a certain trumpet, the walls of other castles do not necessarily come tumbling down. By contrast, American frontiersmen expect sudden and satisfying results—gold in the pan for those who wade in, scoop up, and shake.

But the "New Frontier" is a misnomer. That era is over. Even as a wish-fulfillment of the radical right, no amount of TV Westerns, with their Goodies readily distinguishable from their Baddies, and their simple Bang-Bang solutions, can bring it back again. The new directions of the Kennedy programs are bounded by taut fences of barbed wire. Both to president and to people, such confinement is irksome. To some of the people, it is sufficiently unexpected to cause vigorous but futile kicking against the pricks.

The change has been very sudden. For three centuries, Americans enjoyed unhindered economic expansion across vast territory. It was an era of rapid becoming, and it lasted until after World War I. Then during the Roosevelt period, the horizontal expansion undertaken at private initiative was complemented by a vertical expansion undertaken at private initiative. It spread purchasing power through new layers of American society and gave a steep economic pyramid the new shape of a Christmas tree. This too was a time of becoming. And at the end of World War II, the expansion of technological knowledge gave the United States a brief monopoly of unimagined power.

Then, in a little over a decade, external barriers solidified around American life. Space, which had been two-dimensional and buffered by broad and empty oceans, became three-dimensional and occupied. The wild blue yonder turned into crowded skies; flight, manned and unmanned, arched over the old geography, compressing time; the overshadowed earth became a small planet. New forms of political organization, comparable in size and strength to America's own, and in several cases unfriendly, established surrounding sovereignties over great aggregates of land mass, resources, and peoples. Then in the winter of 1961 the physical limits to United States action were suddenly dramatized by the wall bisecting Berlin.

The restraints on United States policy-making caused by these new conditions can be quickly demonstrated. The dollar is no longer self-determining. American monetary policy can no longer be made solely in response to the requirements of the domestic scene. Internally, it may be desirable to stimulate growth and reduce unemployment by increasing the supply of credit; but if United States interest rates are not kept in line with the world money market, gold flows out of the country and the dollar weakens. In his 1962 "Economic Message," Mr. Kennedy specifically stressed the exigencies of this "narrow middle course."

Similarly, military strategy cannot be devised unilaterally. Strength must be sought through allying the free world, and the alliance must not look like a white man's club to the uncommitted formerly colonial areas. Foreign aid cannot rest on a simple transfer of know-how to the revolution of rising expectations. The United

States has a group of client states that depend on it to excess, but these would collapse if unaided. It has collaborators in military defense whose die-hard colonial policies ignore the writing on African walls. Behind the iron and bamboo curtains, it has competitors who offer economic assistance for political purposes. These pressures can compress a simple purpose into curious and at times forbidding shapes. What in its original form would find broad and ready acceptance among Americans often appears distorted and arguable by the time it is expressed as specific policy. Few top level executive decisions represent clear-cut choices; they have reached the top exactly because the supporting analyses that recommend their adoption and those that counsel against it balance each other so closely that a feather tips the scales. Out of such niceties, it is hard to compose a sense of direction. There is much to be said, therefore, on behalf of the view that the present uneasiness is a frustration that is due to external circumstances, rather than to the persons who are trying to cope with them.

Nonetheless, even deeper difficulties *do* concern persons rather than circumstances. To live effectively in today's conditions, Americans require no less than a new and deeply realized national style. If claustrophobia is to be shaken off and excellence is to lead, the country must develop a new way of life for both governed and governors, one suitable to an enclosed society. In a democracy, excellence is a complex interaction. Top policy makers, whether in government offices, executive suites, sensitive laboratories, or intellectual think-shops, must themselves be capable of excellent performance. Nevertheless, if they are to demonstrate their capacities, the men and women at the lower levels of American society must sustain, and in many cases choose, this kind of leadership; and if they are to do so, they must be able to comprehend through their own experience the broad outlines of their leaders' purposes.

The old American style was part and parcel of the frontier. It was a historic necessity and, in the framework of its times, a generous success. The early American arrivals, particularly those who came seeking religious liberty, had a set of inner values as important to them as life itself. Such freedom-seekers knew what they meant by freedom. To their descendants, the resources of the old West took on a more than material significance. In the New World, the Old-World trinity of natural rights was altered: life, liberty, and property became life, liberty, and opportunity. The first American Bill of Rights phrased it as "life and liberty, with the means

51

of acquiring and possessing property, and pursuing and attaining happiness and safety." Thomas Jefferson condensed this into "the pursuit of happiness." On the frontier, the relation of work to reward was close enough to carry a moral significance, long preserved in the idea of America as the land of opportunity.

To successive waves of newcomers adopting this American style, the past was prologue. They were eager to put it behind them and get on with the action of the play. Without a common heritage, the common denominator of the new country came to be an agreed external norm—symbolic as well as material—known as the American standard of living. In attaining this norm, the newcomer became naturalized. Over the years, however, their unique geographical position enabled Americans to take their freedoms more and more for granted, and, with advancing industrialization, the nonmaterial values of opportunity became lost among the out-puts of the assembly line. From then on, into our own time, Americans progressively became hollow men, living external lives from which significance had departed. In an expanding world, surrounded by copious commodities, their hollowness did not show; but when they run into today's barriers, they crumple. Even in the domestic enclosures constituted by large institutions, inner emptiness has become progressively apparent: the organization man, the lonely crowd, the affable and the affluent.

The American dream can no longer be based on the values that went with the frontier. Component after component of the American way of the nineteenth and early twentieth centuries has vanished. The offer made in the verse engraved on the pedestal of the Statue of Liberty,

> . . . give me your tired, your poor,
> your huddled masses yearning to breathe free,

has become as much of a period piece as the Statue itself: immigration has been shut off for a generation. The great open spaces where yesterday's immigrants found free land are occupied. Racial discrimination clouds the promised opportunity for all. The worldwide image of the United States betrays these disappearances. And so does the domestic malaise of Americans not quite sure of who they are.

Until recently, moreover, the contrast between the American way and that of Communism provided several comforting comparisons: Russia has never had a democratic political revolution; Russia is a backward country; Russia lacks technological know-how.

Today, only the first of these contrasts stands. With a rate of economic growth consistently more rapid than that of the United States, Russia is fast catching up. In important sectors, Russian scientific capacities are greater than American. Americans who used to boast that in the United States everything was bigger and better now find themselves in the position of Texans since Alaska achieved statehood. The new (or newly realized) minority position of the United States in the world refers to geography, resources, population, race. At the turn of the century, the creation of a modern state covering half a continent was unique. Today, there is Russia, China, India, and the New Europe. The resources of these political units surpass those of the United States. In each one, the population is larger. In the family of man, the white race outnumbers only the red Indians.

These are startling facts, and they do much to explain the country's current state of shock. While the frontier lasted, the American way offered a common denominator to the varied nations of mankind and led Americans to assume that, since their society included people from all nations, their way was a normative standard, and the ways of other nations could be considered as incomplete fragments of that standard.

The generation on the way out are singularly ill-equipped to shift over from the world that is gone to the world of current reality and to find a sense of direction again. They may have run up tens of thousands of miles of air travel, but most of them have seen the rest of the world only from the outside. Their lives have been intensely local, and in their localities they have believed that the customer is always right, not one, but all the customers—do they not refer to the latter as the influentials? In a political context, they have believed that the constituent is always right, not one, but all the constituents, especially in an election year. In the university, they have believed that the alumni, the dean, the department heads are always right. They may summon the power of positive thinking, but the power of positive decision is beyond them. They exemplify what men below them on the ladder say: "Who, me? I just work here."

The new American style must be sought, not among these aging fat cats, but among their sons. They are the cool cats, and they are of a different breed. To their fathers, conformity was an end pursued consciously, avidly, and with a certain amount of painfully obvious trial and error; to them, having grown up knowing to what

53

to conform, conformity is a reflex; they have quite naturally bought the right clothes (dark of color, conservative of cut), owned the right cars, gone to the right universities, used the right credit cards at the right night spots, married suitable girls, and enhanced the population explosion in the right suburbs.

The cool cats are wary. They show what they think, sparingly; what they feel, never. They listen. They are tide-watchers. When they were children, many of their parents snatched a living from the flotsam and jetsam of the shore; but their sons are accomplished navigators; they launch themselves on the flood, and keep dry doing so. Behind their poker faces is a will to arrive, and a skill as well, but it is based on timing rather than on substance, on being agreeably if unobtrusively present, competent when asked to do a piece of work, available when something further is needed. They are neither beat nor off-beat.

Besides these differences between a generation that made its way up and a generation whose conscious experience began in comfort after the family had arrived, there is a further difference that is of great moment to Americans. The cool cats are fascinated by ideas. They are cautious about admitting an idea as being their own; they take readily to brainstorming and gamesmanship, for in such sessions everyone knows that tossing out novel proposals is merely good clean sport. But the cool cats are well informed. The paperback companies are discovering with pleasure and profit that supplying the fat-cat market with Westerns and whodunnits is not the only sound basis for large sales. From classics to contemporary commentary, the cool cats read, and read understandingly. They know the score, but they prefer not to be involved in the scoring. They are the American neutralists.

If the country is not moving again at a rate anticipated in Kennedy's first year, it is because the fat cats don't understand their world and the cool cats want to keep out of it. Communication between the seasoned young intellectuals who have accepted Federal executive posts of responsibility and others of their generation across the country is not at all difficult in the area of reportage. The hard assignment is to communicate a sense of purpose and a commitment to that purpose in terms, not of words, but of acts. All the right words are available; but they are heard as truths without consequences.

It may be charged that within the administration itself there are too many executives whose past experience has been chiefly with words, whether in academic life, in foundations where the giving of a grant entails no responsibility for its execution, or in research facilities on projects whose application becomes someone else's business. To an extent the charge is true. But the reason why the intense activity of these executives (and no Washington administration has ever worked harder) does not communicate a sense of purpose is a reason that applies also to their fellow intellectuals who are not in government—the absence of an American style suitable to the times. The ranks of a democracy composed of neutralists, though crammed with bodies, form a hollow square. The malaise of a lack of commitment, like an engine running but not in gear, is what has baffled the country in the early part of the Kennedy administration.

How quickly can America find a style in which she feels herself as sure as in the days of the great open spaces—a style, moreover, that will be recognized with equal clarity by the world at large? It is anybody's guess. Yet there is new evidence that a considerable number of Americans are experiencing a renaissance. This rebirth is taking place in an unexpected area. For a long time —initially because of Puritan disapproval, subsequently because of an economic hurly-burly centered in materially useful things—the arts had a thin time in America. The he-men scorned them; the matriarchs took them up as one aspect of their control over consumption and display. Now in mid-century, however, across America from coast to coast, new orchestras, new museums, new theatres appear, directed and financed by knowledgeable local boards. And many of their backers not only appreciate art but are themselves practitioners and encouragers of young practitioners. In painting, writing, playing musical instruments, they struggle with their chosen medium and give it form. True, some of these activities had their beginnings in therapy, and some (as has happened down the ages) in the *snobisme* of keeping up with the Joneses, after the Joneses, who have everything, acquire interests beyond the standard American standard. Yet for every art-collecting tycoon who becomes a check-writing device for a hired connoisseur, many have made it their business to find out what unhired connoisseurs find good.

Among cool cats, impeccably neutral though they may be during office hours, there now are many who not only know what the Western heritage comprises and what other cultures, old or contemporary, have created, but who have their own inwardly understood criteria and preferences. These they explain and defend with skill and even with feeling.

This is the end of the external standards of an earlier America, of norms accepted without question by newcomers merely because they found them present when, whether by immigration or by social advancement, they arrived. This is the beginning of a sense of form, of selection by an individual on his own terms, through the application of criteria which he not only understands but affirms as having significance. The underlying assumption of a society founded on norms is that uniformity and averageness are desirable; a society founded on form assumes the desirability of uniqueness and excellence.

The promise offered by the sudden quickening in the arts in America is pertinent to the achievement of a national sense of direction in economics and politics because such a change cannot be compartmentalized—a renaissance, a renascence, a rebirth, like birth itself, is of the whole man. The United States can never again offer a norm to the world. Only through the development of a style of its own, one deeply realized by its people, will it advance to the greatness suited to the present age.

JOHN CONWAY

Standards of Excellence

THE IDEA of the excellent is one shared by all civilizations; but the notions of what is the excellent, the best, vary over a wide range. In considering the concept of excellence in contemporary America the temptation is to take for granted certain cultural and philosophical presuppositions inherent in our society and to measure excellence solely in terms of them. This would be an error, for it would get us no nearer to an understanding of what constitutes our notion of the best. We would be discussing not excellence but skill. Excellence has to do with values and ideals rather than the expertness with which they are implemented. It is the *summum bonum* of any culture at a given time. For the civilization of the high middle ages it was sanctity and heroism. The saint and the knight were the ideal types against which the ordinary man measured his life and achievement. The abandonment of worldly success and material objects— or rather the attainment of a perspective which made such an abandonment the only rational course of action—has been common in various cultures at various times. The Emperor Charles V abdicated and entered a monastery. Racine retired from a brilliant career to prepare himself for death. Still today the Hindu merchant may leave his business and family for the begging bowl of the mendicant. What governs and in fact creates the idea of excellence in a society is its vision of reality, that which it considers to be true.

Now, what is our idea of excellence? What do we consider to be the highest good toward which all effort should in the end, at least ideally, direct itself? Certainly not sanctity. Certainly not withdrawal from the world. Nor is heroism in its classic sense the value we most esteem. And yet we do have, as we must, a concept of the highest that gives vitality and creativity to our culture. I would like to suggest two propositions. The first is that our concept of excellence emerges from distinctive American historical and social experiences colored and shaped by the secular and almost exclusively activist tone of the twentieth century world. Second, in this concept, as in so much else, we have been pioneers. What constitutes for us the idea of excellence is rapidly becoming the common property of all of Western European civilization, at least.

In order to ascertain the *summum bonum* of contemporary America, then, we must begin by examining those characteristics which are peculiar to this country and have therefore profoundly affected its system of values. Of these, it seems to me, the most important is the pluralistic nature of the society, a pluralism which is without an exact or even a close parallel in the world today. There is, to begin with, the pluralism inherent in the diverse geography of this half-continent. A potato farmer in Maine, a citrus grower in southern California, a cattle rancher in the southwest, a plantation owner in Mississippi, an industrial worker in Detroit or Chicago, all have much in common, and it is the purpose of this essay to find out, if possible, what general attitudes and beliefs can be shared by such diverse elements of the population. We can start by saying that if such a sharing did not exist the American Republic would not have been a viable political entity for as long as it has been. Still, the differences brought about by variations in climate, occupation, and physical environment are clear. These variations over a period of time affect values, because from place to place and from occupation to occupation the physical and emotional demands made by the environment vary. The life of a fruit-grower in the Sacramento Valley is, no doubt, rigorous. But the kind of rigor it imposes is different from that demanded of the Gloucester fisherman, who for his livelihood must sail in mid-winter to the Grand Banks. And both are different from the kind of discipline required of the New York business or professional man and his counterpart in Chicago or San Francisco. Instances of this fundamental economic, climatic, and environmental dissimilarity could be multiplied almost indefinitely. It is sufficient to point out that this is the first factor to be considered in any examination of our values respecting excellence and leadership.

A second aspect of American pluralism comes from the wide range of historical experience which has been responsible for creating the nation and its institutions. This is implicit in the theory of states rights. The New England legacy is different from that of the South. In the one case, a set of Puritan beliefs, now secularized, forms the basis of notions of excellence and concepts of leadership.

The westward movement spread these beliefs in a somewhat diluted form throughout the country. They are certainly the single most effective element in shaping the national outlook. "God hath sifted a whole nation," wrote one early colonist, "that he might send choice grain into the wilderness."[1] And another wrote, "We are as a city set upon a hill in the open view of all the earth, the eyes of the world are upon us, because we profess ourselves to be a people in covenant with God."[2]

The theme of mission and special selection remains strong in American history to the present day. The more aristocratic and Anglican tradition of Virginia and the Old South was of a different order. Although it was defeated in the Civil War, it continued alive and has been effective in shaping the distinctive outlook of the Southwest. It is worth noting in this connection that the roster of distinguished American generals contains few New England, many Southern and Southwestern names. Military achievement as a value in itself is alien to the commercial and literary culture formed in New England and disseminated across the Northern States. It was, and remains, however, a natural product of the agricultural and aristocratic society of Virginia and that part of the United States colonized by the South. New England and the old South, these are the two fundamental forces that have created and shaped American values. Originally, they were in large part the result of migration from Europe because of religious persecution in England. The passage of time and the success of the North American venture removed from the descendants of the original settlers the psychology of persecution. The American Revolution and the establishment of the Republic transformed the opinions of a minority group into an affirmative political philosophy with universal aspirations.

The agreement between New England and Virginia was not long-lasting. Economic and ideological factors, the tension between the industrial North and the agricultural South, with the accompanying problem of slavery ended the harmony that had permitted the creation of the Republic. The victory of the North however did not mean the destruction of Southern values. By reason of nostalgia and migration through the Southwest they remained strong. At the close of the Civil War, characteristic American attitudes can be said still to have been, although modified by time and circumstance, those of the two groups that had first come to these shores. The pluralism was distinct but simple.

The flood of European immigration which now began and con-

tinued in ever-increasing numbers until the outbreak of World War
I introduced a new dimension to the problem of historical pluralism
and rapidly put an end to the basic simplicity of the American outlook. Irish, Italians, Jews, Germans, Slavs, Scandinavians, Armenians
arrived in their millions, each group bringing its own set of values
and its own national or racial memory. That memory was rarely very
similar to the historical experience of the early dominant groups,
Anglo-Saxon, Protestant Christian, Puritan or Anglican. Since nine-
teenth- and early twentieth-century migration was a response to a
labor shortage in the industrialized North, the problem of confront-
ing these different cultural groups and effecting some sort of recon-
ciliation between their beliefs and mores and those of traditional
America fell to New England and that part of the country influenced
by it. The agricultural South was left relatively untouched by this
phenomenon, and its point of view therefore remained uninfluenced
by the impact of alien attitudes. It is interesting, however, to note
that adjustment to the newcomers was made more easily by Anglican New York than by Puritan Boston and the adjoining mill towns.
New York produced an Al Smith at about the same time that Boston
was producing a James Curley.

The idea of the elect, even though by the late nineteenth century it expressed itself in terms of commercial success and literary
culture rather than religiously, could not easily be extended to the
illiterate or semiliterate newcomers with their foreign customs and
their often violent and exuberant temperaments. The immigrants
from northern continental Europe were absorbed most easily, for
they were usually Protestant and agricultural. Their transition from
the old world to the new took place in areas remote from the large
urban centers. The assimilation of these newcomers into the two
dominant old groups is not yet complete. Two forces have acted as
obstacles, although not necessarily insuperable obstacles, to such
assimilation. First, the original groups themselves by no means spon-
taneously embraced the new Americans; on the contrary, for a long
time they excluded them. Second, the newcomers in many instances
were reluctant to give up their own racial and historical traits even if
such a surrender would buy them a place in the old established order. In a situation of such complexity the problem of leadership was
not easily soluble.

The third aspect of American pluralism that bears upon this question arises from the religious differences which are the result of a
century of immigration. It is customary to speak of the country re-

ligiously as consisting of Protestant, Catholic, and Jew, a satisfactory method of classification up to a point, although it contains a considerable oversimplification, since these categories have probably at least as much to do with ethnic and historical patterns as with real religious convictions. This classification, moreover, has several shortcomings. It ignores the many who are passively or actively agnostic. It also ignores the diversity contained within Protestantism. The eastern Episcopalian, the southern Baptist, the mid-western Methodist, the Mormon, the Christian Scientist, the New England Congregationalist, the Unitarian, the member of one of the many splinter sects, cannot easily be grouped together theologically except in the negative and not very helpful sense that they are all non-Roman Catholic. The classification in addition suggests the dubious assumption that the members of the various communions are active and committed rather than merely formal subscribers to their creeds.

Nevertheless, with these reservations in mind, the usual way of describing the country's religious diversity serves a useful purpose. And this religious diversity is of great importance. It has to do not only or mainly with a method of worship. Theoretically, it is concerned with differing concepts of the nature and destiny of man, and therefore with notions of social justice, of the national purpose, and even of the foreign policy of the country. To what extent this theoretical position is related to actuality will be discussed in a further paragraph.

The final element of American pluralism comes from the eighteen million Negro citizens, whose origins and historical memory are very different from those of the majority. This central fact of American history and politics is too well known to require any further comment or emphasis.

Now, it should be realized that this pluralism is unique to America in two respects. First in its multiplicity, second in the fact that it occurs within a setting of a democratic and egalitarian political and social philosophy. The Soviet Union has an equally dramatic contrast of climate and geography, but it has no effective religious diversity and no democratic conviction. Religion is barely tolerated and is hardly a factor in the political calculations of the Soviet rulers. Values are set by the Marxist orthodoxy and are inculcated uniformly throughout the schools and the universities.

Great Britain has a fairly broad range of religious diversity, very broad indeed if the Commonwealth and what remains of the old Empire are included in such a consideration; and it has long experience in dealing with nonwhite peoples. But, however democratic in a political sense Great Britain has become as a result of the changes which culminated in the introduction of the welfare state by the Labour Party, socially there has been little departure from historic forms. The fact that the Crown is, at law, the Sovereign continues an ancient political perspective in which the American variety of democratic faith has, despite the protests of the angry young men, no place. The British world is still hierarchically organized. More than that, there seems to be no evidence that the great majority of the British people wish it otherwise. The failure of as gifted and committed a man as Aneurin Bevan to communicate successfully his own passionate egalitarianism even to his own party would seem to indicate that Great Britain, in the decline of her world power, intends to keep those values which were the accompaniment of her greatness. Politics will remain the highest profession. The gentleman will be the leader even when that leadership is called upon to produce an economic revolution which seems to threaten the foundations of the idea of the gentleman. The Established Church with the monarch at its head will continue to provide a formal public philosophy by which standards of excellence will be set and to which public men must, even if only negatively, adhere.

France has experienced religious disagreement of a bitterness which has hardly existed here; and as a legacy from the Revolution, a political disagreement which has not yet been entirely healed. Yet all Frenchmen share the same history and form a unified culture. Indeed, a vivid awareness of the *mission civilatrice* unites clerical and anticlerical, authoritarian and radical democrat. The French pyramidical school system with the universities and the École Normale at the apex is evidence of at least one agreement among the many divergent elements in the country, that is, that leadership shall come from the most gifted members of a highly educated and cultivated group which, by definition, must be a minority, steeped in the faith in France's unequaled cultural greatness. The persistent Jacobinism in French political sentiment has yet to produce a working-class political leader for a working-class cause. French academic categories are scarcely less exclusive in their way than British class categories.

This cultural and historical unity, seen perhaps at its strongest in France, is common to the rest of non-Marxist Europe. Beneath differences in politics and religion, there is a common agreement about Germany, about Italy, about Denmark or Norway or Sweden. There is a consistent image of what the country was and is, a commonly shared notion of the qualifications for leadership, an almost equally well-defined concept of what constitutes excellence. All European countries, excepting Great Britain, have experienced the forcible imposition of alien values by invasion and conquest. These experiences have been temporary and have served in the long run only to define more fully the national image and the national values. The wars between Germany and France are the classical example. It is only the American democracy which, by reason of its own definition of itself, has had to receive and welcome, at least as a nation, large numbers of people from cultures alien to its own. In this sense, the United States has been and to a certain extent still is a process, and it has been required to produce concepts previously derived only from settled cultures. It is not surprising that this has been a difficult task.

It is, then, in relation to this pluralism that American ideas of excellence and leadership have been developed. And yet the use of the word "pluralism" can be deceptive, for, although the United States has a pluralist problem, it is not a pluralist country. Canada is. The old Austro-Hungarian Empire was. Canada has two languages by law. Either language can be used in Parliament. Official publications must be in both. A citizen can plead in either language in the higher courts. The country exists as a political fact by reason of the acceptance of two cultures, two languages, two religions. The Austro-Hungarian Empire rested on a like basis of accepted and legalized multiplicity. The British Commonwealth and Empire in a somewhat similar way dealt with the problem of diversity. It has been otherwise with the United States. Originally, it can probably be said that federalism represented a cultural as well as a legal concept. But the Civil War put an end to this, and the immigration of the latter part of the century introduced complications which were resolved in a distinctive fashion by the political beliefs on which the Republic rested. The American democracy, without any question, contains a substantial Rousseauistic component, as does any system which contains the concept of the sovereign people. This being so, there is present the idea of the general will, which presupposes a cultural and ethnic homogeneity, if not now, then ideally in the future. At any rate, such an idea cannot easily tolerate really fundamental diversities of value and outlook and belief in the entity known as the sovereign people. The pressures, therefore, have been toward dissolving the differences between the groups in the interests of achieving a higher synthesis in which all, discarding their original characteristics, can participate. It is this higher synthesis that, I think, has produced and is producing American conceptions of excellence and leadership.

Does such a synthesis involve a religious similarity as well? This is a difficult question. On the one hand, we have the unchallenged doctrine of religious toleration. On the other, we have, perhaps, its irrelevance, at least at the moment: its irrelevance in the sense that there seems to be a doctrine, more than simply political, to which all Americans subscribe. President Kennedy's anxiety during the campaign to delimit very carefully the area in which his own religious convictions would operate seems to point to the existence of a generally held socio-political creed, with, in the anthropological sense, some religious overtones. The logical end of Rousseauism is a civic religion. Rousseauist democracy is, however, only part of the American political legacy, and this point should not be pushed too far. It does, however, help to explain why the thirty-five million Roman Catholics in the country have failed so far to produce a distinctive culture or even to maintain in their institutions what might be called a Catholic cultural, as against a Catholic spiritual, atmosphere.

The same considerations apply to the other religious groups in the nation. Whatever American civilization may be, it cannot be described with any accuracy as pluralist or, in the traditional sense of the word, religious. The many faiths that are represented in the country are the private concern of the citizen. They do not, except in a most general sense, shape the national values. They are negative, not positive, forces; that is to say, they prevent or attempt to prevent public acts that would be detrimental to their beliefs and interests. They do not and, in the nature of things, cannot attempt to define the direction in which the country is going and the principles that should govern its conduct. This function is performed by a monistic set of propositions which, since they cannot be defended by strictly rational methods, as Joseph Schumpeter was fond of pointing out, must be described as a faith. The real religious tension in the country is not between Catholic and Protestant or between various Protestant groups; it is between the traditional faiths on the one hand and the new democratic and secularist humanism on the other. A gifted young graduate student in describing his meeting with young people in the Middle East and in Africa wrote recently: "They, or may I say we, are idealists and materialists, secularists yet men of faith. Our faith is in the power of man, and from this faith surges a conviction that the future holds more joy and less suffering, more prosperity and less privation, more self-respect and less indignity than the past."[3] It is this kind of emergent belief put usually into the context of political democracy that is becoming, I would suggest, generally prevalent and subsumes into itself what can be termed the particularist beliefs which are often so influential in the private life of the citizen.

The foregoing comments will be interpreted as strictures only by those who like to believe in a perfect world or by those who prefer to ignore problems. Given the premises of the American democracy and the difficulties which have confronted it in the past century, the monistic outcome was probably unavoidable. Whether it has been desirable is another question. In any case, it is with us, and it defines public as distinct from private notions of excellence.

I think that the concept of excellence which we have developed under these circumstances can best be described as Nietzschean, because Nietzsche's thought and teaching come closest to explaining it and giving to it some sort of philosophical foundation. I need hardly say that this has nothing to do with the superman or theories of racial supremacy or any of the other doctrines that are commonly and often incorrectly attributed to Nietzsche. I mean that, in the absence of a commonly shared religious faith in the old sense, we have substituted, on the highest levels of our interpretation of human experience, an aesthetic for an ethical standard. We evaluate and judge a man not on the basis of his moral life—how can we with so many differing ideas of what the correct moral life is?—but instead on the basis of his gifts and the skill and integrity with which those gifts are realized. We judge him on the completeness and line of the trajectory of his performance. This does not by any means exclude moral considerations. On the contrary. They are an important component but they have meaning only in so far as they affect the aesthetic totality. They are not primary. They derive their validity from their relation to the pattern of performance as a whole. The poor lawyer has no excellence either because he has no talent or because he has failed to fulfill it. The brilliant dishonest lawyer fails in excellence because his performance constitutes an aesthetic affront. He does not present that harmony and unity and single-minded intellectual drive which his duty to his talent demands and merits. The observer experiences, not a moral shock in the old sense, but the shock, to borrow a particularly apt English expression, of bad form.

This subtle but profound shift in emphasis is probably best illustrated in the area of sexual mores. The impact of Freud's teachings has thrown our inherited convictions about sexual morality into confusion, with the result that, as a society, we have certainly no common belief about what is right or wrong in sexual matters. In the absence of belief about this and other moral concerns, we seek about for and have found another standard by which to judge people and their actions. Let me hasten to add that in my view this new standard is demanding. I am not suggesting a decline of the West or a collapse of our civilization. I do argue, however, that this change in fundamental standards has taken place. Private standards which continue the old traditional beliefs remain very strong. However, what is important is that they operate not in a congenial but in a neutral or hostile public atmosphere. More and more the law (as is evidenced by the decision here and in England to allow the publication of *Lady Chatterley's Lover*) reconciles itself with what, for lack of a better word, must be called an aesthetic standard of justification. We no longer agree about the good man and what to expect from him. We do, however, agree about the gifted man and what to expect from him. And this has become our point of departure. It explains our competitiveness and our achievements as well as our conformism and a good many of our neuroses.

What is most admired then, what constitutes our concept of excellence, is talent and its triumphant fulfillment. The kind of talent admired varies from level to level of literacy and cultivation. All levels have in common the concept of fulfillment, that is, success. The talent admired may be athletic (this runs through the whole range of our society) or literary or scholarly or artistic. It may be the capacity to compose music or play or conduct it or to write a novel or a poem or a distinguished work of scholarship. It may be the gift of the scientist or the doctor or the lawyer, or it may be the simple gift for making money. The point is that in a certain sense all these objects of admiration are the same. They do not differ philosophically. The difference comes from the varying levels of education in the society and the varying temperaments of individuals. They are all material goals. They should all be achieved; that is, the practitioner should be successful in what he sets out to do. They are all activist, for our view of excellence makes impossible a true concept of leisure in our society. The preoccupation of the American world with athletics is significant because this activity presents in its purest and most abstract form a skill and its simple realization. The game is the type of all talent, an example of the commonly held notion of excellence which can be appreciated by everybody, irrespective of education or background or individual gifts. It is an allegory of the way we live and the values we live by. The measure of its force and centrality in the American view of things is its wholehearted and uncritical adoption by religiously based schools and colleges.

Our universities and the rest of our educational system foster, strengthen, interpret, and teach this concept of excellence, and in this respect the greatest university is exactly like the least. It is useless to contrast the football preoccupation and thoughtless anti-intellectualism at a state university with what Sir Charles Snow has called "the splendour" of Harvard, if by contrasting them we mean that they are in some real sense different. They are not. Their objectives are the same. The only difference is the accidental one of resources, faculty, level of cultivation of the community, the quality of the student body, and the power of the university tradition to impose its values on young people. But all are trying to do the same thing. Our best universities do it extremely well. Other institutions less well.

What is this common concern? It is probably best stated in Matthew Arnold's definition of criticism: "*A disinterested endeavour to learn and propagate the best that is known and thought in the world.*"[4] This eclectic endeavor involves primarily an aesthetic criterion, although here again the word "best" introduces ancillary moral considerations. But only ancillary. Taste, in the highest and most vigorous sense of that word, is what dominates. This being so, undergraduate studies at good colleges tend to have a strong literary bias, for it is in literature that the best, not only in poetry, the novel and the drama, but in history, political theory, and philosophy (in the old-fashioned sense of that word) is to be found. Literature, an art form, teaches the great lessons, philosophy now being preoccupied with the task of finding out whether the words used in this or any other essay mean anything. Science we leave to those undergraduates who happen to be gifted in these special areas, not because we are opposed to science—our scholarly methods derive from it—but because the drive of our educational system is necessarily elitist. To each man the scholarly discipline most suited to his talents. Snow's well-known thesis about the two cultures has much less applicability here than in England. In England the idea of leisure, St. Thomas' teaching that the end of action is contemplation, has still considerable vitality and is, I suppose, bound to come into conflict with scientific pragmatism. With us the victory of the scientific point of view has been if anything too complete.

We have developed a rubric to correspond with our idea of education. It is explained, I think, by two factors: our deep distrust of traditional dogmas and the sense of mission which has been a continuing characteristic of American belief. We therefore pursue a rather selective course through the history and culture of the past two or three thousand years. We are at home with the Greeks, not only or perhaps even mainly because of the magnificence of their achievement, but because they were sceptical and because they conceived of *arete*, which is certainly closer to our own idea of excellence than anything that has appeared since. We are at home with the Romans because of their laws and because they produced the classic example of a Republic, although we are repelled by their harshness and brutality. We are ill at ease with the ages of faith because they were dogmatic and contemplative, and we therefore wend our way in a rather gingerly fashion through the foundations of European civilization until we emerge, considerably relieved, at the Renaissance and the Reformation.

From there on the going is fairly easy. The Puritan Revolt, the frustrated aspirations of the Levellers, Locke, the Enlightenment, the American and French Revolutions, John Stuart Mill, Karl Marx and ourselves—the whole buttressed by the great body of English literature. Continental literatures, as far as education (as distinct from scholarship) is concerned, are for the accidental or deliberate specialist. The educational achievement at our best colleges—and one can only judge any system fairly by its best—has been splendid. Snow chose the right word. It has reintroduced *arete* as a standard of excellence, a standard around which all the multitudinous variations of the American world at their most intelligent can rally, for it is above and beyond them all. It has provided a value system that is almost transcendent.

It has also solved the difficult problem of leadership. The problem of leadership was difficult for a good many reasons. In the first place, the American political philosophy, emerging as it does in part from the teachings of John Locke, contains a negative rather than a positive view of government. Society, politically and economically, is, or rather was, supposed to run itself, government being set up only to remedy the slight defects in the state of nature. Ideally, the President was to emerge from his proper role as private citizen to preside for four years over a government that had minimal powers because it had minimal needs. After having discharged this civic responsibility, like Cato he was expected to return to the ordinary and proper concerns of the citizen. Sovereignty was not vested with mystery, with ceremony, with a semisacramental significance.

Second, the problem of leadership in an acute sense is of recent origin in the United States. In the first century and a half of its existence the Republic was faced with only two crises of a profoundly dangerous nature, the war for independence and the war between the states. At other times it mattered little in the long run whether Millard Fillmore or Chester Arthur or Grover Cleveland was in the White House. Given the American political and social philosophy the country, for better or worse, ran itself. Even World War I called for an academic rather than a real leadership. American participation was relatively slight, and Woodrow Wilson's assumption of a dominant role in the peace negotiations reflected his own personality and his own private philosophy rather than American needs or American convictions, as the electorate was soon to make clear. As late as the nineteen-twenties, Calvin Coolidge with more time on his hands than he knew what to do with was in many respects the ideal President. Thus there was a coincidence between what Americans believed to be the proper role of the President and what the situation required. It is perhaps not going too far to say that the people neither wanted nor believed in political leadership in the sense in which the term was defined and accepted in Europe. Theodore Roosevelt's assertion of American power was, as with Wilson, an aspect of his own character and private faith, the whim of a colorful and gifted man which an indulgent and confident public tolerated and enjoyed all the more readily since jingo imperialism had to a slight extent affected the Jeffersonian idyll at the heart of the national life.

Third, mass immigration introduced a new complication into the problem. This complication is best illustrated by an incident in the life of Edward Sheldon. Sheldon, in 1924, proposed to Edith Wharton that he should write a dramatized version of *The Age of Innocence*. Mrs. Wharton at first was most interested. She was less interested when she learned about the changes Sheldon proposed to introduce into the story. The central character, Newland Archer, in the novel a characteristic young man-about-town of excellent background and connections, in the play was to be a young political reformer with a taste for adventure.

Both Mrs. Wharton and her sister-in-law Mrs. Cadwalader Jones were shocked at the idea. Mrs. Barnes, who has discussed the changes with Mrs. Jones, acting as proxy for the remote Mrs. Wharton, wrote to Sheldon: Mrs. Jones and Mrs. Wharton feel absolutely with the van der Luydens [characters in the play] that a genteel young man would not dabble in politics. She [Mrs. Jones] said "Edith thought he would not have been so vulgar" meaning so vulgar as to have fought Tweed. And they also thought it would have been a bit common to join up with Custer to fight Indians. They feel a U. S. Senator is "very distinguished" so the political career can be left in—just the mud and sweat toned down a bit.[5]

Such a view of leadership would be inconceivable in Europe. But then Europe had no immigrants. The educated classes on the east coast of America were dismayed at the problems which the immigrants had introduced into what had been a fairly well understood and cohesive society, and since the new Americans were almost always alien in customs, values, religion and even language, one understandable reaction by the elite was to withdraw from a situation in which leadership seemed to be impossible. This reaction has by no means entirely disappeared. There was another reaction however and Sheldon may have had a better understanding of his time than the intelligent expatriate New Yorker. The Puritan sense of responsibility remained vigorous. As Edith Wharton said, "A U. S. Senator is very distinguished," and there were always plenty of candidates for such honorific posts from the old groups. But withdrawal was by no means as universal as Mrs. Wharton's gentility led her to believe. Impelled by the rigors of Andover and the optimism of Yale as well as by his own Calvinist sense of duty, the young Henry Stimson threw himself into New York politics. Endicott Peabody's Groton prepared Franklin Roosevelt for a career of public service. C. C. Burlingham organized the New York reform league. Wilson and Taft were fully prepared to enter the maelstrom of politics. I would argue, however, that this was not leadership in the true sense, although it kept the idea of leadership and public service very much alive. It is significant that Sheldon thought of his character as a young reformer. Stimson, Roosevelt, Wilson, Taft, and Burlingham were reformers. Leadership in the true sense does not come about until the situation to be reformed has in fact been corrected, for the notion of leadership can only be based upon some approximation of unity. There has to be a good degree of identity between the leader and the led.

This unity is a development of the past thirty years, and it is still precarious. Its setting has been the social and technological changes which have taken place since the end of World War I. Ease of transportation and communication has minimized the parochialism imposed by the diverse geography of the country. The American passion for education has resulted in more and more Americans receiving a college education and therefore sharing in the common set of values. The New Deal summed up and put into a political philosophy the efforts of the reformers at the turn of the century. It seems unlikely that this philosophy will ever be discarded, for it has become the platform not only of the Democrat but of any Republican who hopes to lead the country.

Very importantly, the tide of immigration has ebbed. The grandson of the Sicilian peasant, if he is able enough, goes to a good college and then to a professional school. The exclusiveness of the older universities has broken down as the new idea of excellence has grown and taken strength. President Conant's policy of National Scholarships has radically changed the character of the Harvard student body, and there is no good university that does not aspire to be representative of all parts of America and all elements of American life. These diverse and largely unrelated potentialities for unity have been synthesized by the two great crises of the age: the economic crisis of the great depression that threatened the economic well-being of every class and group; and the international political crisis that threatened and continues to threaten the physical existence of the country. America has become what she never was before and never intended to be, the legatee and leader of Western civilization. A unity more accidental than planned has allowed a new concept of leadership to appear. It is, as might be expected, closely related to the dominant idea of excellence.

The fact that a change was taking place was obscured first by the brilliant charismatic personality of Franklin Roosevelt, by the despondency and alarm in the country which permitted and required him to assume a role and powers at variance with the historic idea of the presidency, by the involvement of the country in the preliminaries of World War II and then by the war itself, and by the assumption that there was somewhere a normality to return to. It was obscured further by the optimism which attended the immediate postwar period and the success of the Marshall Plan, as well as by the reassuring homespun quality of Mr. Truman. General Eisenhower, presiding over a period of great prosperity, seemed to embody the normality which the citizen always hoped would appear once again. He returned to the classic image of the presidency. That was part of his popular strength, and, at the same time, the greatest weakness of his administration. The recent election has produced for the first time the new concept of leadership as it has been grasped and defined by the able young men who surround President Kennedy and by the President himself. The great majority of these men have been educated and shaped during the 'thirties and 'forties. The pre-1914 world has had little influence in forming their political values and convictions. Presumably, that is why among other reasons it never occurred to General Eisenhower to make use of them.

The new idea of leadership is strongly conditioned by the pluralist problem and by the dominant idea of excellence. Canada can have as Prime Minister a St. Laurent or a Mackenzie King, the one campaigning unambiguously as a French Catholic, the other as a Presbyterian Anglo-Scot, each expecting and obtaining majority support in the other ethnic, religious, and cultural group. This cannot happen in the United States, for the Rousseauistic assumption of homogeneity requires a neutral image which reflects likeness rather than difference. President Kennedy is not identifiable with a particular group as Al Smith was. In appearance and speech and in his approach to problems, he might be any one of a number of highly trained men who have received their education at an eastern preparatory school and at one of the major universities. If there is any flaw in his neutrality, it is not that he represents Catholicism and bases his social or political philosophy on papal encyclicals, but that he might alienate the mid-West by an over reliance on university faculties for his advisers. His administration might seem to be too closely tied to the eastern elite. Franklin Roosevelt had Cordell Hull and Harold Ickes and Frances Perkins to keep his cabinet representative of various national types.

The neutral image which reflects likeness, however, must be the highest common factor, the expression of the idea of excellence. It must demonstrate skill and intelligence of a high order. On reflection, it should cause no surprise that the President should have drawn so heavily on the universities for assistants. They provide the expertness that is needed to deal with the complications of contemporary foreign and domestic affairs. But, in addition to this practical consideration, the universities—alone in the country—are where the orthodoxy of public values by which the country lives is defined and stated. They may be the subject of derisive epithets like "egg-head," but this criticism is as much the acceptance of the orthodoxy as it is an attack upon it—rather like the anti-clericalism of the middle ages. It is in the secular universities and schools that the civic religion is being shaped and taught. That the President's enormous subventions for education are to be directed exclusively toward them should reassure anyone who doubts the existence of a higher doctrine, well-established and safe from the encroachments of traditional faiths.

Governments in the Western tradition have always drawn heavily on the clergy of the Establishment for advice and assistance. The sociological pattern remains the same, even in the American democracy. Only the innocence that was part of our isolation allowed us to believe for a long time that an Establishment could be permanently avoided; or, to put it in the language we like so much, that Church and State could be permanently separated.

I would like to make two further comments about this problem of political leadership. First, the neutrality with respect to the country's diversities has tended to emphasize what might be called the mythic aspect of the Presidency. The President, as classically conceived, emerged from one of the two original groups of which the country consisted. In becoming President he did not cease to be part of that group; he was identified with it. Jefferson was as characteristic and avowedly a Virginian as John Quincy Adams was a New Englander. This valuable element of realism has been largely dissipated by the need to construct a separate, dispassionate, and somewhat inhuman world in which the President must, politically, live. He is cut off from his roots and exists in a category by himself. Second, the President is both monarch and Prime Minister; that is to say, he bears the weight of both symbolic and executive authority. The British monarch is the expression of the traditions and greatness and achievements of her realm and thus has great emotional power. She has very little executive power. On the other hand, the Prime Minister has executive power but no symbolic role. Until the crises of the twentieth century broke in upon the great American peace, there was no need for such a symbolic figure; as we have seen, there was little enough need for the executive figure. But increasingly since 1929 there has been a need, familiar to old countries, for the rallying point toward which the emotions of a troubled people could be directed. A distinguished American journalist, writing in 1956, referred to the Presidency as "the most august position in the world."[6] The choice of the adjective is interesting for it introduces a new attribute of the Presidency—a certain measure of controlled Caesarism.

This unplanned, unintended but inevitable augmentation in the idea of the Presidency leads us to the heart of the problem of political leadership in the country today. The answer is easy to state; difficult, perhaps, to implement. It is simply that we must learn to accept the idea of leadership itself, as we never have before excepting in a time of crisis, as a permanent part of our political philosophy. So long as the main function of the President was to preside over an isolated, expanding, and prosperous society, protected internationally by the British navy, he was an administrator rather than a leader. The most that could be expected from him, the most that was wanted from him, was an imaginative insight into the society of which he was—the nomenclature is significant—the Chief Executive. The answer had been arrived at, and it was his task to execute it. But we no longer live with the eighteenth-century problem or with the nineteenth-century problem that can be taken care of by the eighteenth-century formula. We live with the unprecedented problems of the twentieth century, which can be solved only by as creative a vision as that which brought the Republic into being.

Such a vision is the product of one man or a few men, not of masses of men. It is in this sense that we must, with all due caution, accept the necessity of leadership. An executive, even a Chief Executive, is not a leader. A leader is a man who is leading a people to a preconceived goal which he, and not always they, can see. Thus it was with Washington and Lincoln and Franklin Roosevelt. It is infinitely more important today that someone should envisage the desirable world of two generations hence and lead the nation, through constitutional means, toward that world. This means a serious modification in our habits of political thought and, in particular, in that habit of thought that considers the politician primarily as the representative and spokesman for the wishes of the electorate. This change, however, is not as radical as it might at first seem; it means only to concede that there is more wisdom in Edmund Burke's letter to his electors at Bristol than democratic individualism has been accustomed to allow; that Paine's political outlook, satisfactory enough in many ways for his own time, no longer holds in its entirety when the dimension of world history is added to the American perspective.

True, there are dangers to this position, but they are surely minimized by American law and history. And in any event we live in an age in which we have only a choice of risks, not a choice of certainties. It seems unlikely that such a concession to the principle of leadership would lead to the establishment of a dictatorship in this country. The far greater danger lies in the fact that if we do not realize that creative action is necessary and that creative action is indissolubly allied with this concept of and acceptance of leadership, the power to mold the future will pass from our hands into those of men and nations who have solved the problem of leadership once and for all by the simple and brutal device of destroying freedom.

REFERENCES

1. Perry G. E. Miller and Thomas H. Johnson, *The Puritans*. New York: American Book Company, 1938, p. 246.

2. *Ibid.*, p. 198.

3. Unpublished letter from Robert Socolow to the Dean of Harvard College, dated 1 July 1960.

4. Matthew Arnold, *Essays in Criticism*, 1st series. New York: Macmillan and Company, 1898, p. 38.

5. Eric Wollencott Barnes, *The Man Who Lived Twice*. New York: Charles Scribner's Sons, 1956, p. 154.

6. Richard H. Rovere, "Letters from San Francisco," *The New Yorker*, 1 September 1956, p. 44.

D. WILFRED ABSE and LUCIE JESSNER

The Psychodynamic Aspects of Leadership

Introduction

IN 1932 Freud wrote:[1] "I have told you that psychoanalysis began as a therapeutic procedure, but it is not in that light that I wanted to recommend it to your interest, but because of the truths it contains, because of the information it gives us about that which is of the greatest importance to mankind, namely, his own nature, and because of the connections it has shown to exist between the most various of his activities."

Psychoanalytic investigation of emotional disturbances has led to the recognition of hidden unconscious motivations for human behavior in general and for its origin in early experiences. These findings also illuminate the motives of those who seek leadership and of those who seek a leader.

The human infant is at first completely dependent on his parents for survival. During this period grandiose images of the parents are formed. In these early images, the parents are endowed with omnipotence and omniscience, and the child gains strength by identifying with them. They become an integral part of himself, and he imitates their gestures and their sounds, thus participating in their power. In the further course of development, with increasingly discriminative perception of self and not-self, these earlier distorted images recede into the background, and the foreground is occupied by a more realistic perceptual appraisal of the parents. In pathological conditions, this corrective development is impeded. But for everyone there yet remains a longing to find again, or to be, a godlike personage, unlimited in power and wisdom.

To some degree the potential leader fulfills this wish. Thus the leader has to possess real or alleged superior qualities which the potential follower wants to possess. Certain attributes of the leader, such as having been born in a log cabin and having suffered hardships, facilitate identification with him and attenuate envy and rivalry.

The follower's wish for a changed self-image, one of greater strength, can be fulfilled only if the leader appears as an idealized *alter ego*, which then can become a part of the follower. In order to permit this idealization, a selectivity of perception is necessary, and this is often instigated and maintained by the leader's choice of self-revelation. Sometimes equally important is what he keeps secret about his own person.

Readiness for devotion to the leader is especially high when feelings of emptiness or discontent with drab trifles of daily living, or states of despair are prevalent. The relation of the follower to the leader may resemble infatuation, and like falling in love, this enriches life. Unlike falling in love, however, this interaction arouses feelings that are not consciously sexual; on the contrary, sexual aims are suspended, they are inhibited, as in the parent-child relation.

Freud[2] has shown that if several persons have set the same image as their ideal model, they consequently identify with one another and develop tender feelings toward one another. The first kind of identification with an ideal model leads to the second kind of identification with one another. This in turn is associated with affectionate feelings, while aggressive feelings are diverted away from the group so formed. But group formation depends on the initiative of a leader who is a suitable ideal model for many. It is also to be noted that in any social group, whether of animals or humans, adults or children, a hierarchy of dominance and status soon develops.[3, 4, 5, 6, 7]

In its most extreme form, even in caricature, one may say, the leader-follower relation exists in the rapport of hypnotist and subject. The cardinal event in the process is the thorough occupation of the subject's mind with the hypnotist. This *engourdissement d'esprit* results in a reduction of the span of consciousness, a selective, concentrated, and expectant attention devoted to the hypnotist and his behavior, and a simultaneous indifference to even massive excitations emanating from anyone else. The procedures for inducing this state of mind are basically appeals to *awe* and to *love*. In the first of these, matters of decisive importance are the social and professional prestige of the hypnotist, his imposing behavior and his self-assurance in issuing commands. In the second of these, a mild and friendly attitude, a low monotonous voice, and a restful atmosphere, including perhaps a darkened soundless room and soothing, light stroking, are important ingredients. Sándor Ferenczi[8] has shown the connections of the first method with the child's conception of the firm, infallible, and all-powerful father, whereas the second or "maternal" method is reminiscent of scenes in which a mother woos her child to sleep by singing lullabies. The "paternal" and "maternal" inductions may be mixed. Appeals to awe and love characterize the efforts of some leaders to fascinate their audience and to secure a following.

Since followers have dominance needs as well, C. A. Gibb[9] suggests that such satisfaction may come about vicariously through identification with the leader or with the total assertive group itself, or it may occur directly by virtue of the hierarchical organization of the group, which gives to almost every member both a submissive and a dominant role. As we have indicated, the leader is also the potential incarnation of the glorified, provident mother.[10] Moreover, he may also symbolize the son or daughter, who becomes what the follower aspired to be.

Character-Disorder and Leadership

Freud[11] has explained in *The Interpretation of Dreams* that "what we describe as character is based on the memory-traces of our impressions; and, moreover, the impressions which have had the greatest effect on us—those of our earliest youth—are precisely the ones which scarcely ever become conscious." These early impressions result in sustained patterns of behavior, patterns which are relatively stable and resist change. Certain character types[12, 13, 14] are expressed in behavior that is habitually intimidating or encouraging toward others.

Otto Fenichel[15] writes: "In general it can be stated that those who strive passionately for power and prestige are unconsciously frightened persons trying to overcome and to deny their anxiety." There is an especially marked trend in such persons to turn to activity in relation to others in order to avoid anxiety. Alternatively, and similarly, encouraging others may also be reassuring, and indicative of the kind of treatment the individual wishes for himself. The need to intimidate or encourage others stems in such cases from unconscious identification with a powerful aggressor or an omnipotent provider, originally the early parent imagoes. In character disorder of this kind, external power is sought as a means of protection against inner dependence and passivity, which, should they reach consciousness, would be frightening and detrimental to self-esteem. This kind of mastery of anxiety may become an all-consuming task for some leaders; in others the mastery of guilt feelings may become paramount. Such a leader may conduct a "moral" campaign against scapegoats, for instance, a minority group, on whom he projects his own "badness." The followers come to share this self-righteous attitude and gain a similar relief from their guilt feelings.

We have described these pathological types of character, because they have been and are dominant in authoritarian regimes. They constitute a menace for democratic societies, not only as a voracious threat from the outside. Their capacity to arouse and to sanction primitive drives, which are dormant in everyone and only painstakingly controlled by civilization, is a potential temptation also within a democratic state. Understanding these powerful figures who, to use a phrase of de Gaulle, "see and comprehend the world only through the distortion of their frenzy," can be a first step on the difficult road of speaking and dealing with them.

The Charismatic Leader

Infantile cravings and irrational motivations as such are not incompatible with leadership in a democracy; they may even indeed be an ingredient necessary for an appeal to deep longings. This is most obvious in the figure of the charismatic leader. His main weapon (and armor) is charm. His charm conveys not only his magic power but also his delicate need for love and protection. He yearns to be not only a man, but a woman at the same time; his inner balance is precarious because of the concurrence of active domineering and submissive seductive strivings. It is an eternal wish of mankind, expressed in the mythic idea that once man and woman were one. Darwin[16] describes how "in the great classes of the animal kingdom the males are ornamental with infinitely diversified appendages, and with the most brilliant or conspicuous colors, often arranged in elegant patterns, whilst the females are unadorned. . . . In almost every great class, a few anomalous cases occur, where there has been almost complete transposition of the characters proper to the two sexes; the females assuming characters which properly belong to the males."

It is evident that Man is one of the "anomalous cases" in which there has been an almost complete transposition of secondary ornamental characters to the female. However, both sexes have some of those bodily characteristics which Darwin shows are more generally possessed by the males of other species, and which are the biological basis of charm used in the service of sexual union. The biological basis of charm and the modes of mutual attraction, shared by bodily characters in the male and female of the human species, are relevant to the psychological characteristics of the charismatic leader. For he fascinates by a display of both male and female qualities, simultaneously or more often in more or less rapid alteration, just as in some hypnotic procedures.[17]

The charismatic leader needs his followers as much as the actor needs his audience. In this interdependence he maintains the cohesion of the group largely by keeping aggressiveness in suspense and by diverting it toward out-groups.[18]

Such irrational motives, as stated, do not exclude sound leadership in a democracy, if a sense of reality and devotion to social aims are superordinate. Some degree of personal insight can be a check on the intoxication of power. In Thornton Wilder's *Ides of March*[19] Julius Caesar writes about himself:

> Nothing seems to me to be more dangerous—not only for us rulers, but for those who gaze upon us with varying degrees of adoration—than this ascription of divine attributes. It is not difficult to understand that many persons will feel at times as though they were inflated by unusual powers or caught up into currents of some inexorable rightness. I had this feeling frequently when I was younger; I now shudder at it and with horror. How often I have had it thrown back at me, generally by flatterers, that I said to the timid boatman in the storm "Have no fear; you bear Caesar." What nonsense! I have had no more exemption from the ills of life than any other man.
>
> But that is not all. The history of nations shows how deeply rooted is our propensity to impute a more than human condition to those remarkable for gifts or to those merely situated in conspicuous position. I have little doubt that the demigods and even the Gods of antiquity are nothing more than ancestors about whom these venerations have been fostered. All this has been fruitful; it expands the imagination of the growing boy and it furnishes sanctions for good manners and public institutions. It must be outgrown, however—outgrown and discarded. Every man that has ever lived has been but a man and his achievements should be viewed as extensions of the human state, not interruptions in it.

Group Dynamics and Leadership

Evaluation of qualities of personality, including dominance needs in terms of character structure as we have briefly considered them here, is in isolation insufficient to command comprehension of a leader in action. Even a firm grasp of the social, economic and historical conditions which foreshadow particular group phenomena, though greatly assisting our understanding, by no means completes it. We need also to take into account more adequately the nature of group processes.

Some of the conspicuous features of more primitive and of more highly organized groups have been described, notably by Gustave Le Bon[20] and William McDougall,[21] and these features have been discussed and given richer meaning by Freud.[2] The intensification of emotion, the lack of emotional restraint, the incapacity for moderation and delay, and the tendency to rapid action, together with a collective inhibition of intelligence form an ensemble characteristic of rudimentarily organized groups. The more highly organized group, with a greater continuity of its existence, with traditions and customs, and with specialization and differentiation of the functions of its constituents, procures for the group precisely those features more characteristic of the individual. This congeries of features, varying especially with the degree and kind of organization of a group, has given rise to the concept of "group mind," about which there has been considerable though largely semantic dispute. Like other useful concepts, it can, of course, be abused; and, often enough, this has occurred by a kind of mystical elevation, which itself is related to the release in group phenomena of impulses and aspirations which remain repressed and unconscious in the individual.

In the more organized group, the "group mind" approaches a likeness to the mind of the leader, a likeness which is cast in the form of a magnified reflection of his characteristics, especially those expressed under the conditions of group excitement. Not only is there a spectrum along which groups may be placed according to the degree of organization, but in time a group may move along from one end of the spectrum to the other. Indeed, there may be many tentative group formations, even many misfires, until a group becomes well-established and later more organized. In the course of such events, there may be a change of leader. In *Moses and Monotheism*, Freud[22] attempted to reconstruct such a change, explaining it as a response to the group's regressive longing for an earlier belief in a Father-Image represented by the bloodthirsty demon-god Yahweh. The prophets later struggled to overcome this cruder

81

worship and to reinstate the nobler conceptions of the original Moses.

In a rudimentarily organized group, as for instance a mob, the individual is extraordinarily credulous; he thinks in images unchecked by considerations of reality, and the notion of impossibility recedes, together with doubt and uncertainty. There is a grossly exaggerated feeling of strength and unity as a temporary surge in a mob which easily dissolves. However, a leader may highly organize a group at this very primitive level and thus become more enduringly its primal father, taking upon himself his followers' individual responsibility and thus weakening the restraints of individual conscience. He may provide a new morality, a "parasitic superego," which demands as well as sanctions the acting out of dormant cruelties, the diminishing of guilt feelings and the fear of retribution. For example, Hitler in initiating brutal action kept repeating to his followers that he took full responsibility. Characteristically, Eichmann's main defense consisted in portraying himself as one who merely carried out orders. He confessed that he could never stand the sight of blood and therefore could not become a physician, while the execution of mass murder and atrocities did not ruffle him.

In contrast, the leader can heighten the moral strength of his followers, instead of attenuating it. Gandhi, with his insistence on independence, responsibility, and truth, is a supreme example of this kind of leadership.

In the group, the individual is indeed readily inclined to extremes. Moreover, in groups the most contradictory ideas can exist side by side, as is the case in the minds of primitive people and in the unconscious mental life of the more cultivated. In short, there is an unmistakable picture of regression of mental activity to those ways of thinking and being-in-the-world characteristic of childhood. It is evident that anyone who wants to assume the leadership of such a group need only rely upon this heightened suggestibility. He would thus avoid logical arguments, would instead paint concrete pictures in lively colors; he would exaggerate and repeat the same thing again and again.

In our own times, through modern technology, the level of organization which an essentially primitive group can achieve is quite unprecedented. Besides new means of communication, a leader has at his disposal experts in mass suggestion whose methods of diffusing the public image he favors can rapidly widen his influence. Our technological mastery is accompanied by competing ideologies which are readily both disseminated and assimilated, often in a simplified and distorted way. Because of the high degree of specialization and the complexity of modern science, the resources of adequate criticism are diminished.

Ideology and Disillusion

Literature both reflects and influences the spirit of the times. Within the brief compass of this article and in conformity with our clinical approach which first concerns itself with *dis-ease*, a conspicuous motif in current literature is of immediate interest. This occurs both in works of more or less overt political concern and in books which seem to ignore public affairs. John Strachey in "The Strangled Cry" [23] expertly concerns himself with this very motif as it is more explicitly revealed in the works of Arthur Koestler, Whittaker Chambers, and Boris Pasternak. He points out that these authors reveal not merely a reaction against the values of present-day Communism, but also a reaction against hundreds of years of burgeoning rationalism and empiricism. From our point of view, it seems that Communism and dialectical materialism, like many other ideologies of the modern era, already contain the germ of an escape from a genuinely scientific attitude into a system of certitude, which attempts to replace the crumbling foundations of medieval religion. In attempting this replacement, however, many of these ideologies, such as dialectical materialism and fascism, purvey a mystique which seeks to persuade that a scientific approach is incorporated within their particular systems of thought.* Strachey [23] writes,

> The desperation in these books is not put on: it is justified by the times and the predicaments of their authors. Moreover, what force the literature gains from the fact that it has been written by men who worked and fought in the great struggles of our time: by men who collided with events and were shattered by them, and then somehow or other, and to some extent, put themselves together again. "Only a participant can be a profound observer," said Trotsky.

In *Nineteen Eighty-Four*, George Orwell [24] depicts Communism as well as Fascism as patently irrational. Strachey [23] writes of this book, "The lesson of his book is *not* that the catastrophe which Com-

* We do not doubt that many of these ideologies also express valuable points of view: their "world-view" however, is vitiated by "half-truths" calculated to convince their converts, and quite removed from the fundamental openness of the scientific attitude.

83

munism has suffered proves that reason carried to its logical conclusion leads to horror; that consequently we must retreat from reason into some form of mysticism or supernaturalism. On the contrary, what Orwell is saying is that the catastrophe of our times occurred because the Communists (and, of course, still more the Fascists) deserted reason."

Within the scope of this essay, only this political facet of the process of disillusion can be briefly discussed. In the course of the vast socio-economic changes concomitant with technological advances and population growth, in the face of educational progress which results in large numbers of semiliterate individuals, in the reorientations to the world and the self to which scientific knowledge challenges those who are more literate, anomic conditions are created in the social process;[25] and these conditions result in confusion and feelings of helplessness. The omniscience and power of the "gods" no longer serve to delete these feelings of helplessness. Meanwhile, the turmoil in men's minds, increasing with the underlying regressive longings, creates opportunities for new leadership.

Mein Kampf repeatedly makes the point that a genius is selected by Providence to lead a people out of their time of troubles to renewed greatness. Hitler remarks, "It nearly always takes some stimulus to bring the genius on the scene. The world then resists and then does not want to believe that the type, which apparently is identified with it, is suddenly a very different being." This leader thus remarks on the "resistance" which reason opposes to his seizing power, and he remarks, too, on the metamorphosis the potential leader undergoes through the stimulus of the emotional hunger of others and the resonance within himself of his nascent fantasies of becoming their hero. The resistance may indeed have already been seriously impaired by the chaos in human affairs and the longings for a magic helper.

When reason apparently fails, a whole people may turn more and more toward their ancient mythology in a desperate attempt to renew their strength. This mythology, evidence of which may abounding in literature, art, and music, lives *pari passu* with their official religion and might appear as a mere plaything in the culture. In conditions of *anomie*,[25] the game becomes dangerously real, and the deluded or unscrupulous leader has his greatest opportunity. A nation's myths, as Karl Abraham[26] has shown, are susceptible to interpretation through the knowledge gained by Freud's technique of individual dream interpretation. The myth may be treated as the dream of the masses of the people. There is an intimate relationship of dream and myth in regard to both form and content and in regard to the unconscious forces that find expression in their manifest details.

In psychotic disease of the individual, we recognize clearly the withdrawal from reality, and the remodeling of it in accordance with the frustrated wishes, formerly only discernible in the disguises of dream life. The psychosis is in many respects a waking dream, as Kant first disclosed. In a comparable way, the mythology of a nation can move from its place in art and fantasy to the remodeling of social reality, with horrible consequences. Hitler believed that the "world-historical individual" was a blend of the practical politician and the thinker. We may revise this idea by qualifying "thinker" in his case as an "irrational thinker."

Otto Rank[27] has shown by a review of many hero myths, including those of the Babylonian Sargon, the Hebrew Moses, the Hindu Karna, the Greek Oedipus, the Persian Kaikhosrav, the Roman Romulus, the old Norse Siegfried and several others, that there is a common groundwork from which, as it were, a standard saga may be constructed. Usually, the royal father receives a prophecy of some disaster, threatening him through the expected son. Then it is the father who causes the exposure of the boy to the elements. But the father is finally vanquished. Through the myth of the hero, the individual is vindicated for his own revolt against his father. The revolt against the father may be partly understood in our present context as the revolt against the traditional masculine world with its intellectualism and rationalism.

The Strength and Hazards of Leadership in Democracy

We have so far emphasized the more regressive elements in leader-centered groups, and the pathological phenomena which may emerge. Beneath the level of conscious adult cooperation in groups for the performance of social tasks, we have wanted to draw attention to those unconscious dimensions of interaction which strongly influence the course of manifest events. Little detail can be supplied within this brief scope, but we have referred to the factors of the transference of parental dependency, of vicarious satisfaction through unconscious identification, of reduction of guilt by the usurpation of the individual conscience by the projected image of the leader, and of the wish for transformation. There are, however, factors within a democratic society which counter the regressive process and heighten resistance to the acceptance of an irrational type as leader.

As David Krech and R. S. Crutchfield[28] have shown, the authoritarian leader must maintain segregation within the group and must see that intragroup communication is kept to a minimum, except in so far as it is expressed through him and focused on him. Thus he makes himself indispensable, the key to all group action.

Authoritarian leadership in an authoritarian culture reduces the group's participation in decision-making to a minimum. Per contra, as Gibb[9] writes,

> Because it shares decision-making and other responsibilities, democratic leadership enables a group to make maximum use of the relevant individual differences existing within it. It releases creativity in group members because it can tolerate temporary or specific transfer of power and influence in a way that authoritarian leadership cannot. The authoritarian leader seeks to retain power by monopolizing knowledge and initiatory action, whereas the democratic leader gains strength by utilizing the full capacity of the group.

Gibb[9] also points out the necessity to recognize the facts of individual inequality. In the democratic system of values, men have equal rights, but they are not equal in ability, personal development, and education. A democracy which promotes illusions in this respect is undermining its own strength: its power to foster and release the different talents of its individual members.

The promotion of crude notions of equality readily becomes equated with the desirability of sameness. This desire has its roots in the nursery, where a child gradually overcomes his wish to be loved exclusively or to be the favorite, and his jealousy and envy of his competitors, by insisting that everyone be treated alike. Social justice, an important ideal of democracy, is a gradually achieved value, but it sometimes betrays the original reaction-formation against jealousy by an irrational insistence on a literal sameness of qualities of thought and character and of reward and punishment, just as is evident in the behavior of children during their struggle to make concessions to others and to belong to the group of their coevals.

In industrialized society, the competitive aspects are partially resolved in the social process by the creation of an illusion of actual equality and the coercive demand to be the same as others. Anxiety about being different then instigates arrests in development and inhibitions in special talents. Paradoxically, social engineers, who are enthusiastic about human relations and impressed especially with the rootlessness, or anomy, of the worker in industry, have encouraged techniques to recreate feudal belongingness. [29, 30, 31] The upshot in many places has been a premium on mediocrity. As William H. Whyte writes[32]: "Anti-authoritarianism is becoming anti-leadership. In group doctrine the strong personality is viewed with overwhelming suspicion. The cooperative are those who take a stance directly over the Keel; the man with ideas—in translation, prejudices—leans to one side or, worse yet, heads for the rudder." In such instances ambivalence toward a potential, mature leader, indeed sometimes toward the notion of leadership, has exceeded all useful proportions.

At high levels of leadership in a democratic society, on the other hand, it is a special responsibility to recognize the complex emotional currents and counter-currents which so largely derive from unconscious forces. The cultivation of a level of adult cooperation, rather than a level of pandering to magic craving, the encouragement and tolerance of criticism, the respect for individual differences, the necessity for vigilance in keeping open channels of communication,* these are the policies which in our society counteract deeper regressive and pathological reactions. The checks on power which democratic society has painfully evolved, the avoidance of cataclysmic changes which produce anomic conditions, are major safeguards against irresponsible and irrational leadership. In particular, anomic conditions in society result in disillusion and despair, accompanied by an inward disturbance of identity, in many individuals to the extent of a threatened loss of self-concept. Such an individual is especially vulnerable in groups to the blandishments of irrational and megalomanic leadership.

The application of psychoanalytic knowledge in the therapy of groups is slowly making progress, and in the future might add considerably to our understanding of the motivations underlying a choice of leadership and of the personality structure of chosen leaders.[33, 34, 35] In group analytic psychotherapy, there are limits set to regression. The activity of the conductor in this connection may

---

* We see here another problem for democracy, namely, the insistence of a group to keep nothing hidden from the public eye. It is obvious that in dealing with opponents outside, a certain degree of secrecy is sometimes necessary. Also, in this instance, infantile motives are at play, namely, the insatiable curiosity of the child and his resentment of parental secrecy.

be a useful model of responsible democratic leadership. There are, of course, essential differences: in such a therapy group the stage is set, and maintained, for the release of feelings through verbal interaction, for testing reality, and for the acquisition of insight. There is no other occupation of the group, in contrast to naturally occurring groups with an orientation toward objective tasks. However, in a democratic culture, these task-oriented groups provide opportunities for the release of feelings (including hostile and aggressive feelings within the group), which tends to set limits to the hate of out-groups in the larger social fabric. The variations in the mythology of the nation, based on its particular history and geography, can be remodeled in accordance with the current demands of reality, rather than becoming remodeled in reaction to the personal history of a particular leader. Here in this country we may be moving toward new frontiers, but these are set in terms of the conquest of outer space. It is also reasonable to hope that democratic society will continue to provide the foundation for man's efforts to understand himself, now so urgently important for his survival.

We are keenly conscious of the need for further psychiatric and psychoanalytic work in this area. In this short article we can only refer to the work in progress that is related to problems of leadership. The new type of excellence in leadership, in our opinion, may be an old type of excellence, now, however, more urgently necessary than ever: the power of self-understanding. Without an enhancement of man's power to understand himself and his relation to both his human and nonhuman environment, the conquest of other "new frontiers" will not avail.

The relation of inspiration to personality, especially in connection with geniuses and their creativity,[36, 37] is a problem which democratic society cannot afford to ignore. As Paul Schilder[36] writes: "The genius is a discoverer of object-structures in the scientific, artistic, or ethical realm: he encompasses parts of reality which are not easily amenable to others." And he adds, "Actually the lives of great men show greater or lesser deviations from the so-called normal." Some of those transactions which result in a new apprehension and transformation of reality take place unconsciously and liberate thinking from rigidity. This kind of originality may occur in those whose everyday life is unconventional, a toleration for which should be possible in a democratic culture. This toleration is a major asset in the competitive struggle of the democratic way of life with that of authoritarian cultures. Within a democratic society, however, subservience to a demand for conformity often prevents those who come bearing gifts from taking leadership or even from getting involved in public affairs. There is much yet to be understood about the relation of early traumatization to intellectual leadership, and to scientific and artistic achievement.

After all, however, as Plato requires for his guardians,[38] the genuine leaders must not only hate to tell lies, but also hate to be the victims of false ideas, and show the facility for dialectic, the power of "seeing things together."

Conclusion

The principal contribution of psychoanalysis to the study of cultural problems has been to illuminate the darkness in the sphere of human motivation, and especially to show those regressive irrational forces, and their relations, which impede the struggle for mastery. The insights hard-won from the therapy of individuals have led to hypotheses which can be tested in psychotherapy. In the application of these theories to cultural problems, there remains the adventure of surmise, but not so far a possibility for verification. Nonetheless, some light has been shed, though fitfully, on cultural problems. Moreover, with the advent of analytic group psychotherapy, as we have already mentioned, further possibilities have emerged, of new discoveries and of the confirmation or refutation of hypotheses, or of testing the usefulness of hypotheses. So far we have tried to show some of the unconscious forces connected with leadership and the selection of leaders which relate more to neurotic gratification than to the testing of reality and to the goals of democratic society. Unwelcome though some of these complexities may be, they aid in defining the problem of achieving and maintaining the goals of our society; and the definition of a problem is often a necessary preliminary step to its solution.

In our era, in the realm of political leadership, the style of a leader may be located along a continuum from predominantly authoritarian control with minimal freedom at one pole to a democratic sharing of decision and responsibility at the other. The former invites and exploits primitive unconscious needs and fantasies, while the latter seeks to exert influence through an appeal to reason. The Founding Fathers of American democracy attempted to establish government, as Jefferson stated, "not in the fears and follies of man, but on his reason, on his sense of right, on the predominance of the social over his dissocial passions." As William Miller states:[39] "To his followers, persons counted more than wealth, debate more than dictation, consensus more than conformity. Jeffersonian democracy was not an enthronement of the people, but simply of leaders with profound respect for them."

The appeal to reason, of which Jefferson speaks, does not avoid suggestion, but it encourages people's own judgment. The toleration of opinions which are at variance with those of leaders or of the majority is the hallmark of democracy. However, this toleration necessitates a constant vigilance, because cravings for a magical fulfillment of primitive longings are ever present and sometimes take a form inimical to democracy and to our ideals of freedom. Their suppression by means of authoritarian methods can itself threaten the foundations of democracy. An understanding of their significance may sometimes suggest better ways to prevent their becoming epidemic. We have stressed that the earliest relationships of the child are crucial to the eventual diminution of a later readiness for the arousal of magical wishes and fantasies concerning political leaders. We also believe that later formal education has an important influence on character formation and often succeeds in modifying earlier impressions. To induce an immunity to the mass arousal of fantasies that are destructive of democratic values, these values have to be made explicit. Moreover, the inner discipline necessary to safeguard these values has to be built up. We have to ensure that in the struggle between the authoritarian and democratic countries something wholehearted (however repulsive to the democratic mind) does not face the halfhearted. As Sir Richard Livingston[40] writes: "To be successful, we must realize that we are in the midst of two revolutions: a social and economic and political revolution; but also a spiritual revolution—the weakening and dissolution of the traditions and beliefs which for many centuries have ruled Western civilization and held it together." Sir Richard quotes an untitled sonnet by Robert Bridges. We can do no better than quote it in conclusion:[41]

> Who builds a ship must first lay down the keel
> Of Health whereto the ribs of Mirth are wed:
> And knit, with beams and knees of Strength, a bed
> For Decks of Purity, her floor and ceil.
> Upon her masts, Adventure, Pride and Zeal,
> To fortune's wind the sails of Purpose spread:
> And at the prow make figured Maidenhead
> O'erride the seas and answer to the wheel.

And let him deep in memory's hold have stor'd
Water of Helicon: and let him fit
The needle that doth true with heaven accord:
Then bid her crew, Love, Diligence and Wit
With Justice, Courage, Temperance come aboard,
And at her helm the master Reason sit.

REFERENCES

1. Sigmund Freud, "Explanations, Applications and Orientations," in *Introductory Lectures on Psychoanalysis*. London: Hogarth Press, 1933, Lecture 34.

2. Sigmund Freud, *Group Psychology and the Analysis of the Ego*. London: Hogarth Press, 1948.

3. A. H. Maslow, "The Role of Dominance in the Social and Sexual Behavior of Infra-human Primates," *Journal of Genetic Psychology*, 1936, *48*: 261-277.

4. Sir Solly Zuckerman, *The Social Life of Monkeys and Apes*. London: Kegan Paul, Trench, Trubner and Company, 1932.

5. Konrad Z. Lorenz, *King Solomon's Ring*. New York: Thomas Y. Crowell Company, 1952.

6. Eugenia Hanfmann, "Social Structure of a Group of Kindergarten Children," *American Journal of Orthopsychiatry*, 1935, *5*: 407-410.

7. Paul Deutschberger, "The Structure of Dominance," *American Journal of Orthopsychiatry*, 1947, *17*: 343-351.

8. Sándor Ferenczi, "Introjection and Transference," in *Sex in Psycho-Analysis: Contributions to Psychoanalysis*. Boston: Richard G. Badger, 1922, ch. 2.

9. C. A. Gibb, "Leadership," in Gardner Lindzey (editor), *Handbook of Social Psychology*. Cambridge: Addison-Wesley Publishing Company, 1954, Vol. 2.

10. Edith Weigert-Vowinkel, "The Cult and Mythology of the Magna Mater from the Standpoint of Psychoanalysis," *Psychiatry*, 1938, *1*: 347-378.

11. Sigmund Freud, *The Interpretation of Dreams*. Translated by John Strachey. New York: Basic Books, 1955.

12. Karl Abraham, "Character Formation of the Genital Level of Libido Development," in *Selected Papers*. London: Institute of Psychoanalysis; Hogarth Press, 1927.

13. Wilhelm Reich, *Die Funktion des Orgasmus*. Vienna: Internationaler Psychoanalytische Verlag, 1927.

14. Sigmund Freud, "Repression," in *Collected Papers*. London: Institute of Psychoanalysis; Hogarth Press, 1924, Vol. 4.

15. Otto Fenichel, "Character Disorders," in *The Psychoanalytic Theory of Neurosis*. New York: W. W. Norton and Company, 1945.

16. Charles Darwin, *The Descent of Man, and Selection in Relation to Sex*. London: John Murray, 1871.

17. Konrad Z. Lorenz, *op. cit.*

18. Joachim Flescher, "Political Life and Super-ego Regression," *Psychoanalytic Review*, 1949, *36*: 416-428.

19. Thornton Wilder, *The Ides of March*. New York: Harper & Brothers, 1948, p. 169.

20. Gustave Le Bon, *La Psychologie des Foules*. Paris: F. Alcan, 1925.

21. William McDougall, *The Group Mind*. Cambridge: The University Press, 1920.

22. Sigmund Freud, "Moses and Monotheism," in *Collected Papers*. London: Institute of Psychoanalysis; Hogarth Press, 1924, Vol. 23.

23. John Strachey, "The Strangled Cry," *Encounter*, November, 1960.

24. George Orwell, *Nineteen Eighty-Four*. New York: Harcourt, Brace, 1949.

25. Emile Durkheim, *Suicide: A Study in Sociology*. Translated by John A. Spaulding and George Simpson. The Free Press of Glencoe, Illinois, 1951.

26. Karl Abraham, *Dreams and Myths*. Monograph Series No. 15. New York: Journal of Nervous and Mental Diseases Publishing Company, 1913.

27. Otto Rank, "The Myth of the Birth of the Hero," *Journal of Nervous and Mental Diseases*, 1914, *41*: 51-56; 110-117.

28. David Krech and Richard S. Crutchfield, *Theory and Problems of Social Psychology*. New York: McGraw-Hill, 1948.

29. Elton Mayo, *The Social Problems of an Industrial Civilization*. Boston: Graduate School of Business Administration, Harvard University, 1945.

30. W. L. Warner, *The Social System of the Modern Factory*. New Haven: Yale University Press, 1947.

31. J. P. Marquand, *Point of No Return*. Boston: Little, Brown, 1949.

32. W. H. Whyte, Jr., *The Organization Man*. New York: Simon and Schuster, 1956.

33. Fritz Redl, "Group Emotion and Leadership," *Psychiatry*, November, 1942, Vol. 5, No. 4.

34. S. H. Foulkes, "Introduction to Group-Analytic Psychotherapy," in *Studies in the Social Integration of Individuals and Groups*. London: William Heineman Medical Books, 1948.

35. S. H. Foulkes and E. J. Anthony, *Group Psychotherapy: The Psychoanalytic Approach*. Harmondsworth, Middlesex: Penguin Books, 1957.

36. Paul Schilder, "Geniuses and Their Creativity," in *Medical Psychology*. Translated and edited by David Rapaport. New York: International Universities Press, 1953.

37. Ernst Kris, "On Preconscious Mental Processes," in David Rapaport (editor), *Organization of Pathology of Thought*. New York: Columbia University Press, 1951.

38. R. L. Nettleship, *Lectures on the Republic of Plato*. London: Macmillan and Company, 1937.

39. William Miller, *A New History of the United States*. New York: George Braziller, 1958.

40. Sir Richard Livingston, *Education for a World Adrift*. Cambridge: The University Press, 1944.

41. *Robert Bridges, The Poetical Works of* (London-Toronto: Geoffrey Cumberlege-Oxford University Press, 1953), Sonnet 15, from "The Growth of Love," p. 194. Reprinted by permission of the Clarendon Press, Oxford.

GERALD HOLTON

Models for Understanding the
Growth and Excellence of Scientific Research

THE FACT THAT an important social invention has occurred, one that is destined to transform a part of society, sometimes goes unrecognized for a surprisingly long time. A case of this sort was the nineteenth-century development of science as a small but worthy profession for individuals in its own right. Another case exists at present. It is to be found in the particular way by which scientists have come to organize and coordinate their individual research pursuits into a fast-growing commonwealth of learning.

The new pattern for doing basic research in science is worth studying for its intrinsic merits. This essay hopes to spell out what it now means to be active in basic scientific work; it also is an attempt to find a coherent pattern among the individual characteristics of contemporary science, each of which is obvious enough by itself—above all the rate and the excellence of research output, the size of the funds that are needed and made available, and the spectacular applications of science in industry and the military establishments.

There are more important reasons still for sketching here the operation of this new commonwealth of learning. One reason is the fact that this pattern carries specific lessons for the conduct and organization of effective scholarly work in any field, no matter how different or remote from science it may be and must remain; one such lesson should be in the definition of a scale for measuring the adequacy of support. The second reason is, conversely, the realization that scientific work may best be understood as one of the products of the general intellectual metabolism of society, and hence that in the long run the growth of science depends critically on the growth of all fields of scholarship.

I stress this point of view because of the wide currency of two

94

related preconceptions involving science: first, that its spectacular efflorescence is the result of forces so unique to science that other fields cannot hope to apply its lessons to their own benefit; and second, that science in turn is nourished by a system of its own whose health does not depend significantly on the state of all other scholarship. Both these conceptions are false.

The Stimuli for Growth

As a profession, science has been remarkably little studied, except for a handful of books and reports that seem to be covered over by the growing flood of changing statistical data. I shall choose basic research in physics as carried on today in the United States to characterize some common features of all the sciences. The choice is quite appropriate from several points of view. For example, the number of its academic practitioners has not grown at an inordinate rate compared with other fields of study. In the year 1914 there were only 23 doctorates awarded in physics in the United States out of a total of 505 for all fields, 244 of which were in science.[1] Thus some fifty years ago the Ph.D. degrees granted in physics amounted to 4.6 percent of all Ph.D. degrees for the year, or 9.4 percent of those in all the sciences. Remarkably enough, the most recent year for which good figures are available, 1959, shows virtually the same proportions. The 484 Ph.D. degrees in physics accounted for 5.1 percent of all Ph.D. degrees, and for 9 percent of all those in science.[*]

The great rise of research output in physics in the last half century did not entail a corresponding loss of numbers in other areas. Indeed, in a sense, there has been a relative decrease in the number of basic-research physicists, since now one-half of all new Ph.D.'s in physics are heading for governmental or industrial research and administration employment for which there was no equivalent in previous years and where a much smaller fraction of men are doing basic research than are in academic employment.[2] Thus the remaining group of Ph.D.'s in physics is of intermediate size—that is, it is comparable to the graduating Ph.D. classes in history, political science, mathematics, religion, or English literature.[3] Those who do not stay in the academic life serve, of course,

---

[*] *Statistical Abstract of the United States, 1961* (82nd edn.), pp. 130, 539. The total number of Ph.D. degrees in science in 1959 was 57 percent of all Ph.D. degrees versus 48 percent in 1914—a noticeable but not unbalancing shift.

GERALD HOLTON

to link physics to applied science, as is also the case in the larger fields of chemistry and biology.

Physics is a good profession to choose for this analysis because there exists an immense variety in the group, from the man in the small college who, with two or three colleagues, does all the work of the department and still finds time to think about new physics, to the man whose full time is spent in the laboratory of a large research institute. Any two physics-research projects picked at random are likely to have less in common with each other than does the statistical average of all physics research compared with the statistical average of almost any other experimental science. And yet there is in this group, taken as a whole, a strong sense of cohesiveness and professional loyalty. Despite the variety, despite the specialization that makes it difficult to follow what is being done in the laboratory next door, despite the important differences between basic and applied, large and small, or experimental and theoretical physics, its practitioners still clearly conceive of themselves as doing in different ways work in one identifiable field. There are no large cleavages and disputes between sizable factions representing fundamentally different styles.

If we first focus specifically on the professional life of a representative physicist, it is essential to remember at the outset the brevity of time in which basic research on a significant scale has been done in this country, or, for that matter, anywhere. The word "scientist" itself did not enter the English language until 1840. Until about the turn of the century, the pattern was that of work done by isolated men. Experimental research was often financed with one's own funds. Even in a relatively large department, advanced students were rare. Thus, Harvard University, one of the earliest in the United States to grant Ph.D. degrees in physics, had a total of six theses before 1900, and thereafter an average of about two per year until World War I. During that war, it has been reported, "there was no classification of physicists. When the armed forces felt the need of a physicist (which was only occasionally), he was hired as a chemist."[4] Having an adequate laboratory space of one's own in most universities was an unfulfilled wish even for the outstanding experimentalist—though this applied more to Europe than to the United States. For example, in 1902, at the peak of their research, four years after their discovery of polonium and radium and after many years of pleading for more space in which to do their extensive chemical and physical work, the Curies still had only their old

96

wooden shed at Rue Lhomond and two small rooms at Rue Cuvier. On being proposed for the *Légion d'Honneur*, Pierre Curie wrote to Paul Appell: "Please be so kind as to thank the Minister, and inform him that I do not feel the slightest need of being decorated, but that I am in the greatest need of a laboratory."

The growth of science between the wars needs little discussion. The driving force was in part the needs of an increasingly sophisticated, technologically oriented, competitive economy, and in part the sheer excitement induced in more and more students (drawn from a widening base in the population) by beautiful ideas ever more rapidly revealed, such as the quantum theory and early nuclear physics. But the rate at which exciting ideas are generated is correlated with the ability of a field of study to "take off" into self-amplifying growth.

To the economic and intellectual stimuli of earlier days the Second War added the new stimulus of the threat of power in the hands of the Germans, who had been the foremost nation in scientific achievement. Einstein's letter of 1939 to President Roosevelt (so like that of Leonardo to Sforza!) dates the moment after which the scale of research support changed in a surprisingly short time by more than an order of magnitude. Since 1940, Federal funds for science alone have grown over one hundred-fold.*

What mattered here, however, was really not so much the hot war and the cold war, for wars by themselves had not in the past unambiguously promoted the growth of science. Rather, it was a development unprecedented in recorded history: the demonstration that a chain of operations, starting in a scientific laboratory, can result in an event of the scale and suddenness of a mythological occurrence. The wide-spread fascination and preoccupation with science—in itself an essential element in its continued growth— find here their explanation at the elemental level.

In our society there had always been a preoccupation with the scientific hero who comes back with a major revelation after having wrestled with his angel in self-imposed isolation (Newton, Röntgen) or in relative obscurity (Curie, Einstein). Now, a whole

---

* Great care must be taken not to use any easily counted measure (money, persons, pages of articles, energy of accelerated particles) to stand for increases in what really "counts," namely, in the qualitative understanding and the qualitative rate of increase of that understanding. The numbers are useful to a degree, but the effects of numerical increases in hands, minds, and tools for science are highly nonlinear.

secret army of scientists, quartered in secret cities, was suddenly revealed to have found a way of reproducing at will the Biblical destruction of cities and of anticipating the apocalyptic end of man that has always haunted his thoughts. That one August day in 1945 changed the imagination of mankind as a whole—and with it, as one of the by-products, the amount of support of scientific work, including accelerators, field stations, observatories, and other temples.

To a physicist, nothing is so revealing as relating qualitative changes to quantitative changes. Man can cope surprisingly well with large rates of change in his environment without himself changing significantly. His psyche can take in its stride rapid rearrangements in the mode of life—collectively, for example, those owing to a large increment in the life span, and, individually, those owing to great deterioration of health. Precipitous changes of condition during quite short periods are well-tolerated. But the traumatic experience of *one* brief, cataclysmic event on a given day can reverberate in the spirit for as long as the individual exists, perhaps as long as the race exists. Hiroshima, the flight of Sputnik and of Gagarin—these were such mythopoeic events. Every child will know hereafter that "science" prepared these happenings. This knowledge is now embedded in dreams no less than in waking thoughts; and just as a society cannot do what its members do not dream of, it cannot cease doing that which is part of its dreams. This, more than any other reason, is the barrier that will prevent scientific work from retreating to the relative obscurity of earlier days, even if some turn in our civilization should bring all other phases of our lives back to their earlier levels.

Who Are the Scientists? A Representative Case

The element of discontinuity in the general experience of our time merely reinforces the discontinuities in the experiences of contemporary science. The rate at which events happen is again the important variable. For, when a field changes more and more rapidly, it reaches at some point a critical rate of activity beyond which one has to learn by oneself, not merely the important new ideas, but even the basic elements of one's daily work. This is now true of many parts of physics and of some other fields of science, not only for the most productive and ingenious persons, but for anyone who wishes to continue contributing. The recent past, the work of one or two generations ago, is not a guide to the future, but is prehistory.

Thus the representative physicist is far more his own constantly changing creation than ordinary persons have ever been. His sense of balance and direction cannot come from the traditional past. It has to come from a natural sure-footedness of his own—and from the organism of contemporary science of which he strongly feels himself a part. None of the novels or the representations in the mass media which I have seen have portrayed him with success, perhaps because they missed the fact that this is the component that really counts.

Though I am referring to statistical data, the man I have selected to typify my comments is not a statistical average but rather a summary of traits, each of which is well-represented in the profession and all of which, taken together, will be generally agreed to among physicists as representing a worthy and plausible specimen. I go into some detail, partly because not only the novelists but even the anthropologists have so far failed to penetrate this part of the forest to provide a good description of the new tribe. But I also want to make a basic point about the humane qualities of training and professional life. First of all, I note that our man, like the majority of his colleagues, is young, perhaps thirty-five years old, or just three years short of the median age of fulltime-employed scientists in the United States.[5] Even so, he has already had nine years of professional experience and increasingly creative work, having finished his thesis at the age of twenty-six, after a study period of about four and a half years.[6] In completing this work, like 25 percent of all physics graduate students in the country,[7] he was supported by fellowships, in his case by National Science Foundation fellowships for the first two years.* During his last two years he worked on a research assistantship, helping an experimental group in the construction of a new type of beta-ray spectrometer and submitting as his thesis early measurements he made with it in connection with this work.** Thus, like the majority of graduate students in physics,

* The present number of such National Science Foundation awards for graduate study, offered in all the sciences, is 2,500, at stipends of $1,800, $2,000, and $2,200 for successive years, plus full tuition, a family and travel allowance, and a cost-of-education allowance to the institution; in addition, there are a number of other substantial fellowship programs in science.

** More than one-third of all graduate students in experimental or theoretical physics held research assistantships in 1959-1960, and 31 percent were holding teaching appointments while studying. This, with fellowships and

99

his education was financed from the outside and proceeded without significant delays.

After graduation, he hoped to obtain a postdoctoral fellowship—perhaps the best way for the really good scholar to consolidate his grasp of his material and to map out a field for himself before plunging into the routine of professional life. But there are not yet enough such programs, and he did not receive an award. He therefore chose among the two or three suitable offers of a job and went into a middle-sized university. In selecting academic life—the only aspect of the profession to be treated here—he has become one of approximately 8,000 physicists in colleges and universities, as against twice as many working in industry and half as many in the government.[8]

He knows the pull toward industry to be strong because he compares offers that regularly reach him. The present median income for all college and university physicists of his rank and approximate age is $8,000[9] (somewhat better in his particular case), whereas the median income in industry is $3,000 higher,[10] and the usual offer he receives from industry is higher than that. Moreover, the pull may be expected to be much stronger over the next years. While the needs for physicists in educational institutions and in the Federal government are expected to grow by 66 percent respectively, the figure for industry is 130 percent.[11]

These facts help to explain his lack of deep concern as to whether the forthcoming discussion of his promotion to a post having tenure in the present university will go well. He knows from folklore that fifteen years ago there were only a few really good departments of physics in the United States; but now there are some thirty universities with research programs lively enough to yield between five and forty-three theses each year,[12] and there are many more good small departments. The availability of funds has helped to spread excellence in basic research widely and rapidly. He would have an even larger choice in liberal arts colleges, but he has become rather used to cooperative experimental research of the size and with the tools that are usually associated with the larger universities. Significantly enough, there are twice as many physical scientists on the faculties of universities as in liberal arts colleges; they form a larger fraction of the total faculty on campus; and—most important for this par-

scholarships, means that only a relatively small fraction was not helped one way or the other, though 30 percent reported that inadequate finances were still a retarding factor in their graduate work. Source: Interim Report, Ref. 6.

ticular experimentalist—whereas the average liberal arts college employs one nonfaculty professional staff person in physical science for every ten physical science faculty members, at the average university the proportion is better than one to one.[13] This implies much better backing from technical personnel in universities, particularly for those inclined to do large-scale experimentation; however, this ratio will probably soon improve, when the regional joint facilities now being developed among colleges in several areas are completed.

Our physicist has to his credit a number of publications—several short papers and one long review paper. He is considered a productive person, interested in one of the main excitements (which to him has recently become an experiment in the field of high-energy physics), and, to some degree (less than one would perhaps like) in his undergraduate students. These he meets relatively rarely by the standards of his predecessors. One course, more rarely two, is a typical class schedule for a physics professor at a major university; it allows sufficient time for work, for contact with graduate students, and for the long seminars with colleagues in which one carries on one's continuing self-education. For the same purpose, his research leaves, sponsored by one of several national programs, come rather more frequently than sabbatical years used to do. Summers are given by the members of his small group to research on the same contract with the government agency that sponsors the project. During these months there is extra salary for faculty and assistants. When necessary, there are trips to one of the seven major laboratories sponsored by the Atomic Energy Commission but administered for unclassified academic research by a regional group of universities.*

These circumstances, to repeat, are not typical of all scientists, but representative of a type of new scientist now often encountered. What is emerging is the picture of a research-minded scholar who lives in a world that has arranged fairly adequate support to help him carry through his ideas wherever such help is possible.

* One example is the Brookhaven National Laboratory, where approximately half the operating time of the principal accelerators is reserved for the resident staff, and the rest is for visiting groups from universities and other domestic and foreign institutions. The present budget of the Brookhaven National Laboratory is $18,700,000; the total budget for all seven such laboratories in the United States for the next fiscal year is $135,000,000. (See *Background Information on the High Energy Physics Program and the Proposed Stanford Linear Electron Accelerator Project.* Report of the Joint Committee on Atomic Energy, 87th Congress, 1st Session, 1961, p. 38.)

This help shows up in a number of other important (or even quite trivial) ways. For example, postdoctoral fellowships bring good research talent at no extra cost to the project, for a year or two at a time. Or when an important-looking article in a foreign-language journal appears (one not among the many journals regularly translated by the American Institute of Physics and other organizations), funds for a translating service can be found.

Our physicist's current research grant happens to have been negotiated with the Office of Naval Research, after some extended discussion and troubled waiting. An insight into the sources from which basic-research sponsorship usually comes and the places where the work is done may be obtained by a quick count of the acknowledgments cited in the program abstracts for the most recent meeting of the American Physical Society.[14] Of the 480 papers contributed, 18 percent are from colleges and universities without indication of foundation or government support; 43 percent acknowledge such support (from the Atomic Energy Commission, the United States Air Force, the United States Naval Research, the United States Army, the National Science Foundation, the National Aeronautics and Space Administration, or others); 21 percent are papers on basic research done in and largely financed by industry; 16 percent were done in government (including national) laboratories by persons employed there; and the remaining 2 percent include sponsorship from private foundations such as Sloan and Ford.

Our man's Navy-sponsored contract, therefore, is financed quite typically; it is not a large contract, and of course no part of the work is hampered by restrictions on publication nor, indeed, does it have any directly foreseeable applications to Navy activities.* The amount of the grant available to our man and to a senior colleague and collaborator who is acting as "principal investigator" is perhaps $46,000 for a two-year period. About half this sum is for the purchase and construction of equipment; the rest is largely for serv-

---

* Basic-research sponsorship by the Navy, Army, Air Force, Atomic Energy Commission, and other branches of the government (and in other countries by their equivalents) is generally justified in such terms as these: the project is one "with which the Navy should be in communication lest a breakthrough of vital importance occur. A classic example of the latter was early Navy work in nuclear physics which ultimately permitted more rapid utilization of nuclear power for ship propulsion. It is not possible to define firm boundaries as to Navy interest because of the unpredictability of basic research results and the complex interrelationships between fields of science." (*Basic Research in the Navy*, vol. I, p. 53.)

ices, including graduate student research assistants. Though the Navy cut down the original request for funds, there is still enough for the machine shop, electronics technicians, secretarial help, work by the draftsman's office or the photographer, and for publication and reprint charges. The contract support, therefore, is adequate.

Our physicist is better off than a considerable number of other academic physicists in less convenient circumstances. Many, in smaller colleges particularly, are hard-pressed. And, on the other hand, this man is perhaps not differently situated from many an equally talented and productive young man or woman in fields outside the sciences. Nonetheless, it is clear by the standards of the recent past in physics itself that here is a new type of scholar. Indeed, he and each of many colleagues like him has available for life the security, means, and freedom to do research that Alfred Nobel hoped to give by his prize to the few outstanding persons in the field. Most significantly, our new scientist is new in that he does not regard himself as especially privileged. The facilities for doing creative work are being accepted and used by him without self-consciousness and with the same naturalness as one accepts the convenience of a telephone.

This is the point. For whatever reasons, right or wrong, that society has chosen to make this possible, the circumstances exist for getting scholarly work done by more people than might otherwise do it, and for providing humane conditions of training for the on-coming generation.

There is at once a number of urgent objections, of course. One might say that it is not difficult to construct utopias for any field, given enough money. On the one hand, the money involved is easily afforded, the amount small on any scale except that of depression-reared experience or the starvation-oriented practices in all too many other equally worthy fields of scholarship;[15] on the other hand, this is not a paper utopia, but a working system for employing people's minds and hands in the time-honored mission of adding to the sum of the known.

Alternatively, the opposite objection may be heard: that really good ideas do not flourish without an element of personal hardship. But, despite the support intended by well-known stories (true, false, and sentimentalized), the evidence now is altogether the other way round. The once-in-a-generation ideas may still, as always, come from the most unexpected places; yet, throughout history, transforming ideas, as well as great ideas only one magnitude less high, have not appeared in science at a rate equal to a fraction of the present rate. The sacrifice implied by the sum of thousands upon thousands of wretched student and research years under inadequate conditions in the past can surely be no source of satisfaction, even if the additional expenditures had not, after all, shown a better yield in science. I suspect that another Marie Curie, a Kepler, even a Roger Bacon, would not be damaged by more help, or by the availability of cooperative research facilities for those inclined to use them.

I will refrain from elaborating on the point that the new scientist now seems to have at least as much time and energy for other socially valuable activities as previous generations did. For example, a large number of distinguished scientists participate prominently in national voluntary advisory or citizens' groups, or give thought and help to one of about ten current national elementary and high school or college programs for improving curricula in science.

Because in themselves they are either not new or not intrinsically unavoidable parts of the present pattern of science, I shall equally refrain from elaborating here some of the persistent and well-known complaints raised by scientists themselves: the volume of material to digest, the imbalance between different special fields, the encroachment of bureaucracy and of military technology, the need for keeping some "big science" efforts big and in the news by artificial means, the poverty of many teaching efforts.[16]

I shall also neglect here the occasional pirate who is drawn to the scientific field, as in earlier times a man of talent with a like soul would have found scope for his aspirations in the service of a queen or a Boniface III. The obligations and opportunities of power and all it entails now lie on many of the most outstanding scientists, and abuse is exceedingly rare.[17]

There remains a third major objection. Has this useful and often pleasant arrangement not been bought at too high a price? It is popularly suspected that somewhere in the background there is a group of high military officers whose interest and decision ultimately control, from year to year, whether or not academic research shall flourish, just as the Renaissance patron determined whether the studio would continue or not. If tomorrow it were discovered how to destroy multitudes by reciting poems, the physicists would have to move into the garrets, and poets would be enticed into the laboratory space. It is not, after all, only the intrinsic merit of the subject that now gives it vigorous life, but also the weapons-aspect of its occasional by-product, vigorously exploited by applied scientists and engineers in industry and government. As the student newspaper, *The Tech,* at the Massachusetts Institute of Technology said not long ago in a plaintive editorial: "Most of the students at M.I.T. will, at some time in their lives, work for the government on military projects."

This is of course frightening and confusing ground. In part these widely held conceptions are not true, or at least no longer true. The influence of government (particularly that of the military branch) on science has not been without an effect in the opposite direction. As some scientists have become increasingly effective and trusted in their roles as advisors, a noticeable educative influence has made itself felt in Washington. The rising role of certain agencies such as the National Science Foundation and the National Institutes of Health have vastly improved the picture in the last decade. The research effort, when carried on above a certain minimum level, becomes an autonomous part of the system, as certain long-resisting industries are also beginning to discover. Even if any group now wanted to turn off the Federal support of science, it could not be done. On the contrary, it is nowadays more typical for scientific advisors to try to turn off what appear to be hastily conceived projects initiated by the Pentagon.

And yet, the deeper intent of the objection cannot be either disproved, or evaded, or sustained. It is at the same time bitterly true and false, as would be a refusal to sanction the rising standard of living in our present, artificially sustained economy. The problem posed is at bottom the same for the academic scientists as it is for anyone from grammar school teacher to legislator who participates in the life of a nation which is so closely geared to an arms race with a determined antagonist. And while the hope of gaining indirect or long-range benefits from basic science motivates those agencies that support physics, the large majority of academic scientists themselves have clearly declared again and again their eagerness to work toward a peaceful resolution of the crisis that is to a degree responsible for the high level of their support. In fact, it is largely from the work of such scientists that one may hope for the development of ideas, understanding, and techniques that will help in achieving what mankind never before took to be a serious task, the control of armaments and of international aggression.

GERALD HOLTON

Requirements for Growth
Mobility, Organization, Leapfrogging

While it would not be either possible or necessary in this context to describe in detail the research project that engages our physicist's attention, let us turn from his personal background to the general rules of action of the profession. We leave him as he is contemplating a possible modification in the use of a liquid-hydrogen bubble chamber, a device for making apparent the passage of elementary particles such as those generated in accelerators. The triggering event for this thought was a brief article, the heading of which is duplicated in Figure 1.

It will be instructive to study this figure with care. It contains a great deal of information about the metabolism of a lively field of scholarship, denoted even in the very name of the journal. The *Physical Review* is perhaps *the* definitive physics journal in America, though it is only one of the many good journals in which basic research in physics is published. In 1958, the sheer bulk (7,700 pages in that year), the continuing rate of expansion, and the delay between the receipt and publication of articles made it necessary to detach from the *Physical Review* the "Letters to the Editor," in which brief communications are made. This resulted in the separate, quickly printed, semimonthly publication, *Physical Review Letters*. The article indicated in Figure 1 came out a month after its receipt; under the older system it might have taken twice as long.

VOLUME 7, NUMBER 6   PHYSICAL REVIEW LETTERS   SEPTEMBER 15, 1961

HELICITY OF THE PROTON FROM Λ DECAY[*]

J. Leitner, L. Gray, E. Harth, S. Lichtman, and J. Westgard
Syracuse University, Syracuse, New York

M. Block, B. Brucker, A. Engler, R. Gessaroli, A. Kovacs, T. Kikuchi, and C. Meltzer
Duke University, Durham, North Carolina

H. O. Cohn and W. Bugg
Oak Ridge National Laboratory, Oak Ridge, Tennessee

A. Pevsner, P. Schlein, and M. Meer
Johns Hopkins University, Baltimore, Maryland

and

N. T. Grinellini, L. Lendinara, L. Monari, and G. Puppi
University of Bologna, Bologna, Italy
(Received August 16. 1961)

[*]This research is supported in part by the Office of Naval Research, U. S. Atomic Energy Commission, Office of Scientific Research, and the National Science Foundation.

Figure 1. The heading of a short announcement of results in *Physical Review Letters*, 1961, 7: 264.

106

Why is this speed so important? One explanation could be that this profession is made up of fiercely competitive people. It is true that egos are strong and competition naturally present. But in the United States, at least, it proceeds in a low key; personal relationships, though perhaps lacking some color and warmth, are almost invariably friendly.

There are three explanations for this fact. First, the authority of scientific argument does not lie in personal persuasiveness or in personal position but is independently available to anyone. Second, there is the general loyalty to the common enterprise, mentioned previously. And most importantly, scientists as a group seem to be self-selected by a mechanism that opposes aggressive competition. Anne Roe, in summarizing her long studies in this field, reports in an essay, "The Psychology of Scientists,"[18]

> Their interpersonal relations are generally of low intensity. They are reported to be ungregarious, not talkative—this does not apply to social scientists—and rather asocial. There is an apparent tendency to femininity in highly original men, and to masculinity in highly original women, but this may be a cultural interpretation of the generally increased sensitivity of the men and the intellectual capacity and interests of the women. They dislike interpersonal controversy in any form and are especially sensitive to interpersonal aggression.

Thus the theory of aggressive competition is not likely to be correct in explaining the speed often felt to be necessary. Rather, one must look to other causes. I will select two quite obvious ones, which seem to me among the most important. One is the intense interest in what has been found. The other is the natural desire not to be scooped by other groups known to be interested in the same topic. And here it is important to note a major cause for this possibility—the fact that research is usually carried out in the open. It would be inconceivable for a typical academic physicist not to instruct any visitor who shares his interests on the detailed current status of his research, even if, and precisely because, this same visitor is working on the same "hot" lead. This principle of openness is one of the basic aspects of the scientific ethos.

We now read the names of the authors given in Figure 1, and are perhaps surprised by their number. To be sure, a commoner number of collaborators would be two, three, or four, although ten percent of the authors of the other papers in the same issue of the journal are sole authors. Yet it is neither the longest list of authors to be found, nor is it unrepresentative. Here let me signal three points. One is the cooperation in research that is implied within each group, as well as among widely dispersed groups; another is the distribution in this country (and indeed internationally) of the cooperating enterprises (some long established, others not known as little as twenty years ago to have had strong research interests in physics); the third is the authors' remarkably heterogeneous backgrounds that are implied. The list of names makes the point more bluntly than could any comment of mine.

This last point is perhaps the most important of these factors in explaining the growth of science in our time. Nowhere else can one find a better *experimental* verification of the general worth of the democratic doctrine, which is often uttered but rarely tested seriously. Social and geographic mobility in a field of work, as in society itself, is the essential prerequisite for a full exploitation of individual talent. The success of contemporary science all over the world despite the great variety of social and political settings is merely a striking case study of this proposition.

It is somewhat ironical to note how the need for talented individuals in science is discussed by people who speak about it in very different ways. For example, Academician A. N. Nesmeyanov, president of the Soviet Academy of Sciences, said in closing a celebration on the first anniversary of the launching of Sputnik: "We may be confident that in the name of the great ideals of humanity, our people, under the leadership of the Communist Party, will accomplish new and ever more notable feats. Our guarantee of this is the socialistic structure of our country, which gives wide rein to the development of science and ensures the bringing out of the notable talents of our people."[19]

This comment was cited by L. V. Berkner,[20] president of Associated Universities, Inc., which administers the Brookhaven National Laboratory. He added: "We have one great advantage, and that is the immense freedom that is enjoyed by each of our citizens. This freedom challenges the individual, without being pressed by his government, to do his part in bringing the free society of men in which we live to a position of unquestioned leadership. For in a free system, it is the individual, not the government, that determines the competence of the system."

The important fact is of course that regardless of their deeper differences the two systems share a preoccupation with the nurturing of individual scientific talent, and as a result are more or less on a par with regard to the quality of their scientific output.*

* It follows that any relaxing of social, economic, or other barriers which

The gathering of talent brings not merely rewards proportionate to the amount of talent but also rewards that are, at least in the early stages of a new field, nonlinear and disproportionate. In other words, the contributions of n really good persons working in related areas of the same field are likely to be larger (or better) than n times the contribution of any one of them alone in the field. This is true of a group as well as of individuals who do not work in physical proximity to one another.

With respect to the former, the particular way group work or cooperative research functions was long ago discovered and exploited by industrial laboratories and by medical researchers. Although some group research existed as far back as the seventeenth century, and beginnings of cooperative research even on something like the present scale of groups had been made, notably in the Cavendish Laboratory and E. O. Lawrence's laboratory at Berkeley, physicists did not really understand its full merits until the creation of the World War II laboratories (the Manhattan District, the Massachusetts Institute of Technology Radiation Laboratory, the Harvard Radar Countermeasures Laboratory, and others). Not only did they learn what it means to do science when the rest of society is really backing science (a lesson not forgotten); more particularly, they discovered how to work together in groups, despite the fact that a member may be neither particularly inclined to gregariousness nor even informed in detail on the subject of his neighbor's specialization.

What took place here was analogous to impedance matching, the method by which an electronics engineer mediates between the different components of a larger system. That is, special coupling elements are introduced between any two separately designed com-

---

prevent talent from finding its proper scope is to be encouraged. Physicists would do well to ponder whether the amazingly low number of women in physics (2½ percent) in the United States is not indicative of such barriers, particularly in view of the larger fraction typical of other technically advanced countries. Disturbing and not unexpected difficulties of another kind are discussed in Russell Middleton, "Racial Problems and the Recruitment of Academic Staff at Southern Colleges and Universities," *American Sociological Review*, 1961, 26: 960. On the other hand, the obvious distribution of the authors' names in Figure 1 sets a certain norm for any field. The standard of social mobility implied by this case has very little to do with respect to science per se, but everything with respect to the seriousness of one's interest in the excellence of scholarship.

ponents, and these allow current impulses or other message units to pass smoothly from one to the other. Similarly, in these quickly assembled groups of physicists, chemists, mathematicians, and engineers, it was found that the individual members could learn enough of some one field to provide impedance matching to one or a few other members of the group. They could thus communicate and cooperate with one another somewhat on the model of a string of different circuit elements connected in one plane, each element being well enough matched to its immediate neighbors to permit the system to act harmoniously. While an applied organic chemist, say, and a pure mathematician, by themselves, may not understand each other or find anything of common interest, the addition of several physicists and engineers to this group increases the effectiveness of both chemist and mathematician, *if* each scientist is sufficiently interested in learning something new.

That this system worked was a real discovery, for the individual recruits had come largely without any experience in group research. And while during the war the system of cooperative research was tried out successfully on applied, or "mission-directed,"[21] research on a large scale, it was continued after the war in many places in basic science, at first on a much smaller scale—and it was still found to work to great advantage.

Another and even more important effect of group work on the growth of a field exists among eager groups in the same field who are, however, not side by side but located at some distance from one another. One research team will be busy elaborating and implementing an idea—usually that of one member of the group, as was the case with each of the early accelerators—and then will work to exploit it fully. This is likely to take from two to five years. In the meantime, another group can look, so to speak, over the heads of the first, who are bent to their task, and see beyond them an opportunity for its own activity. Building on what is already known from the yet incompletely exploited work of the first group, the second hurdles the first and establishes itself in new territory. Progress in physics is made not only by marching, but even better by leapfrogging.

To be sure, this method of locomotion is the way that interplay in the work of individuals can help to assure rapid advances; and the most valuable scientists are precisely those who can leapfrog by themselves farther than groups can. Yet, in sum, the presence of groups assures that their imagination and combined follow-up

110

potential will allow frequent long jumps ahead into qualitatively different territory.

We can turn for a specific illustration to accelerators, not because they are glamorous or unique, but because quantitative data are easy to find there. Ernest Rutherford suggested in 1927 that the nucleus should be explored by bombarding it with artificially accelerated particles, because the natural projectiles available from radioactive sources are neither continuously controllable in speed nor of high enough energy. This gave rise at the Cavendish Laboratory in the early 1930's to the design and construction by J. D. Cockcroft and E. T. S. Walton of an accelerator for protons. Its first successful operation is represented by a black circle near the left edge of Figure 2.[22] Improvements since then have increased the top operating energy, e.g., in the proton linac, from the original one million electron volts (1 Mev) to about 60 Mev (note the nonlinear, i.e., logarithmic scale on the ordinate). But in the meantime, a profusion of new machines of quite different types have made their appearance, one after another. The cyclotron of E. O. Lawrence and M. S. Livingston (1932) was a radically different machine, and it immediately rose to higher operating energies; but this curve later flattened out (owing to the impossibility of a fixed-frequency resonance accelerator of this type to impart effectively more energy to particles when these have already achieved a significant relativistic mass increase).

The electrostatic generator, initiated by Van de Graaff at the Massachusetts Institute of Technology, entered the situation at about this time, with less energy but with useful advantages in other ways. It differed from its two main predecessors qualitatively (i.e., in the fundamental method of achieving the accelerating voltage), as indeed these differed from each other. In 1940 the betatron—again a fundamentally different machine—started with a design by D. W. Kerst at the University of Illinois, and then entered regions of higher and higher energies, where new phenomena could be expected to occur. New machines are continuing to come from different groups and widely dispersed laboratories; the leapfrogging process is clearly at work and opens up more and more spectacular fields for basic research.

One cannot help noticing an unexpected but crucial result in Figure 2. The heavy straight line (which would be an exponentially upturned curve if it were on an ordinary plot instead of on the semilog coordinates) of course indicates roughly the approximate

GERALD HOLTON

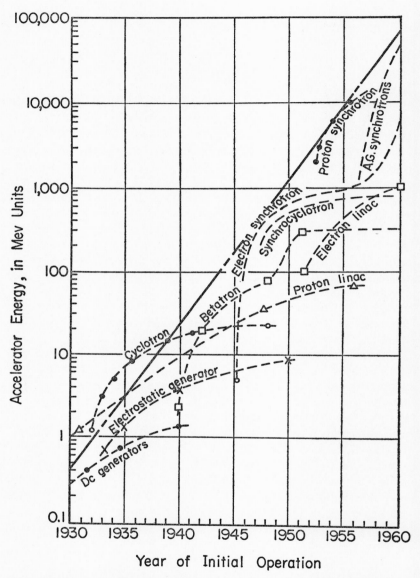

Figure 2. The rate of increase of operating energy in particle accelerators. (Courtesy of M. S. Livingston.)

112

maximum accelerator energy available to physicists in any year. This line shows that the top energy increased on the average by a factor of about ten every five years—for example, from about 500 Mev in 1948 to about 5,000 Mev (i.e., 5 Bev) in 1953. At this rate, the 33,000 Mev Alternating-Gradient Synchrotron at the Brookhaven National Laboratory, first operated on 29 July 1960, was ready none too soon. The possibility of going into the next higher range by means of two large accelerators whose particle beams will collide with one another is now being discussed.

This ten-fold (i.e., order-of-magnitude) increase in energy every five years entails a corresponding opening up of interesting results and new fields of work, each of which will keep research projects going for a long time. The multiplication of fields and results constitutes a graphic example of what is meant by an increase in scientific activity in one area. This, too, is a particular and peculiar pattern of physical science—although, of course, the time for a doubling of range or scale is not so short in most other areas of physics.* The driving force here is in large part a simple and general psychological one: Particularly when the more onerous material constraints on the realization of an ingenious new idea are removed, the really original person is not likely to be interested in spending his creative energy on something that produces much less than a three-fold, five-fold, or preferably an order-of-magnitude change. This has always been true, even when the financial considerations prohibit the realization of the idea, or when costs are inherently no great factor. A five- to ten-fold increase in accuracy of measurement or of prediction; an extension of the accessible pressure range from 2,000 atmospheres to 10,000, then to 50,000, then to above 200,000; an eight-fold increase in the volume of space seen by a new telescope—these are obviously interesting and worthy goals. On the other hand, to increase the precision or range in an area by, say, 30 percent is good, but is not likely to generate special enthusiasm in an individual or a particular group.

The natural pace, therefore, is that of doubling (or more), and of doing so rapidly. As in developments in the military missile field,

---

* Exponential increases in range or accuracy have long been a part of scientific advance, but the doubling rate was smaller. Thus between 1600 and 1930, approximately, the accuracies of measuring time and astronomical angular distance each increased fairly consistently at an average doubling time of about 20 years. For data, see H. T. Pledge, *Science since 1500.* New York: Harper & Brothers, 1949, pp. 70, 291.

the urge is strong to design an accelerator which will be beyond the one now being readied for its first tests. Leapfrogging has become somersaulting. But not all physics is accelerator-bound, just as not all science is physics, and so a balance is preserved in the large.

These considerations apply directly only to experimental physics, and even then only to those research projects that go after an extension of knowledge that can be associated with an increase of some numerical index such as range or accuracy. It therefore does not refer to such experimentation as the investigation of G. P. Thomson, which was intended to confirm whether or not an electron beam exhibits wave properties, and it also does not refer to much theoretical work. Models to deal with these cases are nevertheless possible—for example, by using as a quantifier the criterion of the inclusion in one framework of previously unrelated elements, and the production of new, unrelatable entities—and such models produce the same general conclusions concerning the increase of pace.

Diffusion Speed and Critical Rates

Nothing is more striking in a high-metabolism field such as physics or experimental biology than the usefulness of the present. For example, M. M. Kessler[23] has found that 82 percent of the references cited in research papers published in the *Physical Review* during the last few years are references to other recent articles in scientific journals. Half of these articles cited are less than three years old! Reference to the more distant past decreases quite sharply; only 20 percent of all references are seven years old or more.

After journal citations, the next most frequent references (about 8 percent) are to private communications, unpublished or to be published; if the latter, they are usually in preprint form, the old standard method of communicating in a specialty field, a method which has now grown markedly. References in *Physical Review* articles to books turn out to rank only third, or 6½ percent (the remaining 3½ percent of references being to industrial reports, theses, etc.). Even these books seem increasingly often to be edited volumes of various articles. The net effect, then, is that of the diffusion and use of information at high speed.*

* Not surprisingly, the speed of advance implies a degree of waste, and a number of simultaneous efforts along virtually identical lines. I have discussed

114

There are other ways in which scientific information diffuses and is used. Nothing, surely, is a more viscous medium for diffusion than the educational system of college and high school. How do the advances of science fare there? We know that the situation is not yet satisfactory, and we can understand the difficulty that must arise whenever the diffusion time is radically different from the natural pace of research. An example is the treatment of special relativity theory in a long-established senior-level physics text, such as F. K. Richtmyer's *Introduction to Modern Physics*. In the first edition (1928) the theory of relativity occupied about a page. Six years later came the second edition, with twelve pages on this topic, gathered in an appendix. The third edition, eight years later, had a separate, regular, thirty-page chapter in the text. And in subsequent editions of this outstanding text the material has properly spread throughout the book so that it is meaningless to make an estimate of the actual space given it. But then, little had been added to special relativity theory as a separate research topic since long before 1928.

Alternatively, by making a cut through the educational system another way, one can follow the progress of ideas as they move from the research desk down to the schoolroom. The emanation electroscope was a device invented at the turn of the century to measure the rate at which a gas such as thorium emanation loses its radioactivity. For a number of years it seems to have been used only in the research laboratory. It came into use in instructing graduate students in the mid-1930's, and in college courses by 1949. For the last few years a cheap commercial model has existed and is beginning to be introduced into high school courses. In a sense, this is a victory for good practice; but it also summarizes the sad state of scientific education to note that in the research laboratory itself the emanation electroscope has long since been moved from the desk to the attic. The high rate of turn-over of ideas in science presents almost insoluble problems for a conventional educational system in which information about the events at the top are propagated slowly and without a short-circuiting of any of the intermediate elements below.

In order to have a better model of the process by which

---

elsewhere other reasons for the necessity of some wastefulness and for synchronicity in scientific work; for example, in the *American Scientist*, 1953, *41*: 89-99, and the *American Journal of Physics*, 1961, *29*: 805-810. Nothing here should be taken as a defense of much that is merely expensive large-scale gadgetry, but which passes for science under such labels as "Space."

knowledge in a research field advances, we must think about the rate of diffusion along yet another dimension. In all fields of scholarship, the inputs for a lively research topic are not restricted to a narrow set of specialties, but can come from the most varied directions. In physical science it is easy to document this process of the diffusion of knowledge from many sides, over a period of time, into one research area—on the part of individuals, and quite independently of the effectiveness of groups dealt with earlier. Figure 3 is a schematic design intended to give, in rough approximation, both a feeling for what may be meant by the "growth of a field" and an overview of the cumulative effects of contributions from various scientific specialties.[24]

The field chosen is that of shock waves. It is a "classical" research subject that originated in 1848 when the British mathematician and physicist G. G. Stokes and the astronomer and mathematician J. Challis communicated their struggles with solutions of the equation of motion in a gas as developed by Poisson in 1808. Stokes was led to propose, on theoretical grounds, that a steep gradient in velocity and density should exist in the gas if a large disturbance were propagated in it. Both their contributions are represented by the two arrows at the far left, the directions of the arrows indicating the specialty fields involved.

The successive events are similarly indicated. For example, further basic work in the mathematics of wave propagation by Riemann and by Earnshaw follows in 1860, and other arrows placed on the "General Research" line refer to contributions in mathematics by men such as Hadamard (1903), Chandrasekhar (1943), and Kantrowitz (1951), or in physics by Mach (1876, 1887, 1889), Bethe (1942), von Neumann (1943), and Truesdell (1951). New specialty fields branch off as shown from time to time, some having pronounced technological orientation; but it is illustrative of the difficulties of clear separation that a branch such as magnetohydrodynamics (where the initial arrow indicates the work by Alfven in 1942) now plays a fundamental part in both basic and applied fusion research. The increasing activity is evident throughout. As these lines go forward, one may well expect further branchings at the growing edge from any of the five present lines, and fundamental contributions along any of the four dimensions. It is becoming more and more evident that departmental barriers are going to be difficult to defend.

Another illustrative interpretation of cumulative growth is

116

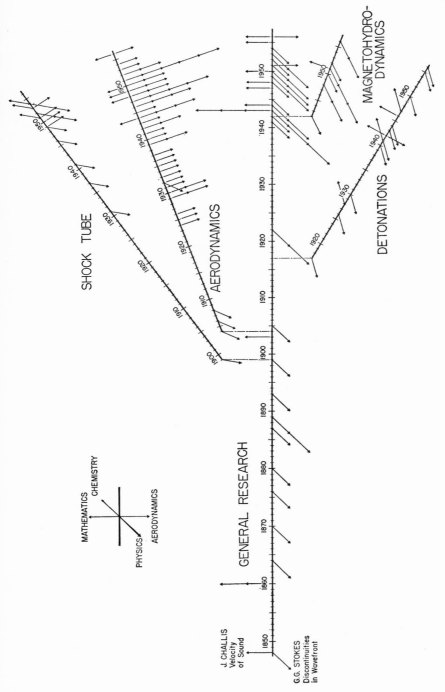

Figure 3. A representation of the development of basic research and of some applications. Each arrow represents a major contribution. Its direction indicates the specialty field involved (see coordinate system at the left); for example, an arrow rising perpendicularly from the time axis represents mathematics.

obtained by following, on a shorter time scale than Figure 3, the effect and interrelationship of a few particularly creative and stimulating persons within a field. Figure 4 represents the results of a recent study,[24] tracing in general terms the rise of the fields of molecular beams, magnetic resonance, and related work in pure physics. In particular, it is focused on one part of the extensive achievement of I. I. Rabi, both in developing the original molecular beam techniques, and in selecting and stimulating a group of productive associates or students (whose names are underlined on the chart in Figure 4).*

This description is analogous to making a large magnification of a small part of the previous figure to determine its "fine structure." After working with Otto Stern in Hamburg, Rabi in 1929 effected a branching-off from previous lines of research (analogous therefore to Alfven's arrow for 1942 at the head of the magnetohydrodynamics line in Figure 3, or the arrow on the aerodynamics line for Prandtl in 1904). It can be seen that soon after, both in independent laboratories as well as in those of Rabi and his associates, the applicability of the early techniques, and the originating of new questions now suggesting themselves in neighboring parts of the same fields, provoked a rapid branching into several new directions. The excitement of this field as a whole and its fruitfulness are attested by the large rate of inflow of new persons, including many outstanding experimental and theoretical physicists.

The course of the future is clearly going to be a continuing multiplication on the same general pattern. And although the growth is more eye-catching at the end portion of each branch, there is still a fruitful harvest in many of the lower boxes in Figure 4. Thus, molecular beams themselves remain important in current research. Finally, the connections with the technological exploitations of these advances have not been represented; but one should be aware that such connections almost invariably exist, and in this case they could be shown at several points (for example, maser, atomic clock).

A Simple Model for the Growth of Research in Science

We may now correlate the descriptive details in a simple qualitative model of the growth process of scientific research. It is too

* It should be understood that this chart does not pretend to an exhaustive description of all work in this field, and in particular does not indicate any work by these persons in other fields.

ambitious to expect such a model to tell us "how science works," but it should help us to understand its more bewildering and spectacular aspects.

A hypothetical construction should start with a "zeroeth-order" approximation; that is, we know it to be inadequate from the beginning, but we also know how to improve it to attain a first-order approximation and, if possible, higher-order approximations later. Such a start is provided by Newton's analogy of having been on the shore of the known, "while the great ocean of truth lay all undiscovered before me." Scientists do indeed seem generally to think about basic research in terms of some such picture. They often have described it as if it were a voyage of discovery launched on uncharted waters in the hope of reaching a new shore, or at least an island. To be sure, neither research nor a sea voyage is undertaken without some theory that serves as a rough chart. Yet such vague terms are used, even when the promise of end results would strengthen the cause of the hopeful explorer. Thus during a recent Congressional inquiry to ascertain the large financial needs for future accelerator constructions, the scientists—quite properly— gave Congress no more definite commitment of returns on the considerable investment it was asked to undertake than this:*

> It is, therefore, likely that the next decade will see the discovery of unexpected phenomena as well as the development of hitherto unknown techniques of particle detection and identification, and new means of particle acceleration and containment. Since it is impossible to predict the nature of these developments, it is very difficult to take their effect into account in any ten-year cost preview.

Taking the analogy of the voyage of exploration as sufficiently suggestive for the moment, we see that on the average a single searcher will expect the number of new islands he discovers to increase with time, perhaps more or less linearly. The same will be true if his is not the only ship that has started out, and if we assume the expeditions to be still few and not yet in contact with one another so as to affect the individual search patterns.

Hence the number of unknown islands yet to be found in a finite ocean (that is, the number of interesting ideas—not "the facts"—

---

* "A Ten-year Preview of High Energy Physics in the United States. Detailed Backup for Report of Ad Hoc Panel of the President's Science Advisory Committee and the General Advisory Committee to the A. E. C., December 12, 1960," in *Background Information on the High Energy Physics Program, op. cit.*, p. 24 (see p. 101 above).

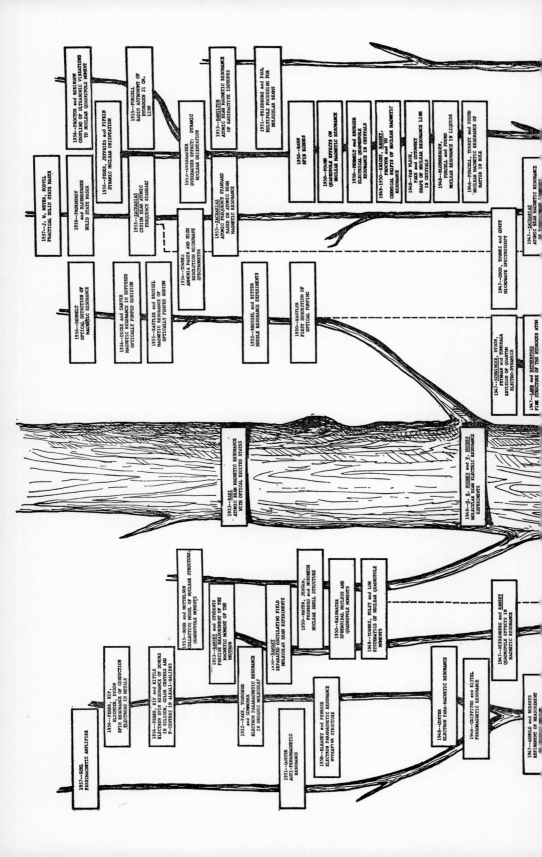

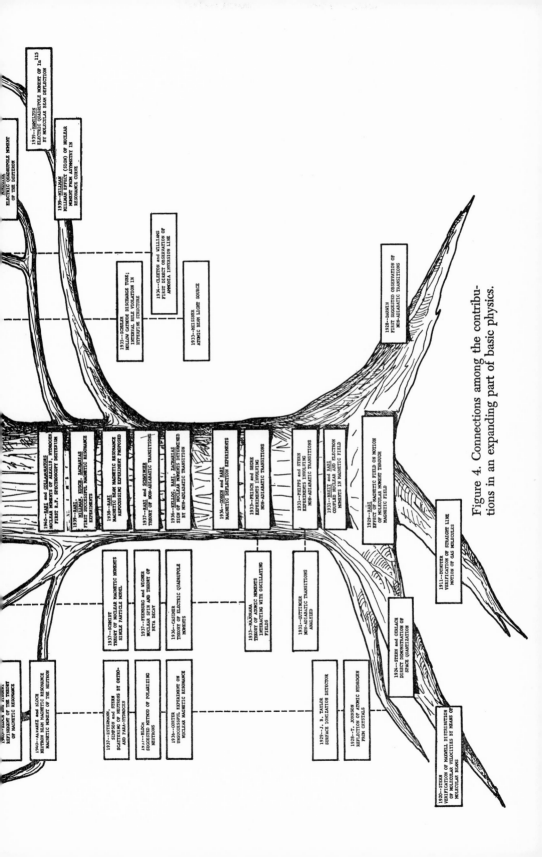

Figure 4. Connections among the contributions in an expanding part of basic physics.

supposed to be still undiscovered in this pool) will be expected to drop off in time, somewhat as line I in Figure 5(a) does. In devel-

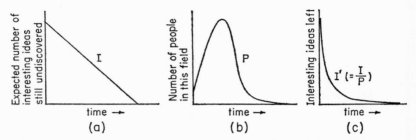

Figure 5. Zeroeth-order approximation for a model of research in a specified area.

oping a model for discovery, we shall now build a series of simple graphs on Figure 5(a) to summarize in an easily perceived form some qualitative trends.

But if Figure 5(a) itself were a proper model for discovery, science, like geographical exploration or gold-mining, would sooner or later be self-terminating. In fact, the end should come sooner rather than later, because the news of discoveries in a fruitful ocean spreads interest in them. New explorers will rush in, as shown by the early part of curve P in Figure 5(b). This influx by itself will assure that the quantity of ignorance remaining decreases with time in a manner shown not by curve I but by curve I' in Figure 5(c); that is, it will drop more nearly exponentially than linearly. If one also takes into account the fact that communication among the searchers shown on curve P improves the effectiveness of each one's search (a main function of communication, after all), then the middle portion of curve I' should really drop off even more steeply, causing I' to have the shape of an inverted sigma; and this is precisely what the data presented in Figure 2 indicate. In either case, however, the specified field will in time become less attractive, and the number of investigators will be decreasing somewhat as shown. Curve P thus indicates directly the size of the profession at any time, and indirectly—by the steepness of the slope of P—the intensity of interest or attractiveness of the field with respect to net recruitment (the inflow minus the outflow of people).

We shall soon have to add some mechanism to explain why science as a whole increases in interest and scope instead of deteri-

122

orating, as in Figure 5. Nevertheless, we already recognize that for some specific and limited fields of science this model is useful. Thus in 1820 Oersted's discovery of the magnetic field around wires that carry direct current, and the theoretical treatments of the effect by Biot, Savart, and Ampère in the same year, sparked a rapidly rising number of investigations of that effect; but it was not long before interest decreased, and by the time of Maxwell's treatise (1873) no further fundamental contributions from this direction were being obtained or even sought.

In fact, the same statement now applies (even in a good program) to virtually every topic presented in depth to physics students throughout their undergraduate training, and to a number of their typical graduate courses—except for students' own thesis fields. So, while Figure 5 may also be applicable to other areas of scholarship, the impressively different feature in physical science is that the time span for curve I' has become quite short when compared with the time span of an active researcher's professional life, and frequently even when compared with the new recruits' period of training.

Figure 6 shows again in curve I' the decrease of ignorance,

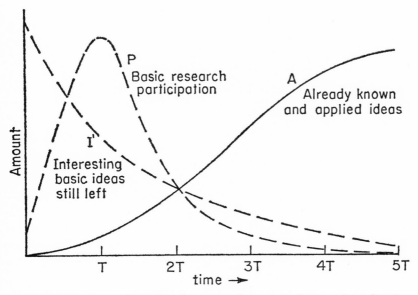

Figure 6. Inverse relationship between the accumulation of application and the interest in a basic-research field.

together with a time scale (T, 2T, 3T, etc.) along the abscissa, drawn in such a way that the amount I′ has dropped roughly to half the initial value when period T has elapsed, to one-quarter after total time 2T, to one-eighth after 3T, etc. T is thus the "half life" of the suspected pool of interesting basic ideas. The statements of the last paragraph imply that T is now short, perhaps between five and fifteen years for a specific, lively field on the frontiers of physical science.* This is also in accord with the data cited earlier, which showed that in reports of new research the references to published work fall overwhelmingly within the most recent years.

While it is not intended here to give an accurate idea of the absolute scales, the relative positions, or the detailed shape of the curves, P has been placed so as to indicate that the number of active researchers will reach a maximum when a large part of the presumed total of interesting ideas has already been discovered. This suspicion and the sense of dwindling time also contribute to the evident pressure and the fast pace. It appears to me that a critical slope for I′ exists. When the rate of decrease indicated by I′ for the specific research field is not so large (that is, when T is of the order of the productive life span of individuals, or longer), the profession organizes its work, its training methods, and its recruitment quite differently than if the value for T is only a few years. There are recent examples, as the case of oceanography, of a science passing from the first phase into the second, taking on many of the sociological characteristics of physics as a profession.

By means of Figure 6 we can briefly consider the application of new findings in basic research, as indicated in curve A. Such applications include use in other fields (for example, radioisotopes in medicine), and use for applied research and development. Curve A is meant particularly for the last of these, for example in the development of an industrial product. Clearly, a curve P′ that would be similar to P could be drawn to show how the number of people engaged in applied research is likely to grow and ultimately to diminish, for it is their work which A traces out.

Such a curve P′ would have the same general shape as P, but it would be displaced to the right of curve P. For it is clear that the longer one waits before beginning to apply fundamental ideas, the more nearly one's work will seem to be based on complete knowledge. Today, however, curve A does not wait to rise until I′ has reached

* Needless to say, one might cite a number of interesting research fields in physics in which the time scale is longer.

very small values. We can readily understand this in terms of three factors: the competitive pressures within an industry, the natural curiosity of talented people, and the needs of basic research itself— which, in experimental physics at least, is now closely linked with the availability of engineering developments of basic discoveries. A curve P' for applied research participation will therefore overlap curve P for basic-research participation, and indeed these two populations will often draw on the same sources. For example, Kessler[23] reminds us that articles in the *Proceedings of the Institute of Radio Engineers* refer with considerable consistency to the publication of basic research in physics; in the case of a relatively new applied field, such as transistors, such references to articles in the *Physical Review* occur not much less frequently than citations to *Physical Review* articles in basic-research journals. In the past much blood has been shed over distinctions between pure and applied research. It may be fruitful to assume that a critical difference lies in the relative positions on the time axis of curve P showing the basic-research population and a corresponding curve P' that could be drawn for the applied research population. The fruitful interaction of basic and applied science will be indicated by the overlap of these two populations, in time as well as in the sources from which they draw their material.

A First-order Approximation

We are now ready to attempt a first-order approximation to improve our model for the progress of scientific research. For this purpose we examine Figure 7(a), where curve D is simply the mirror image of I', plotted in the same plane. That is, whereas I' presented the decrease of ignorance, D presents the increase of total basic "discoveries" made in the finite pool of interesting ideas. The beginning of curve D indicates necessarily the occasion that launched the expeditions in this field, say the discovery in 1934 of artificial radioactivity by the Joliot-Curies while they were studying the effect of alpha particles from polonium on the nuclei of light elements. Up to this point their research had followed a fruitful line, originating in Rutherford's observation in 1919 of the transmutation of nitrogen nuclei during alpha-particle bombardment.

The new Joliot-Curie observation, however, inaugurated a brilliant new branch of discovery. We suddenly see that the previous model (Figure 5) was fatally incomplete because it postulated an

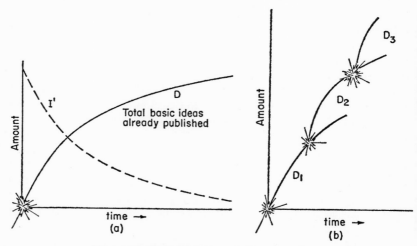

Figure 7. The escalation of discovery lines.

exhaustible fund of ideas, a limited ocean with a definite number of islands. On further exploration, we now note that an island may turn out to be a peninsula connected to a larger land mass. Thus in 1895 Röntgen seemed to have exhausted all the major aspects of X-rays, but in 1912 the discovery of X-ray diffraction in crystals by von Laue, Friedrich, and Knipping transformed two separate fields, those of X-rays and of crystallography. Mosely in 1913 made another qualitative change by showing where to look for the explanation of X-ray spectra in terms of atomic structure, and so forth. Similarly, the Joliot-Curie findings gave rise to work that had one branching point with Fermi, another with Hahn and Strassmann. Each major line of research given by line D in Figure 7(a) is really a part of a series D_1, D_2, D_3, etc., as in Figure 7(b). Thus the growth of scientific research proceeds by the *escalation* of knowledge—or perhaps rather of new areas of ignorance—instead of by mere accumulation.

By means of this mechanism, we can understand at the same time the pace, the proliferation, and the processes of diffusion and branching shown in Figures 3 and 4. When an important insight (including a "chance" discovery) causes a new branch line D_2 to rise, fruitful research usually continues on the older line D_1. But many of the most original people will transfer to line D_2, and there put to work whatever is applicable from their experience along D_1. (Perhaps now the most important thing to know is when to drop

126

D_1 and go to D_2.) If the early part of D_2 rises steeply—because there is now a new area of ignorance that can be filled in at a rapid initial rate—then D_2 will appear as an exciting field, and will be very attractive to researchers. Many will switch to D_2; but the largest source of ready manpower is the new recruits to the field. Hence the lively sciences have a constant need to "grow," or at least to enlarge the profession. This may well run eventually into difficulties as the limitation of available talent sets an upper boundary to possible growth.[25]

The newest recruits, therefore, are likely to be serving their apprenticeship at the newest and most rapidly growing edges. This is an excellent experience for them. But rapidity of growth depends on the inflow of research talent, and at the same time it is also *defined* by the output achieved. Thus there appears a danger of self-amplifying fashions: from a long-range point of view, too many people may be crowding into some fields and leaving others undermanned. One partial remedy has been for the less fashionable fields to set up their own professional specialty organizations and their own training and recruitment programs—a process which, once initiated, further polarizes the narrowing subsections within science as a whole.

With the concept of escalation in mind, let us finally re-examine Figure 2, where we found a leapfrogging progress to ever higher accelerator energies. The two concepts are intimately related; Figure 2 indicates the application of the escalation process of Figure 7(b) to a narrow and particularly vigorous specialty, that of accelerator design.[26] The same analysis may be applied directly to other experimental fields which do not have such strong increases in the value of an easily identifiable variable. But it should again be stressed that advances in most theoretical aspects of science, and in not a few experimental ones, do resist quantification, and that then no analogue to Figure 2 can be readily drawn. Nor should this be unexpected. In the end, what any advance must be judged by is not some quantifiable improvement in a specialty, but the qualitative increase in the depth of understanding it contributes to a wide field. For this reason, our model for the growth of science must, and should, remain qualitative.

We may now summarize. We have described what is considered an adequate system designed to support the pursuit of interesting ideas that add to man's basic knowledge—a system that aids researchers to do this sooner rather than later, and with work and luck to make a large difference to the state of knowledge of their field. We have noted the availability of means, of time, of collaborators, of encouragement by one's fellow-men, and of the stimulus of new results, all of which keep morale high; the open invitation to talent, no matter what real or imagined barriers to it may exist elsewhere; the aid given from student days forward for continued education; the predominantly youthful character of the profession, with the inflow of bright young people that is steadily growing; and the sense of building on the contribution of others.

This, I believe, would be a fair description of the major features of most basic-research sciences as professions in the United States today, whatever their faults may be in detail. But it is to be noted that none of these traits is inherently and necessarily restricted to the profession of science. (Indeed, in the past, perhaps the majority of these traits did not describe any science well.) The description in the paragraph above might well apply to almost any field of scholarship, as it now does to some of them. In this sense I regard this contemplation of the physical sciences as useful, not because their methods are to be imitated, but because they have achieved a state of operation that need have nothing to do with science as science, but only with academic science as a profession in which the achievement of excellence at every level of performance is the overriding criterion for the way the profession organizes its work.

One must of course distinguish between what is unique to science and what is not. It is not to the point to say that historians must be mature men before they can be historians, or that the Romance languages did not help build bombs and have no need of cyclotrons, and that the Navy is not waiting for break-throughs in theology. It is also not to the point to say that science is unique in its attention to quantifiable knowledge, in its need for cumulative growth, or in its luck or its ability to survive periods of acceleration in growth. Certainly, the clamor for more money and more manpower for its own sake is always wrong, even in science, and it can be fatal outside science. Perhaps, indeed, we need no increase in the rate of scholarly production of studies in Byzantine art or even in the history of biology. But even in science, the quantitative aspects of "growth" are merely indices of deepening understanding. Therefore, the question now must be: Given these differences between the needs of special fields of scholarship, what can we do to help each of the particular fields realize its full measure of excellence?

REFERENCES AND NOTES

1. R. T. Birge, "Physics and Physicists of the Past Fifty Years," *Physics Today*, 1956, 9: 23.

2. Byron E. Cohn (editor), *Report of the Conference on Curricula for Undergraduate Majors in Physics*. University of Denver, August 1961, p. 12.

3. *Statistical Abstract of the United States, 1961* (82nd edn.), p. 130.

4. Birge, *op. cit.*

5. *Scientific Manpower Bulletin No. 12*, National Science Foundation 60-78, December, 1960.

6. Interim Report of the American Institute of Physics Survey of Graduate Students (mimeographed). With fellowship or scholarship aid, the median time now taken for the doctoral degree in physics is 4.31 years; without such aid, 4.84 years.

7. *Ibid.*

8. *The Long Range Demand for Scientific and Technical Personnel*, National Science Foundation 61-65, 1961, pp. 42 and 45. All too often the sciences are discussed as though they were all physics. To obtain perspective, the total number of United States physicists of all kinds (under 30,000) should be measured against the total number of professional scientists and engineers in industry alone: without counting scientists in government or physicians who do medical research, the number is 850,000. (See *Scientific and Technical Personnel in Industry, 1960*, National Science Foundation 61-75, 1961.) If government scientists, research-minded physicians, and science teachers are added, the total is 1,400,000. (See *Investing in Scientific Progress*, National Science Foundation, 1961, p. 18.) It had been estimated that only 27,000 in this large group are basic-research scientists, and that 15,000 of the latter are particularly active—the "real" scientists, as it were. (See *Basic Research in the Navy*, vol. I, Naval Research Advisory Committee, 1959, p. 29.)

9. *Scientific Manpower Bulletin No. 14*, National Science Foundation 61-44, 1961, p. 6.

10. *Ibid.*, p. 5. Also A. E. S. Green, "Scientific Salaries," *Physics Today*, 1962, 15: 41.

11. *The Long Range Demand for Scientific and Technical Personnel, op. cit.*, p. 43. The reasons why he will probably continue in a university are significant. The mobility of a good man within the academic system in the United States plays a major part in the decision.

GERALD HOLTON

12. C. B. Lindquist, "Physics Degrees during the 1950's," *Physics Today*, 1962, *15*: 20.

13. *Scientific Manpower Bulletin No. 13*, National Science Foundation 61-38, 1961, pp. 3 and 6.

14. *Bulletin of the American Physical Society*, Series II, vol. 7, 24 January 1962.

15. No fact of science has ever been as difficult to verify as the figure given out as basic-research expenditure. For example, the budget submitted by the President on 19 January, 1962 contains $12.4 billion for "Research and Development" (including that for the Department of Defense, and Space Research and Technology). Of this sum $1.6 billion is said to be for "basic" research and training, including the programs of the National Institutes of Health, the National Science Foundation, and Agricultural Research, as well as large sums for the Atomic Energy Commission, Space, and unspecified items for the Department of Defense. Since in the past years the total sum spent for basic research from all sources has been about twice what the Federal government supplied, one might arrive at a total bill of from $2.5 to $3 billion for basic research in all sciences for the fiscal year 1962, or about half of one percent of the Gross National Product. However, a more likely figure for 1963, particularly if use is made of a stricter interpretation of "basic research," is half this sum (or an average of about $8 per person living in the United States) for all basic scientific research in physics, metallurgy, experimental psychology, medicine, etc.

For comparison, note the latest data in "Funds for Basic Research," *Statistical Abstract, op. cit.*, p. 534. The total expenditures in 1959-1960 are (preliminary) $1.149 billion, and the details list $0.225 billion for basic research performed by the Federal government, $0.344 billion for that performed by industry, $0.500 billion for that performed by colleges and universities (including research centers they administered), and $0.080 billion for that performed by other nonprofit institutions.

16. For brilliant discussions of some of these and related points, see the essays by Merle A. Tuve in *Symposium on Basic Research*, edited by Dael Wolfle (Washington: American Association for the Advancement of Science, 1959,) and by A. M. Weinberg, "Impact of Large-Scale Science on the United States," *Science*, 1961, *134*: 161.

17. A thorough and sympathetic study of the situation is in *Conflict of Interest and Federal Service*. Cambridge: for the Association of the Bar of the City of New York by the Harvard University Press, 1960, chapter 7.

18. *Science*, 1961, *134*: 546.

19. A. N. Nesmeyanov, "A Great Victory of Soviet Science," *Vestnik*, Akademiia Nauk SSSR, 1959, *28*: no. 11, pp. 3-9.

20. *Proceedings* of the Institute of Radio Engineers, 1959, *47*: 1052.

21. This is the place to mention (without entering into it) the debate on the difficult problem of distinguishing among basic research, applied research, development, technology, quality control, and technical services. These

form a continuous spectrum, and precise definitions do not survive the test
of using them and talking about them. Suffice it to say that different panels
of physicists and engineers working together usually manage to discriminate
between these activities on the basis of brief descriptions. For a discussion,
see the essay by D. Wolfle, in *Symposium on Basic Research, op. cit.,* Ref.
16.

22. From M. S. Livingston, *The Development of Particle Accelerators.* New
York: Dover Publishing Company (to be published). Reproduced by per-
mission. A similar chart is in M. S. Livingston and J. P. Blewett, *Particle
Accelerators.* New York: McGraw-Hill Publishing Company, 1962, p. 6.

23. *Proceedings of the Western Joint Computer Conference,* 1961, pp. 247-257,
and private communications.

24. Based on data presented in *Basic Research in the Navy, op. cit.,* vol. 1.
I thank Dr. Bruce S. Old for arranging the release of the material for use
here.

25. See Dael Wolfle, *America's Resources of Specialized Talent.* New York:
Harper and Brothers, 1954, p. 192.

26. The model here proposed may be elaborated so as to deal with other
features of scientific growth, for example, the manner in which work along
lines D_2 and D_3 reflects on continued progress along D_1. Thus, after the
early falling-off of contributions along the original lines of electrodynamics,
interest was revived first by Maxwell's and Hertz's work in electromagnetic
waves, then later by Lorentz's and Einstein's, and most recently by plasma
physics.

DAVID C. McCLELLAND

Encouraging Excellence

AMERICANS HAVE already discovered, and are pursuing with alarm-ing vigor, a system for encouraging excellence. It may be summed up briefly in the following formula: *the best boys should go to the best schools and then on to the best jobs.* The implications of the formula are eminently practical: the nation engages in a country-wide talent search to discover by means of objective psychological tests who the ablest youngsters are. The tests identify the ablest stu-dents regardless of race, creed, color, economic condition, or teach-er's opinion. Once discovered, these students ideally go to the best schools. In order to facilitate the process, the schools, in their turn, participate in the talent search and encourage the best students to apply. Since many of the colleges currently defined as best are in the expensive Ivy League, National Merit Scholarships are provided so that the ablest young people can attend them. Once they are in the best colleges, the students, if they continue to do their academic best, can look forward to being recruited by professional schools or business for the most important positions in developing and serving the nation.

The American formula for encouraging excellence involves a single upward mobility ladder based on academic performance and running from West Redwing, Minnesota, to Harvard, to President of the United States or of General Dynamics. The formula is an attrac-tive one and has always appealed to important American values— like belief in achievement and in giving everyone a fair chance to get ahead according to his merit. Only recently, however, have we been in a position to put it into effect with any real efficiency. We have developed objective psychological tests that can be and have been administered to tens of thousands, if not millions, of students, so that we can discover the ablest ones quickly and within small

132

margins of error. We have begun to get better organized in providing nation-wide scholarship competitions administered by some of
the better universities or independently. Mass communication net-
works—the radio, the press, TV—have knit the country together so
that the talented boy in West Redwing has a better chance of knowing than he did a generation ago that Ivy League colleges exist and
that in the rankings of institutions for academic merit, they stand at
the top. Shouldn't he, as the ablest boy in his town, go to the place
where he can get the best education and have the greatest chance to
realize his own potential and be of most use to his country? Isn't
this the model of success most Americans have in mind when they
think about "encouraging excellence" today? To be sure, local considerations still apply—alumni bring pressure to admit a quarterback, or Alabamans may not want their sons to go out of the state
to school, but such events may be viewed as unfortunate imperfec-
tions in the idealized, rational model in terms of which most thinking people are planning the future of the nation.

In fact, to raise any questions about the rational model is a little
like being against virtue. It is so obviously practical, efficient, democratic, and nonauthoritarian. For, after all, no one is forcing anybody
to do anything. In fact, the model calls only for creating a climate
of persuasion in which excellence is defined, identified, and encouraged to go to the top. Why, then, does it make us slightly uneasy?
Why does it positively give John Hersey the shivers in *The Child
Buyer*? His Orwellian nightmare revolves precisely around what
happens when the ablest boy in a small town is offered the "best"
kind of education (though it is considerably different from Harvard's!) in order to maximize his own potentialities and his contribution to his country. Why does Jerome S. Bruner state with some
concern that "the danger signs of meritocracy and a new form of
competitiveness are already in evidence"?[1] What has led Dael
Wolfle of the American Association for the Advancement of Science
to insist on the diversity of talent?[2]

Let us look at the balance sheet for a moment: what do we gain
by such a system and what do we lose? On the credit side, it has
certainly helped to set uniformly high academic standards everywhere and to provide an upward channel of mobility for talented
youngsters no matter what their social class or racial background
may be. Not even Texans can argue for the superiority of their academic institutions if their students regularly score lower on scholastic achievement tests. And no one can deny that a high test score

and a National Merit Scholarship have given many an underprivileged boy or girl a break they would never otherwise have had. These are important matters: we believe in an open society with rewards given for uniformly high standards of achievement and, to a very considerable extent, we have created one. Access to high-level positions in our society probably depends less on social class background and more on individual merit than in any other country today.[3] Why complain? We do indeed have a great deal to be proud of, and a long way to go in introducing the academic merit system everywhere in the country, yet we must also look ahead lest such a system lead us into a kind of overspecialized excellence that would be as fatal in the long run as the overspecialization of the dinosaur.

If we restrict ourselves to the better colleges, or what are called more euphemistically the "preferred" colleges, the debit side of the merit system is also impressive though less obvious. Consider the extreme case: suppose the better colleges should admit only the academically talented—those whose grades and scores in scholastic aptitude tests are high. The supposition is not unreal for many of them; the Directors of Admissions can proudly report annually that a higher and higher proportion of the freshmen are from the top quarter of their secondary-school classes. What is wrong with such a method of encouraging or rewarding excellence?

The core of the problem lies in the definition of excellence implicit in our current nation-wide attempts to recognize and encourage talent. Ability means, for the purposes of these tests, academic excellence, skill in taking examinations, in following instructions and finding solutions to problems set by others. This is an extraordinarily important type of excellence. It can be discovered by techniques already well developed. It is related to success in many different types of occupations. It deserves and needs encouragement, particularly in lower-class areas as yet untouched by the general American recognition of the importance of academic achievement. But it is not the only type of excellence. It just happens to be the only one that we psychologists can measure at the present time with any degree of certainty, and, therefore, it tends to get more than its share of attention.

If the better colleges go on admitting solely or primarily on this basis, everyone will lose in the long run. The better colleges will lose because they are excluding students whose excellence, though not so obvious, can contribute much to making a college experience more educational for all concerned. Society will lose because young people with very important nonacademic talents will not be exposed to the most liberalizing kind of education. Most importantly, the students themselves will lose—both those admitted and those not admitted—because the system tells them that there is *only one kind of excellence that really counts*: the ability to take examinations and get good grades in school. A single standard of success is being promoted, which, in Riesman's telling phrase, tends to homogenize our cultural value system. Americans all too often, anyway, end up wanting exactly the same thing: the same car, the same standard of living, the same toothpaste, the same wife—all as promoted on television or in the newspapers. Now they must all want the same education—so long as it is the *best* (like the best toothpaste, which is like every other toothpaste only more so) and so long as they can demonstrate what they got out of it, all in exactly the same way, by getting good grades and being promoted upward on the identical ladder of success in the system. So the boy who does not "make" it, who does not get good grades, or get into the "best" college, may well define himself as a failure in terms of the only norm that seems to count. What satisfaction can he get out of alternative paths of life, even out of an alternative kind of education, particularly when he knows that education at a "good" college is increasingly a necessity for leadership in our society? If he is a boy with political talents, and mediocre academic ones, is it likely any more that he can be President of the United States like Harry Truman without a college degree? How can he feel that he can contribute importantly to society if he does not make the academic grade? Or if, on the other side of the picture, a girl happens to have excellent academic talent, how can she feel that she can contribute to society if she marries and has a family, which prevents her from following the professional career that the merit system tells her is the one thing she is ideally suited for? Overstressing academic merit can discourage young people with types of talent that are very important for our society and can create in them a discontent and sense of frustration that lasts a lifetime. Must we not encourage other varieties of excellence along with the ability to do well in course work?

To be sure, there have always been those who have insisted on the importance of musical and artistic talents or athletic prowess. I even know of a case in which a college director of admissions admitted an excellent 'cello player with a "C" average prediction to complete the college string quartet, though nowadays in one of the better colleges he would have been most embarrassed to admit publicly that he had given similar preference to a quarterback. But with all due respect for such visible talents, I should like to focus attention for a moment on less visible, more intangible types of excellence. For the fact of the matter is that Americans are "rating and ranking happy." What they can see and measure on a scale of excellence, they will encourage. They can recognize musical and athletic talent early and, therefore, they find ways of giving youngsters with these talents the encouragement and rewards they deserve. But my concern is with important types of excellence that are not so readily recognizable or so obviously meriting reward.

Let me give three brief illustrations of what I have in mind. For over a dozen years now, I have been concerned as a professional psychologist with understanding the nature of a particular human motive called the "need for Achievement," the desire to do a good job of work. In a crude sort of way, we can measure it, and by now we have developed a pretty fair understanding of what people are like in whom such a need is very strong.[4] To oversimplify a little, they seem characterized by "the entrepreneurial spirit," by a desire and a capacity to do well in situations which challenge their ingenuity and resourcefulness. They are particularly apt to be successful in business, rather than the professions, and wherever a large number of them collect in a particular country at a particular time, the country has tended to show rapid economic development. In short, these men represent a valuable national resource, a type of excellence that should be encouraged. In a very real sense, it is on them that the future economic well-being of everyone in the country rests. Yet their need for Achievement does not lead them to do particularly well in school. Perhaps the reason lies partly in the fact that they like to solve problems set by themselves, rather than those set for them by others; but the fact remains that whatever the reason, they are not likely to be viewed with particular approval by their teachers or selected for help by present tests of academic excellence. Where do they fit in the current system for encouraging excellence?

Or consider another example—curiosity. My colleague Richard Alpert and his students want to measure this important human characteristic and to discover how it can be encouraged by the educational process. But note how it requires a type of behavior in a sense directly opposed to the academic excellence so feverishly promoted by our testing and grading systems. That is, curiosity may be defined as a desire to know, or as the knowledge of, things one is not supposed to know; whereas academic excellence is defined as knowing what one is supposed to know or has been taught. To test for curiosity, one might have to inquire into matters that the student had not been taught at all or that he could not be expected to know because of insufficient background in his previous training or in the test item itself. Such procedures might be unfair to the good and conscientious student, but they tap a type of excellence not currently identifiable or assisted in any way. Let me say again: I do not want to discourage academic excellence or unduly praise curiosity. For the moment I want merely to argue that curiosity is an important type of excellence that we should be concerned with developing.

Finally, let us consider briefly the problem of excellence in the other half of the human race, women. Ours is a male-oriented society. It is so male-oriented that the women, particularly the better educated ones, have tended to accept male definitions of excellence and have felt unhappy about not being able to achieve great success in terms of such standards. A recent nation-wide survey has clearly shown that women are unhappier and worry more than men.[5] They ought to. They are caught up in a system which does not encourage or recognize the types of excellence at which they are best. They enter the competition in academic skill just as the boys do. They receive National Merit Scholarships. They go to the best colleges; but there the system is apt to break down. Their superior academic performance suits them much less for their future role in life than it does the boys. They do not become President of the United States or of General Dynamics, or even very often Nobel-prize-winning scientists. It is small wonder that many of them feel frustrated and unhappy over lost opportunities. They have been gulled. They have swallowed the male definition of excellence, in terms of full-time work, visible achievements, measurable results (e.g., money earned), the manipulation of nature, etc. There are other types of human excellence without which life would hardly be worth living, and I do not mean sewing or the art of polite conversation. I do mean such characteristics as sensitivity to other human beings, compassion, richness and variety of imaginative life, or a lifelong concern for a particular scientific problem, whether one is paid to work on it or not. These are less visible and less measurable types of human excellence, but nonetheless important for all that.

Here we encounter a problem that will shock some and amuse others. Should these qualities be measured? Should we psychologists try to find ways of discovering who are the young people with the highest need for Achievement, the greatest curiosity, the most social sensitivity, or the greatest imaginativeness? The romantic answer is, "no." Must we, after all, bring even these human qualities into the same "rating and ranking" competition that currently marks the field of academic competence? The practical answer, I am afraid, is "yes," for two reasons. On the one hand, no one can stop the psychologists; they are already developing crude measures of many such qualities outside the strictly academic sphere and are likely to be increasingly successful at it in the years to ome.[6] On the other hand, a very good case can be made for the use of such other measures in defense against the exclusive use of academic criteria in deciding what kind of excellence to encourage.

Careful studies have repeatedly shown that, despite the fact that most human judges insist on taking other factors into account in making selections of any kind, their final decisions are almost perfectly correlated with the single quantitative score that they have, namely, some form of academic achievement or aptitude test score.[7] They like to think that they are taking other factors into account, but in actuality they do not, and the reason is simple: the other factors are not expressed in quantitative terms, but come in the form of vague verbal descriptions or recommendations that are very hard to compare in making final choices. So the choices are made in terms of the one available quantitative measure: for academic promise. If we want to encourage a concern for other types of excellence in this merit-oriented society of ours, we have to develop measures of other types of excellence.

But suppose they can be identified. How are they to be encouraged? Does it mean the schools should teach and grade curiosity, the need for Achievement, imaginativeness, and sensitivity? That way lies certain disaster. It is caricatured by those educators who have argued that everyone must be good at something and that therefore the schools must discover and teach that something, whether it be cooperativeness in play or preparation for happiness in marriage. Cultivating other types of excellence need bring no changes in the curricula of the schools, though it may require a change in the attitude of some teachers. Teachers still have to teach content— geology, English, mathematics, or social science—but they can encourage human beings. They can teach in ways that show a genuine respect for curiosity or the entrepreneurial spirit. The schools have always feared that concern for other types of excellence than academic performance would lower standards. Why should it? Suppose a student of algebra is curious and spends so much time picking up odd bits of information about mathematics that he does not learn his algebra. Should he be given an "A" for his curiosity? Certainly not, because he has not learned his algebra. However, it does not follow that the teacher should not encourage curiosity, admire the student's willingness to go off on his own, or perhaps even change the way he teaches mathematics so as to engage the student's curiosity more. The teacher-student relation should not be limited strictly to the grade-giving function, nor should the grade come to summarize all that a student has learned in college or high school.

As a matter of fact, the human qualities we are speaking of do not develop by formal teaching nor do they require the external rewards of grades. How can a student be taught to be curious in the usual way? A contradiction is involved. Can he be taught that he is supposed to learn what he is not supposed to learn? Certain "progressive" schools have come to grief precisely by trying to give instruction in such matters as creativity and curiosity, which almost by definition defy formal instruction, because they involve a student's doing things on his own that are different from what he is expected to do. Or consider the need for Achievement, the desire to do a good job in a situation involving personal challenge. At the present time we do not know how to increase it by formal instruction, nor are we sure that we would want to even if we could. Would it not make the intense competitiveness of the country even worse? Furthermore, research has shown that external rewards, such as grades, are not only meaningless for such people, they may actually be disconcerting. A person with a strong need to achieve works best when left alone to pursue his own goals. Offering him special incentives or rewards only serves to put him off his stride, unlike the person with a low need for Achievement, who needs such rewards to spur him on.

If the usual methods of encouraging excellence—by teaching and grading—do not work for such qualities, what does? Unfortunately, psychologists have only just begun to work on such problems. Their efforts to date have been almost wholly directed to identifying various types of academic talent and measuring the effects of various methods of teaching and grading it. Only a few mavericks have strayed into studying the nonacademic effects of education. However, one conclusion is already fairly well established, even at this early stage in the research. Schools and colleges tend to develop distinctive "personalities," distinctive and persistent climates of opinion that have rather marked effects on students attending them.

R. H. Knapp and H. B. Goodrich have noted this in demonstrating that certain undergraduate colleges excelled in the production of scientists, whereas others produced more humanists, or lawyers.[8] P. E. Jacob has surveyed studies of value attitudes in various colleges and come up with some similar findings.[9] Certain values are more common on some campuses than others. At Haverford the students are more community-minded, at Wesleyan they express a stronger ethical-religious concern, at state universities they are more often interested in promoting their careers than in a general liberal-arts education.

More recent research has pinpointed some of these influences more precisely. For example, academically talented boys were brought together from high schools all over New Hampshire for a six-week summer session at one of the state's oldest and most distinguished private schools for boys. The summer program almost certainly enriched their education in the formal sense, but it also had important effects on their values and outlook on life. For example, before they arrived they had viewed authority as bad, arbitrary, and ineffective. After the summer school experience, they viewed authority as good, strong, and impersonal. They also were more concerned about problems of impulse control or discipline and had developed a sophisticated suspiciousness of the world not characteristic of their fellow classmates who had remained behind in the high schools.[10] Now none of these attitudes or personal qualities was consciously taught by the masters at the private school or consciously learned by the bright students attending it. Yet the effects were very marked, and in the long run they may be more important in the future lives of the boys than the extra amount of mathematics and biology they picked up during the summer.

A somewhat similar study has been started at Harvard University. Preliminary results suggest that Harvard may be having an effect on its students very much like the one people have been claiming it has had for over a hundred years. It turns out students who tend to feel indifferent, superior, and slightly disillusioned. There are very few "committed romantics" among its graduates. Henry Adams' description of the Class of 1858 is still amazingly accurate in 1960:[11]

Free from meannesses, jealousies, intrigues, enthusiasms, and passions; not exceptionally quick; not consciously skeptical; singularly indifferent to display, artifice, florid expression, but not hostile to it when it amused them; distrustful of themselves, but little disposed to trust anyone else; with not much humor of their own, but full of readiness to enjoy the humor of others; negative to a degree that in the long run became positive and triumphant. Not harsh in manners or judgment, rather liberal and open-minded, they were still as a body the most formidable critics one would care to meet, in a long life exposed to criticism.

This is the Harvard style—a type of excellence, if you will, that is strongly encouraged among students who attend Harvard. Not all of them acquire it, of course, but its very existence points a moral. Educational institutions can and do have important influences on the human qualities we have been talking about, in subtle ways that are not as yet understood. Should we not, therefore, encourage varieties of excellence among such institutions as a means of promoting a similar variety in the characteristics of students who attend them? Harvard may promote "objectivity" and a kind of critical sophistication, while Texas produces unashamed enthusiasts. College X may be a haven for the curious, and College Y, a woman's college, may stress the life of the mind, the world of the imagination. Why should it not be so?

There are certain to be those at Harvard who will object to its style, who will think that it should turn out more committed people. But why should a college or any educational institution be all things to all students, or, what is worse, be like every other institution? Harvard encourages a certain type of excellence. Let other colleges encourage other types. It means, of course, that not all the best brains in the country should go to Harvard, however good it may be academically. Society needs brainy romantics as well as brainy critics. The most serious weakness in the argument that the best students should go to the best schools is the naive assumption that the best schools academically can be the "best," too, in the effects they have on character and personality, in shaping other types of human excellence. But let this not be an excuse for easy local pride. No college or university can lay a serious claim to the best students in its area if it is all things to all men and has developed no distinctive excellence of its own.

Varieties of excellence in individuals, therefore, can be encouraged by varieties of excellence in the educational institutions they attend; but one more step is necessary for such a system to work. The institutions must avoid admitting students solely in terms of one type of excellence, namely, academic promise or performance. That is, if our new model provides for a variety of types of excellence encouraged in a variety of excellent ways, then one type of excellence must be prevented from becoming a monopoly and placing a strong restraint on "trade." Academic excellence has very nearly reached a monopoly position, despite the protests of admissions officers that they are still operating in terms of "other criteria." They are fighting a losing battle. The logic is inexorable. Students with the highest predicted grade-point averages are increasingly the ones admitted to any school or college. The last bastion in the Ivy League colleges of the East is about to crumble: alumni sons can no longer receive preference. Sons of Harvard professors have received some preference in the past in being admitted to Harvard, but a recent report on admissions at Harvard has demonstrated that on the average they do less well academically than do boys who are admitted solely on the basis of their academic performance. The report therefore recommends the abolition of the preference for sons of Harvard professors.

Now I hold no particular brief for the sons of alumni or Harvard professors; but I strongly object to the stranglehold that academic performance is getting on the admissions process. So long as there were other means of getting into our better colleges, at least there was a chance of admitting some students who were not marching in tune to the academic lock-step. A Franklin D. Roosevelt or a Chief Justice Harlan Stone might slip in through the side door as a son of an alumnus or graduate of a distinguished private school—though on the basis of academic performance neither could get in the front door today. Yet they represent for me a type of excellence that deserves an education in one of the "preferred" colleges. Yet even if they got in today, they would not stay long, if a practice tried out at Amherst College (where Justice Stone was an undergraduate) spreads. There for a time a student had to live up to his predicted grade-point average or he was expelled, even though he was earning passing grades. Here is concern with one type of excellence with a vengeance. The Amherst professors argue that if a student who should be getting "A's" is only getting "C's," he could better cultivate his curiosity, his need for Achievement, or the life of the mind somewhere else, say, at home watching television or working in the local gas station. Anyway, he is a bad influence on the other boys, who must keep up their performance in the academic lock-step.

It is difficult not to be misunderstood on this point. Academic excellence is a wonderful thing. As a teacher, I much prefer to have conscientious people in my classes who do what they are told, read their assignments, and turn in interesting papers on time. I am annoyed by that boy in the back of the room who comes late to class, never participates in the discussion, and appears to be listening only half-heartedly to the pearls of wisdom I am dropping before him, and I certainly will give him a low grade—but is that all there is to education? Am I or his college having no influence on him except in terms of what is represented in that grade? Does it mean nothing for the future of the country that the scion of one of our great fortunes received such a ribbing from a sociology professor at Yale that it is alleged to have changed his whole outlook on life? He did not graduate, and, probably, with the greater efficiency of our academic predictors today, he would not have been admitted; but is that all there is to the story?

The clock is certainly not going to be turned back. The old leisurely, relaxed, admissions procedures cannot be reinstated with the competitive pressure for entrance into college growing year by year. What can be done, practically speaking? I have a dream about a new type of admissions procedure that I would at least like to see tried out at one of our better colleges. First, the admissions office would set a floor for predicted academic performance. It should not be set too high. For the sake of argument, let us say that it is set at "C," a passing grade at most colleges. Only those boys who on the basis of the usual academic tests had a predicted average grade of "C" would be further considered for admission. Then, within that group, quotas should be set up for various types of excellence. For example, the one hundred boys with the highest academic prediction should be admitted, then the one hundred with the most curiosity, another hundred with the highest need for Achievement, one hundred with the greatest imaginativeness or the most political ability, and so on down the list. The professors would be sure to protest, and perhaps they should get the quota of the academically talented up to fifty percent, but at least the principle would be established that other types of excellence deserve the kind of education that college is giving. For the professors should not have the exclusive say as to who should be educated. Quite naturally they like people who are like themselves, but they do not represent the only type of excellence in the country that is important or needs encouragement. What a revolution in values it would bring if only a few National Merit Scholarships were given for the highest scores on tests of curiosity, creativity, or imaginativeness! I shudder to think of the difficulties of developing such tests and trying to keep the schools and parents from figuring out ways to get round them, but frankly, I see no other effective way in the long run of breaking the stranglehold that academic excellence is getting over the American educational system and the American hierarchy of values. Perhaps some first-rate college will be brave enough to try it out in the short run on a smaller and less public scale.

Our national problem is that we have tended to focus increasingly on encouraging one type of excellence, and a practical, measurable, action-oriented type of excellence at that. Other types of human excellence exist, particularly those involving character and the inner life, and the world of imagination and human sensitivity. They can be measured, if necessary, to combat the stress on academic performance. They, too, need encouragement, and they can be encouraged by less stress on the purely academic side of life and more stress on the unique styles of educational institutions that most influence such other human qualities.

REFERENCES

1. Jerome S. Bruner, *The Process of Education.* Cambridge: Harvard University Press, 1960.

2. Dael Wolfle, "Diversity of Talent," *American Psychologist,* 1960, *15:* 535-545.

3. See for example: W. L. Warner and J. C. Abegglen, *Occupational Mobility in American Business and Industry.* Minneapolis: University of Minnesota Press, 1955. David C. McClelland, *The Achieving Society.* Princeton: D. Van Nostrand, 1961; in press, chapter 7.

4. See for example: David C. McClelland, J. W. Atkinson, R. A. Clark, and E. L. Lowell, *The Achievement Motive.* New York: Appleton-Century-Crofts, 1953. D. C. McClelland, *The Achieving Society.* Princeton: D. Van Nostrand, 1961; in press.

5. Gerald Gurin, Joseph Veroff, and Sheila Feld, *Americans View Their Mental Health.* New York: Basic Books, 1960.

6. See for example: D. C. McClelland, A. L. Baldwin, U. Bronfenbrenner, and F. L. Strodtbeck, *Talent and Society.* Princeton: D. Van Nostrand, 1958. J. W. Getzels and P. W. Jackson, "Career Aspirations of Highly Intelligent and Highly Creative Adolescents," *Journal of Abnormal Social Psychology,* 1960, *1:* 119-123.

7. See the Technical Reports of the research on Fellowship Selection Techniques, supported by the National Science Foundation, Office of Scientific Personnel, National Academy of Sciences, National Research Council, Washington, D. C.

8. R. H. Knapp and H. B. Goodrich, *Origins of American Scientists*. Chicago: University of Chicago Press, 1952.

9. P. E. Jacob, *Changing Values in College*. New York, Harper & Brothers, 1957.

10. See D. G. Winter, Personality Effects of a Summer Advanced Studies Program. Unpublished honors thesis, Department of Social Relations, Harvard University, 1960.

11. Reprinted by permission from Henry Adams, *The Education of Henry Adams*. Boston-New York: published for the Massachusetts Historical Society by Houghton Mifflin, 1918, p. 56.

ADAM YARMOLINSKY

The Explicit Recognition of Excellence

A Survey

THE THESIS OF THIS ESSAY is that the kind of excellence most explicitly recognized in the United States is leadership, and that the reward of recognition is, by and large, more leadership. This recognition occurs both in the private and the public sectors, and in academic circles as well as in the world of affairs. Yet, while the bases of recognition are remarkably similar in different sectors of American society, the structure of recognition is thoroughly pluralistic. Some peaks of recognition are higher than others, but there is little opportunity to leap from peak to peak. We have few national figures in the United States, other than athletes and movie stars, and these almost never earn that ultimate title of respect, the invariable "Mr." before their surnames, which is accorded to senior partners and chairmen of the board. We have even fewer generalists.

America has no Establishment on the British model. An Establishment is essentially incompatible with an open society; it is rather the concession that a closed society makes to talent. The absence of a functioning Establishment is demonstrated by three circumstances of the struggle for recognition: no one is automatically in, no one is automatically out, and there are no obvious indicia of in-ness.

There are no automatic exclusions from the competition. Certain careers exclude the members of certain minority groups, but these restrictions do not operate across the board, and the barriers become progressively less formidable at the more advanced stages of a man's career. It is more difficult for a talented boy from a disadvantaged minority to find his way into college than into a graduate school.

There are no automatic inclusions. The man who earns a First in comparative philology at Oxford or Cambridge can choose a career in the civil service, in politics, in journalism, or in business, and can move about with comparative freedom without endangering either his financial security or his capacity to find interesting work. A *summa* from Harvard or Berkeley, on the other hand, is an automatic passport only to graduate school, and its value diminishes inversely as the square of the elapsed time since graduation. The cut-off point below which opportunities are denied in Britain is undoubtedly a good deal higher than in the United States; but above that point there appears to be a substantially greater assurance of some form of early recognition.

Lastly, there is no common style of manners, speech, or dress that distinguishes the elect in America. The upper layers in any given competitive pyramid have a good deal more in common than a cross-section of the tops of a number of pyramids.

Despite the relative openness of American society—or perhaps because of it—there is almost no automatic lateral transfer from one ladder of success to another. A successful business man may be able to buy himself a minor role in politics (though the converse is even less likely). The successful academician may maintain a consulting practice in industry or government (and the business or professional man may be occasionally invited back to the university to lecture or to contribute to a learned journal an article drafted by one of the bright young men in his office), but most men climb the rungs of their own institutions, and think of themselves exclusively as scholars, or civil servants, or businessmen. A few general exceptions to this rule should be noted: in the natural sciences, the discipline may take the place of the institution, and the man may regard himself primarily as, say, a meteorologist, whether he is working for the Weather Bureau, in a university, or in industry. Lawyers more often in the northeast than in other parts of the country are accustomed to embellish the accomplishments of their private practice with tours of duty in government. This lawyer-public servant is perhaps the closest approximation of the generalist that our society affords.

The common thread that runs through the diverse careers of those who receive explicit recognition for excellence in our society is a kind of hyperactivity, on the way up, and a quality of leadership at the top. It tends to be a form of leadership characterized more by an excess of energy than of imagination. The kinds of recognition cover a range from the almost completely functional—the chief executive post in a company—to the almost completely formal—the honorary degree. In a nontraditional open society, functional recognition is more frequent and more important than formal recognition.

Functional recognition is particularly important in a society that values leadership. The exercise of leadership requires an organization to be led, and without a system to recognize excellence in leadership, the function may be assigned by inheritance, by popularity, or by lot, if it is not acquired simply by force.

The functional recognition of leadership begins at least as early as high school, and tends to overshadow the formal recognition of other kinds of excellence. High schools, and particularly the more elaborate high schools, in the more elaborate suburbs, put a premium on active participation in a number of organizations.[1] Robert Knapp[2] has pointed out that the mid-Western colleges and universities, which at first prepared their best students for scholarly careers, now emphasize preparation for business and professional leadership in the local or regional community. The importance of extracurricular activities and the recognition accorded to them is demonstrated by the appearance, alongside Phi Beta Kappa, of a *Who's Who Among American College Students.*

The activism of students is at least matched by the activism of their teachers. The best index of status in the academic community is the number of air-miles traveled per year. The proliferation of conferences and institutes creates a demand for organizational talent, which is rewarded in kind. And those academicians who are venturing with more and more success into the commercial publishing market discover, as one publisher has pointed out, that the only measurable corollary of a writer's sales-per-book success is his production of books per year.

Academia still offers recognition to the individual scholar, in such forms as distinguished-service professorships, which may even rank with deanships in the university, although not in popular esteem. In government, on the other hand, the special rewards of managers are set like cement in the rigidity of the Civil Service system. In the United States Department of Justice, for instance, a particularly competent trial lawyer who has reached the top of his Civil Service grade can only be promoted to a higher salary, status and office size taking him out of work for which he is best fitted, and giving him administrative duties in organizing the work of others. There is a small island of exception created in the last few years for people with special scientific and technical skills, who may be paid according to their ability, although their other prerequisites will still depend on their places in the administrative hierarchy.

Similarly, large business organizations, although they may be somewhat more flexible, accord primary recognition to ability for leadership, and sheer stamina is a prerequisite for the higher ranks. The top leadership of large corporate enterprises has passed from the engineer to the lawyer, and seems to be passing now to the public-relations expert; but in each group the quality that draws recognition is extraordinary individual energy and ability to organize the energies of others.

In addition to this functional system of recognition, there is the whole congeries of institutions for the formal recognition of excellence, from the four major national academies, through the various professional honorific societies, committees, awards of honorary degrees, and the like.[3] Two aspects of these institutions are of particular interest: the limited extent to which they perform a primary as distinguished from a reinforcing function in the recognition of excellence, and the even more limited extent to which the recognition they accord is generally recognized by others.

None of the American academies waits quite as long as the *Académie Française,* for which longevity is the essential qualification, but there is a gap of decades between the average age of new members of the American academies chosen on the one hand from the natural sciences, and from the world of affairs, on the other. The social scientists and the humanists range between the two extremes. One reason for the range is that historians, for example, appear to produce their master works considerably later in life than do physicists. But another reason is undoubtedly a tendency to recognize those who have already been recognized by the grant of large responsibilities, or because they have achieved public acclaim for creative work in the arts. It is these people, by and large, who lend the academies what popular reputation they possess, which is surprisingly small. Almost any group discussing the recognition of excellence will contain a minority who are not even aware of the identity of all four academies.*

It is at least questionable whether these academies provide substantial incentives to those who are not yet members, since individual aspirations are more likely to be conceived of in terms of functional professional achievement—books written, experiments completed, public offices attained. What they do accomplish for their members is to provide a sense of colleagueship, a reaffirmation of

* They are, in addition to the American Academy of Arts and Sciences, the National Institute of Arts and Letters' American Academy of Arts and Letters, the American Philosophical Society, and the National Academy of Sciences.

faith in one's own potentialities, and not infrequently an opportunity to do useful work, as on the Committees of the National Academy of Sciences, although membership in the Academy is not a prerequisite for committee membership in all cases. Julian Huxley observed that his early election to the Royal Academy gave him confidence to proceed in the line of experimentation that he might not otherwise have undertaken.[4]

For the natural scientist, then, Academic recognition may have more primary significance than for the social scientist or the humanist. But scientific discoveries are disseminated through the scientific community with increasing rapidity, and scientists who show any administrative competence are under increasing pressure to become part of the web of committees and boards that bind together the worlds of science, government, and industry. Thus it is not unusual for the scientist, after completing his first major substantive work, to move into the world of committees, consultations, and Washington commuting, long before he becomes an Academician.

For the scientist, recognition ordinarily means recognition in a professional community that cuts across geographic lines. Others may have to choose between seeking recognition in a community limited by geography, or in one limited by professional background. David Riesman distinguishes, in university communities, between the Home Guard, whose peers are the local professional and business people, and the more cosmopolitan intellectuals who are in closer touch with their colleagues at other universities than they are with their neighbors.[5] Those who choose the community of their discipline rather than that of their institution may move within the hierarchy of institutions largely on the basis of their scholarly achievements. Bernard Berelson has described the function of the graduate schools as offering the young scholar the opportunity to seek a level of excellence in graduate training appropriate to his undergraduate performance (no matter where he did his undergraduate work), and then sending him out to begin his teaching career at an institution matched to the level of his performance in graduate school.[6]

But academic entrepreneurship—a form of leadership involving the ability to organize research and to attract funds and disciples—is an important factor in upward mobility. And the successful academic entrepreneur is likely to be rewarded with even heavier responsibilities, involving the leadership of larger enterprises, and leaving him even less time for his own work. He may produce more then his colleagues who stayed behind at Siwash U., but the rewards of recognition are almost as much of a distraction as they are a help.

One of the more obvious rewards of recognition in a free enterprise society is money. Yet monetary rewards play a remarkably small part in the recognition of excellence. High compensation levels are confined to the business sector of society, where there is little time to enjoy the fruits of one's labors, and salaries tend to become mere counters of success, along with the executive desk and the wall-to-wall carpeting. Very high compensation does not match pinnacles of achievement; rather it measures control of scarce resources. This scarcity may either be accidental, as in the case of the small businessman whose profits, taxed at capital-gains rates, far exceed the salary and bonuses of the large corporate executive, or it may be intentional, as in the case of the star system in baseball or the movies, where the weekly or seasonal salary of a player is one of the ingredients of his popular image.

There is still a good deal of lip service to the notion of financial rewards. In government service, for instance, great care is taken to preserve salary differentials among various levels of responsibility. But these differentials become so small, in the upper ranks, that they may be more than offset by the additional expenses associated with the higher position. In fact, a junior professional employee (or a young assistant professor) may have more free cash than his senior counterpart. And businessmen are impressively willing to give up their high salaries and fringe benefits, and even to forfeit accumulated gains in stock options and other forms of deferred compensation, in order to assume larger responsibilities in government service.

Leadership is a useful kind of excellence to recognize in a democracy. Since it is inevitably in short supply, the most natural way to recognize leadership is to make even greater use of it. Further opportunity to exercise leadership is a highly appropriate form of recognition for the persons recognized. In an affluent society, increments of affluence have little marginal utility. In an open society, honorific titles and distinctions have little significance. In a noisy society, public praise may be heard only by its recipient. None of this should be particularly disturbing. After all, it is an old saying that the reward of a captaincy is not the captain's cabin, but the command.

Yet there are other forms of excellence, and other ways of rewarding them. Properly rewarded, they might be more highly valued, and might produce corresponding contributions to our society. Leisure, for instance, is a reward available almost exclusively to the unsuccessful. Continuous exposure to a single problem is another reward that goes with not being sought after by people with other problems, more important to them, but perhaps not to the problem-solver. The opportunity to shift from one field of endeavor to another, after having reached maturity in the first field, is very seldom available, although the happy results of such shifts are demonstrated in the careers of men like L. J. Henderson and H. A. Murray. Or take the ability to find and foster excellence in others. We have reason to believe it exists to a high degree in certain gifted individuals. But we know very little about it, in part because it has largely gone unrecognized.

In fact, there are whole professions that suffer from a general failure of recognition by the public at large. The social workers, for example, approached one of our larger foundations, through their trade association, with a proposal for a study of their popular image and how it could be improved. (The proposal was not favorably received.)

Our notions of academic excellence also require revision and expansion in order to give a larger place to the reflective and the creative faculties, as David McClelland suggests elsewhere in this book.[7] At the same time, we need to pay less attention to the student's ability to adjust to the school or college environment, now pre-set to recognize and to reward devotion to the postulate that a straight line is the shortest distance between two points; we must give more thought, in Morris Stein's phrase, to "loosening up" the environment so that it can accommodate the widest variety of talents and interests.[8]

In the adult world, too, there are opportunities to loosen up the working environment. Studies by Donald C. Pelz[9] and others[10] indicate, for example, that the productivity of research laboratories can be increased by giving research workers more frequent contact with a "supportive" but not "over-directive" chief.

The current concern with the nature and environmental determinants of "creativity," as illustrated in the work of Morris Stein at Chicago,[11] and Donald MacKinnon and his associates at Berkeley,[12] represents much more than an interest in the processes of artistic creation. It is rather an effort to explore the ramifications of individual capacity to make significant and unique contributions to society.

The tentative findings on the influence of recognition on creativity are supported by the historical evidence of Wolfgang Kroeber, who discovered that geniuses are not distributed evenly throughout recorded history, but are clustered in particular periods and cultures.[13] We need the benefit of all the creative capacity that we can mobilize to comprehend and cope with the problems of our time. The recognition that society affords to the whole range of these capacities may be the measure of our ability to mobilize them as they are needed.

There are all kinds of ways in which recognition can be given to the forms of excellence that do not now find their own recognition in action. One of the simplest ways is to pay public homage to men whose creative powers have outlasted the brief attention span of popular acclaim. Robert Frost on the Inaugural platform, Walter Lippmann on the television screen, or a former Secretary of State serving as an adviser on foreign affairs—these are incidents too rare in our national life. If they were more frequent, they might even serve to encourage younger men to be less frenetic in pursuit of the bitch goddess, in anticipation of a long marriage rather than a brief affair.

The range of other alternatives is limited only by the limits of our imagination. But the common quality of the useful alternatives is that by recognizing excellence they give it scope to operate, whether through a better workbench for the craftsman or a wider audience for the artist. Several years ago, when President Kennedy was pursuing the Presidential nomination with his characteristic vigor, a reporter asked him why he worked so hard at it, and he replied by quoting a Greek proverb: "Happiness lies in the exercise of vital power along the lines of excellence in a life affording them scope." Remembering that the pursuit of happiness is an ancient and honorable American goal, we might apply President Kennedy's proverb to the recognition of excellence in America today.

REFERENCES

1. See James Coleman, "Style and Substance in American High Schools," *College Admissions*, 1959, no. 6.

2. Robert Knapp and Joseph Greenbaum, *The Younger American Scholar*. Chicago: University of Chicago Press, 1952.

ADAM YARMOLINSKY

3. See Appendix A, "The Techniques of Major National Institutions Which Now Recognize Mature Excellence," in Adam Yarmolinsky, *The Recognition of Excellence*. Chicago: The Free Press of Glencoe, Illinois, 1960, pp. 174-205.

4. Yarmolinsky, *op. cit.*, p. 326.

5. David Riesman, *Constraint and Variety in American Education*. New York: Doubleday Anchor Books, 1958.

6. Bernard R. Berelson, *Graduate Education in the United States*. New York: McGraw-Hill and Company, 1960.

7. Pp. 132-45.

8. Morris Stein, Social and Psychological Factors Affecting Creativity of Industrial Research Chemists (mimeographed); paper delivered at the fall meeting of the Industrial Research Institute, Pittsburgh, 1957.

9. Donald C. Pelz, "Motivation of the Engineering and Research Specialist," in *Improving Managerial Performance*. General Management Series, No. 186, of the American Management Association, Inc., 1957; pamphlet, pp. 25-46.

10. Albert Rubenstein, "The Technical Man—Prologue to Technological Productivity," *Industrial and Engineering Quarterly*, January 1959. See also Annotated Bibliography on Human Relations in Research Laboratories. School of Industrial Management, the Massachusetts Institute of Technology, 1956.

11. Stein, *op. cit.*, note 8; Stein, "Creativity and/or Success," in *Conference Proceedings 1957*, University of Utah Research Conference on the Identification of Creative Scientific Talent. Salt Lake City: University of Utah Press, 1958. Also, Stein, *Creativity and Culture*. Chicago: University of Chicago Press (forthcoming).

12. Donald MacKinnon, "Creativity Research." Paper delivered at the annual meeting of the Western Branch, American Public Health Association, San Francisco, June 1959.

13. Wolfgang Kroeber, *Configurations of Cultural Growth*. University of California Press, 1947.

JAMES MACGREGOR BURNS

Excellence and Leadership in President and Congress

PERHAPS IN NO OTHER area have the concepts of excellence and leadership become more closely identified with each other than in current attitudes toward the American Presidency. Increasingly during the twentieth century our chief executives have come to be tested, on the voters' scales as well as the historians', by their moral and political leadership and policy achievement. How well did the President anticipate developing problems? How much of his program did he get through Congress? How effectively did he represent the national interest? How willing was he to risk momentary unpopularity and to exact sacrifice in order to do what must be done? How deeply did he throw himself into the battle for his program? What will be his place in history?

The crucial test of excellence in this kind of leadership is the capacity of the President not simply to *represent* the voters in the narrow sense, but to move ahead of them, to ignore their more transient and petty interests—in a sense, to *mis*represent, at least until the next presidential election comes around. At the same time, however, the President is a constitutional officer elected by the people, accountable to them, and dependent on them for support. On the President's understanding of when he must directly respond to the fleeting interests of the people, and when he must transcend them, turns his ultimate success as a political leader.

This dualism between leadership and representation finds its enduring expression in the relation of President and Congress. For the national legislature is not expected to move ahead of the voters or to defy them; it is expected to represent them in all their economic, sectional, ethnic, and ideological diversity. Hence the functions of the two branches differ sharply. "The executive is the active power in the state, the asking and the proposing power," Walter Lippmann

155

has said. "The representative assembly is the consenting power, the petitioning, the approving and the criticizing, the accepting and the refusing power."[1] Individual leadership is found within Congress, of course, but as an institution the national legislature does not have the active and initiating role of the President; hence the tests of legislative excellence differ from those of excellence in the executive.

The classic dualism between Congress and President is nothing new; it probably has had more attention from journalists and political scientists than any other single aspect of American government. I shall contend here, however, that this dualism institutionalizes two historic and competing solutions to the problem of achieving effective government without endangering minority and individual rights; that it is today deeply embedded in institutional, ideological, electoral, and intellectual forces; and that this dualism has serious implications for the nourishing of excellence and leadership in our democracy.

Madison: A Balance of Checks

The framers of the Constitution wanted excellence in the Presidency, but they viewed that quality in far different terms than we do today. They wanted not leadership but—as every school boy knows—a wise, judicious chief magistrate who would administer a limited government efficiently and who would, along with the indirectly elected Senate, serve as a check on popular forces in the House of Representatives and in the state legislatures.

But the framers went far beyond the task of setting up government departments and parceling out power. They were occupied, above all, with the problem of how to establish a government strong enough to govern without, as noted above, tyrannizing over the citizens and depriving them of their natural rights. Out of these deliberations came the provisions for an elaborate set of checks and balances, which I shall call, for brevity's sake, the Madisonian formula.[2]

What was the formula? Madison was most explicit. First of all—and this was one of his great arguments for national union—the larger the republic, the "greater variety of parties and interests," and the "less probable that a majority of the whole" would oppress individual citizens and minority groups.[3] But this safeguard was not enough in itself. There must also be the dividing up of national power among different officials, legislative, executive, and judicial, "for the accumulation of powers . . . in the same hands . . . may justly be pronounced the very definition of tyranny."[4] But still this was not enough, for what if the various officials got together and pooled their authority? The answer to this question—the checks and balances—became the archpin of the whole constitutional system. "The great security against a gradual concentration of the several powers in the same department consists in giving to those who administer each department the necessary constitutional means and personal motives to resist encroachments of the others. . . . Ambition must be made to counteract ambition. The interest of the man must be connected with the constitutional rights of the place."[5]

It was here that the Madisonians once again showed their genius as political scientists. For the checks and balances built into the engine of government automatic stabilizing devices were sure to balance one another because they were powered by separate sources of political energy—namely, men's clashing interests and ambitions. The ambitions of Presidents and Senators and Representatives and federal judges were bound to collide because each was responsible to separate constituencies in the "greater variety of parties and interests" of the new federal republic. And each, of course, had some kind of constitutional power—for example, the presidential veto or judicial review—that could be employed against the other departments of government and the sectional or economic or ideological interests they represented.

It was a stunning solution to the framers' problem of preventing majority tyranny. Yet there was a serious flaw, or at least an inconsistency, in the thinking behind it. If, as Madison said, the great protection against naked majority rule was the broader diversity of interests and hence the greater difficulty of concerting their "plans of oppression," why was not this enough in itself? Why would not any political party representing such a variety of interests perforce become so broad and moderate in its goals as never to threaten any major interest? Why was it necessary to have what Madison called "auxiliary precautions"? Because, he said, experience had taught mankind the necessity of them. But he did not prove that this experience was relevant to the new kind of "federal republic" that the framers were setting up.

Jefferson: A Balance of Parties

Madison never came fully to grips with this question. The answer to it finally emerged less from current theory than from later

Jeffersonian practice. Only twelve years after the new republic got under way Jefferson became President, as head of exactly the kind of majority that Madison feared. The new majority was a coalition of Western frontiersmen and Southern planters and Northern mechanics and many other groups, all pulled together into the Republican party under Jefferson. Even worse (from the Madisonian viewpoint) this majority promptly undermined the whole system of checks and balances by taking control of the Congress as well as the Presidency and then proceeding to batter the Federalists, who had taken refuge in the judiciary.

According to Madisonian theory, Jeffersonian practice should have ruined the new Republic. In fact, it did nothing of the kind. When Jefferson in his first inaugural address said "We are all Republicans, we are all Federalist," he was making clear that no deep differences of principle did or could separate the two parties. He was implying that any majority in a balanced society would be so broad and so moderate that no minority party or group would be imperiled. He was saying in effect that *social* checks and balances—the great variety of sections and groups and classes and opinions—stitched into the fabric of society would be enough to prevent tyranny by the majority.[6] And that is the way it worked out.[7]

Americans have made so much of Madison's checks and balances that they often forget that Jeffersonian practice stressed checks and balances too. But the two types differed radically. Madison's system turned on the "Swiss watch" concept, as Saul K. Padover has called it, of checking government through major "opposite and rival" interests, any one of which, through "its" branch of government, could stop arbitrary action by the majority. Jefferson's system assumed that no majority or majority party would take arbitrary action because to do so would be to antagonize the great "middle groups" that held the political balance of power and hence could rob the governing party of its majority at the next election. A democratic people, in short, embodied its own checks and balances.[8]

Each system required a reliable mechanism. Madison's assumed that ambition would indeed counteract ambition, that around each government official—be he executive, legislator, or even judge—a web of political interests and ideologies would develop to furnish political backing for that official within the government and outside it. Madison's assumption has been magnificently vindicated. From the stirring days of the early 1800's, when the Federalists rallied around Chief Justice John Marshall's defiance of the Republican majority, to the grim resistance by segregationist Southerners to the Court and President today, strong minorities have used some agency of government to thwart a popular majority led by a strong President.

Jefferson's system, too, turns on a key piece of machinery—the balance of a vigorous, two-party system. His formula assumes that in a varied society each party will compete mightily for the independents, for the men in the middle, for the nonpartisan or uncommitted. At the same time, each party must keep the backing of its hard core, of the partisans, of even the extremists, in order to continue as a going organization. Hence, each party will broaden its appeal to cover a long spectrum of political interests and attitudes.

How has the Jeffersonian formula turned out? It was bound to work to some extent, for it assumed that men would naturally divide into factions but that there would also be a counterbalancing tendency toward coalescence into broader groupings in order to form a majority and win office. But in two interrelated ways the Jeffersonian formula has broken down. The system of federalism—the division of powers between national officials and a host of state and local officials—has made it difficult for the same two-party system to provide for vigorous competition at every level of government and for every office. And the Civil War so distorted the existing balance of parties as to throw the normal party balance awry for many decades.

What has happened is that both the Madisonian and Jeffersonian formulas have been stamped on our political machinery. We have operated a system of checks and balances at the same time as we have tried to operate a system of majority rule. How has this intermingling of the two systems worked out—and what are the implications for political leadership in the United States?

Domestic Blend: Our Multi-party System

It was Madison's brilliant insight that checks and balances *within* the government were not enough, that the "constitutional rights of the place" must be connected with the "interest of the man"—in short, with his political ambition.[9] Formal constitutional authority would be buttressed by practical political power. How far Madison extended this insight is not clear. His concern—almost an obsession—with factions suggests that he well understood the tendency of politicians to collect a group of followers and build a position of power. In any event, the implications of his insight are clear today: around every position established under the new Constitution, whether President, legislator, or even judges and department heads, a circle of subleaders and followers would grow, the size of the circle depending on the importance of the office and the appeal of the leader. Other factions would grow around politicians outside government, striving to get in. To make matters even more complicated, the new Constitution left essentially intact a proliferation of offices at state, county, and local levels; these in turn were the centers of thousands of other little circles of political action and influence.

These office-holders, their rivals, and the circles of subleaders and followers around them comprise a web of influence stretching across the formal governmental system. This is not to deny the importance of political parties and formal groups, of opinion-shaping agencies, and of the thick crust of traditional habits and attitudes, of the ideological and socio-economic forces at work, and of the other factors that we customarily study in political science. It is to say that, given the essential stability of our constitutional system, these offices establish the main structure of political combat and governmental power.[10]

The Madisonian balance of checks functioned from the very start—for example, when Washington lost his majority in Congress. Carried to an extreme, it would have given us a chaos of separated power groups, each blocking and checking the other. But it was never meant to be carried to an extreme, nor would conditions allow it. Whatever their separated posts and personal followings, office-holders and office-seekers had to concert their efforts to gain their larger aims. Moreover, in each state and in the national government, there were supreme executive posts (governorships and the Presidency) around which the struggle tended to polarize. Around Jefferson, for example, there grew up a nation-wide following strong enough to overcome the Federalists organized around Washington and Adams. In a nation lacking deep fissures, save that between North and South, the competition for the Presidency was largely responsible for maintaining a national two-party system.

But if the Jeffersonian formula, too, began to function within a decade of the adoption of the Constitution, inside the developing two-party system the old Madisonian formula was highly operative. Its full dimensions we cannot explore here. In Washington during the early decades of the last century it began to produce a group of Senators and Representatives more or less loosely allied with the President under the broad umbrella of one national party, or more or less opposed to him under another umbrella. At the same time, in most states and in the nation as well, the two parties were roughly competitive. For some years the Madisonian system of checks and balances and the Jeffersonian system of competitive parties were in a condition of vigorous counterpoise.

Then came the derangement of the Civil War. The struggle left a gash across the politics of the country and on the regular workings of the party battle. The result, in sum, was to leave huge sections of the country dominated by one of the two parties—by the Democrats in the South and by the Republicans in the North and Northwest. In an astonishingly short time the balance of presidential politics righted itself; within a dozen years of the war's end the Democrats were winning majorities in popular votes for their presidential candidate. But in most of the states—and in their representation in Congress—one or the other party was overwhelmingly dominant.[11]

Here was the rub: the more unipartisan an area became, the less competitive, of course, were the two parties, and hence the less pressure on the dominant party to moderate its appeal in order to attract the middle-of-the-road, balance-of-power voters. This was especially evident in state and local politics; but also it closely affected the election of United States Senators and Representatives. For legislators from one-party states, re-election hinged not on winning the votes of the independents and middle-of-the-roaders but on keeping the support of Old Guard leaders and the hard-core partisan rank-and-file.[12] Here was precisely a reversal of the Jeffersonian formula; for the men who went to Congress from these states and districts tended to speak for the strong partisans and their narrower interests rather than for the broader, more diverse interests of the nation. Such legislators not only contracted the scope of their own representation but they also inhibited congressional and presidential leadership as a whole. Entrenched on Capitol Hill, moreover, these legislators further narrowed congressional representation as a result of the inordinate influence they gained through the workings of seniority. They came to dominate not only the committees but also the other key institutions of Congress and even its very atmosphere. Ultimately, not only Congress as a whole but also certain committees and factions and even individuals could thwart action by the majority. Here was the Madisonian formula with a vengeance. Presidents, on the other hand, had to follow the Jeffersonian formula of winning or retaining the support of the centrist groups in order to gain or keep office.

The result of all this in the national government was much more

important, and much more complex, than the familiar division between President and Congress. It was the rise on a national scale
within each party of a presidential grouping that included in its orbit not only the President's following in the Administration and in
the country, but also his following (generally speaking) among the
congressmen of his party who came from marginal districts and were
less responsive to the party's hard core. This development took place
within both the Democratic and Republican parties. If, as Dean
Acheson has perceptively noted, the Democratic party "since the
Civil War has made the Legislature the special province of the
Southern Democrat, and the Executive the special province of the
Northern Democrat,"[13] we can also say that the Republicans have
made Congress the special province of rural, conservative forces in
the party, and the Executive the special province of the Eastern, urban, liberal, and internationalist elements.

The Web of Power

This division of the two national parties into two presidential
and two congressional parties is, of course, a simplification. Indeed,
a logical extension of Madison's insight about factionalism would
compel us to perceive 539 national parties—a party in the Capitol
(and in the country) formed around every Senator and Representative, the President, and the Vice-President—plus at least another
539 parties composed of those vying for all these offices.[14] But again
we must consider the compulsion of politicians to concert their interests and band together. The most meaningful pattern at the national level is to be found not in a jumble of hundreds of personal
factions, not (at the other extreme) in a simple two-party system,
but in a four-party system embracing the congressional and presidential wing of each national party. Why? Because institutionally,
ideologically, electorally, and in other ways, the congressional and
presidential parties are as sharply set off from each other as the
Democratic and Republican parties as a whole are from each other.
In more specific terms:

1. *Institutional:* The national party structure shows a bifurcation
between the presidential and congressional parties. The great domain of the presidential party is the national convention, established
originally to shift control of presidential nominations out of the congressional caucus (and hence out of the congressional party). With

the exception of Warren G. Harding, recent leaders of congressional parties have not won presidential nominations, as the experience of John Garner, Robert Taft, Arthur Vandenberg, and Lyndon B. Johnson attests; the great prize goes to the Roosevelts, Willkies, Deweys, Stevensons, and Eisenhowers. But the congressional party often gains a consolation prize in the vice-presidential nomination (McNary, Bricker, Garner, Nixon, and the like). An instrument of the congressional Democrats against the convention system was the famous two-thirds rule, but the presidential Democrats finally abolished the rule in 1936.

The campaign structure of the parties reveals the same dualism between the congressional and presidential parties. Presidential campaigns are conducted through the candidates' personal organizations, such as Volunteers for Stevenson, the Willkie Clubs, Citizens for Kennedy, and so on—in uneasy alliance with the regular Democratic committees, the national committee, and the national chairman, who is the President's man. The campaigns of the more senior Senators and Representatives receive the strongest financial assistance from the Senatorial and Congressional campaign committees. The presidential and congressional campaign committees usually operate separately from each other.

2. *Ideological:* Each of the four parties stands in a fairly coherent ideological and policy position. The presidential Democrats have been generally internationalist in foreign policy and liberal in domestic matters. The presidential Republicans have been perhaps as internationalist behind the leadership of men like Elihu Root, Henry Stimson, Charles Evans Hughes, John Foster Dulles, and Christian Herter, even aside from almost all their presidential nominees during this century. The congressional Democrats have been relatively internationalist in foreign affairs (although this may be changing today with the swing toward isolationism in the South) and moderate or conservative in domestic policy, as in the case of Rayburn, Johnson and the Democratic committee chairmen in House and Senate. The congressional Republicans are generally conservative and isolationist, as in the case of Robert Taft, Everett Dirksen, Charles Halleck, and Barry Goldwater.

Seeing our national politics as a four-party system, with the two presidential and two congressional parties arrayed from left to right, helps us to understand the durability of certain political alliances. For example, the two presidential parties have long worked together under the banner of bipartisanship, so that it was not difficult for

Henry Stimson to join Franklin Roosevelt's Cabinet in 1940 or for Douglas Dillon to join Kennedy's in 1960. And the coalition between congressional Democrats and Republicans is one of the most durable in national politics.

3. *Electoral:* For the presidential parties the key election is of course the presidential, when each of the presidential parties, following the Jeffersonian formula, reaches out for broader support and brings millions of voters into its embrace. In these elections many congressional candidates are swept into the vortex of the presidential contestants; such congressional candidates tend to represent marginal districts, and their fates turn more directly on the success of the presidential candidate. Congressmen from one-party districts, on the other hand, can withstand presidential tides moving against them, as Northern rural Republicans did against Franklin Roosevelt, and Southern Democratic congressmen did against Eisenhower. Still, the presidential candidates dominate the presidential election, if only in setting the whole style and context of the debate over national issues. It is in the off-year elections that the congressional Democrats and Republicans come into their own. The incumbent presidential party almost always suffers a defeat, and the setbacks occur mainly in marginal districts. But half the congressional seats (those in strongly partisan areas) do not change even during electoral tidal waves, and these seats, of course, are the foundation of the electoral power of the congressional parties.[15]

Other significant distinctions among the main parties might be noted. For example, each of the parties attracts distinctive types of newspapers and columnists; i.e., the *Chicago Tribune* is a spokesman for the congressional Republicans, just as William S. White is a perceptive interpreter of the Congressional Democrats; each has foreign-policy biases according to geographic line (i.e., the two Republican parties emphasize Far Eastern problems, the two Democratic, European); each, of course, has its deepest roots in certain sections of the country. It would be useful, too, to trace the workings of the four-party system back through history and to raise some questions: for example, to what extent was the coming of the Civil War a result of the supremacy of the Congressional Democrats in the 1850's, or what was the role of the Congressional Republicans in the Republican fiasco of 1912?

Perhaps enough has been said to suggest the value of viewing political leadership through a four-party lens. Because each party is responsive to its own peculiar set of electoral, attitudinal, and institutional forces, and because these forces tend to reinforce one another, the four-party system is the supreme embodiment in the nation of the Madisonian formula. For it fortifies the whole set of institutional and factional checks envisaged by Madison with ideological and electoral and personal forces that make those checks far more formidable and persistent than they otherwise would be. For our present purposes, the system has crucial implications for leadership and excellence in government. It remains only to spell these out.

Leadership and Excellence: the Presidential Parties

The test of excellence in President and Congress during the 1960's will turn, it seems evident, on their capacity to provide "hard leadership"—that is, to anticipate rising needs and problems and to head them off early by forthright planning and concerted action, regardless of the outcries and opposition of influential segments of society. Let us consider the potential capacity of the four-party system to meet this test of excellence.

By almost every criterion, the two presidential parties are better equipped to meet the test than are the congressional. For one thing, the presidential party has an assured position of power for four years.[16] It can resist transient opposition to hardship measures on the expectation that these measures will have shown their worth by election time, or that the more self-interested and parochial opposition will have abated. But the next election is a sobering consideration, too, for the opposing presidential party will seize on the more durable and perhaps justifiable complaints and store them for the next presidential campaign. Yet the opposition presidential party has its obligations too; a reckless exploitation of grievances and the offering of irresponsible promises will put the opposing presidential party into an untenable position when and if it takes power. Both presidential parties, in short, operate by the Jeffersonian formula, which forces them to widen their appeal. But—and this is the crucial point for the days ahead—the price of widening their appeal is not inaction in the face of minority groups but bold leadership to arouse and attract the support of the balance-of-power elements in the electorate.

Second, the presidential parties attract talent. This, indeed, has been one of their most impressive contributions to government. Presidents and presidential candidates like the Roosevelts, Wilson, Dewey, Willkie, and Stevenson have brought with them into national life men and women with sharpened vision and fresh ideas: Gifford Pinchot, Henry Stimson, Louis Brandeis, Felix Frankfurter, Frances Perkins, to name but a few. To be sure, congressional party leaders like Taft and Johnson and committee chairmen who are building staffs have brought able people into government (as have Supreme Court justices, by plucking the best graduates from law school), but inevitably the congressional parties suffer by comparison on this score. Indeed, at times these parties tolerate anti-intellectualism, as Taft did, and even, as in McCarthy's day, provide a home for it. The presidential parties can hire on a grand scale, and they can offer the right working environment for talent, including access to the leader. Many presidential party leaders have been able to recruit talent on a private basis even when they were not in office, as in the case of Nelson Rockefeller.

The place that intellectuals have found in our presidential parties is vital to imagination and experimentation in government. It also shows that a mass party under intelligent leadership can co-exist with a small, controversial elite. Even more, the mass party and the intellectual elite need each other to achieve the ends of both. The party requires the elite because it requires the elite's ideas and innovations in order to attract future majorities. The elite needs the party, for otherwise it would be almost impotent politically.

Finally (and most notably) the presidential party, whether Democratic or Republican, holds the levers of government administration. By heritage and temperament and by government position it is better equipped than the congressional parties to unify a series of separate efforts in pursuit of common goals. Above all, it has a single leader, the President. Through his political resources and his charismatic appeal the President stands at the center of the political network.[17] He has the intellectuals to supply him with ideas, the experts to equip him with ways and means, the national rostrum from which to pronounce his views, the reservoir of personal influence for pushing his program on Capitol Hill. Nothing can substitute for the Presidency, and nothing need do so. The congressional parties, on the other hand, cannot govern precisely because they lack these qualities of the presidential parties. Usually they do not possess even a single, acknowledged head, but rather operate under the disabilities of a collective leadership that is only loosely unified in opposition and even less so when holding power.[18]

Still, the presidential party cannot govern alone; it must find an ally either in its own congressional party or in the "opposite" presidential party, or both. Because the two presidential parties are so close in attitude, especially on foreign policy, they are constantly under pressure to work with each other. For example, Presidents Franklin Roosevelt and Truman gained backing from presidential Republicans in Congress and they chose leading members of the party for their Administrations. This was bipartisanship in action. But in the four-party analysis—and this is one reason for using it—there are all kinds of bipartisanship, including the coalition of the two *congressional* parties behind relatively conservative and isolationist policies.[19]

The pressures of presidential elections, on the other hand, inexorably push the two presidential parties apart, at least every fourth year. Where else can the presidential party in office find the allies it must have to press through its program? For the presidential Democrats, the only other resort is the congressional Democratic party. Since today the presidential Democrats once again command the White House, it might be useful to conclude by considering President Kennedy in the four-party context.

In his early years in the House of Representatives, Mr. Kennedy looked like a rising young leader of the congressional party, especially since he represented a Boston district that guaranteed him seniority in the long run. But in the Senate he deserted the congressional Democrats and moved steadily toward legislative and symbolic leadership of the presidential Democrats. Like many of his predecessors, he chose a leading congressional Democrat—indeed, *the* leading congressional Democrat, Lyndon Johnson—as his running mate. In building his administration he followed tradition by appointing Republicans to major posts.

As his administration got under way early in 1961, it appeared likely that the new President would face the classic problems of bipartisanship with the congressional Democrats. Certain factors seemed likely to help him during his first year: his own political skills; the cooperation of Johnson and other congressional leaders; and majorities for the Democratic party in Congress. But it seemed inevitable, barring an acute crisis, that at some point he would encounter the relentless workings of the Madisonian formula. Because, as Madison perceived, the checks against Administration action were embedded in political forces, simple mechanical changes would not be enough; it would be possible, for example, to curb the Rules Committee without curbing the forces that lay behind that committee, and these would reappear in the same or in some other institutional form. To be sure, Mr. Kennedy would probably exploit his executive powers, perhaps more than any President since Theodore Roosevelt, especially in the areas of military and foreign policy and civil rights. But the potential of executive action was sharply limited because Mr. Kennedy's central task was to shift spending from the private to the public sector, and this required the cooperation of the congressional Democrats who controlled the economic-policy committees on Capitol Hill. Here again, reforms could be achieved in superficial procedures and powers without changing the underlying pattern of power.

All this is not to say that American government is static. It is changing more than many realize: population shifts from state to state will be reflected in Congress, even if state legislatures gerrymander the new districts. Urbanization and suburbanization proceed remorselessly. While Southern politicians shout their old battle-cry against integration, their region is becoming increasingly nationalized. The enormous growth of the national and state governments itself is having a heavy impact on the structure of government. The people and press not only tolerate presidential leadership: they demand it. Probably the Kennedy administration will experiment with new techniques of government. Above all, the mass media are forcing attention to world problems such as African nationalism and domestic problems such as race relations in the deep South, problems which only a decade or so were far beyond the awareness of the "man in the street." All these forces are producing institutional change.

But how quickly? The pressures on government accelerate swiftly, while the system evolves slowly. As the Kennedy administration settled in, it was an open question whether the old problems of the Madisonian formula could be resolved in the 1960's, or whether the new President could carry the Jeffersonian formula to a new frontier of its own. This much was clear. The solution to divided government and to four-party conflict would not be provided by anything that exacted as a price the watering down of political leadership—of the President's ability to override narrow opposition, to broaden his political base, to recruit talent and expertise, to unite men in and out of government behind great expectations. For in the 1960's, perhaps more than ever before, this kind of leadership was the price of excellence in a democracy.

Perhaps by an act of creative leadership the new President could reorganize the constellation of political forces in the country and

168

lead in the refashioning of governmental machinery on Capitol Hill so that the political forces to which his presidential and the congressional Democratic parties responded would coincide more closely.[20] Or perhaps, like most of his predecessors, he would act in the pragmatic tradition, making immediate advances wherever he could and leaving more fundamental changes to the steady workings of social and economic change. The latter was much more likely—in which case the vital question would be whether the political changes would come soon enough and decisively enough to enable presidential leadership to contribute its full measure toward democratic excellence, or even democratic survival.

REFERENCES

1. Walter Lippmann, *Essays in the Public Philosophy*. Boston: Little, Brown and Company, 1955, p. 30.

2. A note on nomenclature: to call this theory Madisonian is something of an oversimplification, since Madison as a moderate did not carry the implication of his theory to the hilt (for example, he opposed equal representation of the states in the Senate, and later, as a Jeffersonian Republican, he implicitly repudiated his formula). But this term has received general acceptance; see, for example, Robert A. Dahl, *A Preface to Democratic Theory*. Chicago: The University of Chicago Press, 1956.

3. *The Federalist*, No. 10.

4. *The Federalist*, No. 47.

5. *The Federalist*, No. 51.

6. It should be kept in mind that the Jeffersonian formula applies only to societies comprising a mosaic of groups, not to societies in which a great gap, economic or otherwise, exists between classes or sections—not to societies, that is, that are short on "overlapping memberships." See David B. Truman, *The Governmental Process*. (New York: Alfred A. Knopf, 1951.

7. Another note on nomenclature: While a firm believer in majority rule, and later a strong party leader as President (the first and perhaps the strongest President as party leader we have had), Jefferson did not, as far as I know, develop his practice into grand political theory. What I have described here is implicit in both his theory and his practice.

8. For a brilliant development of this point, see Henry Steele Commager, *Majority Rule and Minority Rights*. London: Oxford University Press, 1943. On the role of the middle classes and our two-party system, see Arthur N. Holcombe, *Our More Perfect Union*. Cambridge: Harvard University Press, 1950.

9. *The Federalist*, No. 51.

10. For a wholly different hypothesis, see C. Wright Mills, *The Power Elite*. New York: Oxford University Press, 1950.

11. For a full treatment of one-partyism in the South, see V. O. Key, Jr., *Southern Politics*. New York: Alfred A. Knopf, 1949; for aspects of New England one-partyism, see Duane Lockard, *New England State Politics*. Princeton: Princeton University Press, 1959; and for a searching study of one-party politics throughout the nation, see V. O. Key, Jr., *American State Politics: An Introduction*. New York: Alfred A. Knopf, 1956.

12. The substitution of party primaries for conventions probably exacerbated this whole problem; see Key, *American State Politics, passim*.

13. Dean Acheson, *A Democrat Looks at His Party*. New York: Harper & Brothers, 1955.

14. Ralph M. Goldman, in "Party Chairman and Party Faction, 1789-1900: A Theory of Executive Responsibility and Conflict Resolution," Ph.D. Dissertation, University of Chicago, 1951, defines a seven-party national split, including "Party-in-Senate," "Party-in-House," and parties focused in the presidential campaign organization, in the national committee, and so on.

15. For an illuminating study of recent congressional elections, see M. C. Cummings, Jr., "Congressmen and the Electorate: A Study of House Elections in Presidential Years, 1920-1956," Ph.D. Dissertation, Harvard University, 1960.

16. An exception here consists of the members of Congress who are in the President's party but who have the problem of the midterm elections, as noted above.

17. See Richard E. Neustadt, *Presidential Power*, New York: John Wiley & Sons, 1960, for an admirable exposition of the President's bargaining power and the limitations on his action.

18. David B. Truman, *The Congressional Party*, New York: John Wiley & Sons, 1959, for example, shows little collective leadership to have existed in either party in the 81st Congress.

19. The virtues of bipartisanship are uncritically accepted in this country because it has come to stand for cooperation between the two presidential parties. But bipartisanship, in a four-party system, is also cooperation between the two *congressional* parties. It would be interesting to see what would happen to eulogies of bipartisanship if the Democratic and Republican Congressional parties began to run the government. What the advocates of bipartisanship really support, of course, is not the mechanism itself but the liberal, internationalist policies that they get through it.

20. On the practical and theoretical aspects of this kind of leadership, see James H. Burns, *Roosevelt: The Lion and the Fox*, New York: Harcourt, Brace and Company, 1956, especially chs. 14, 18, and the "Note on the Study of Political Leadership" in the appendix.

DON K. PRICE

Administrative Leadership

ONE OF THE classic anecdotes in the apocrypha of Washington tells how the chairman of the board of a great corporation, many years ago, was brought in as a staff member of the White House. When reporters asked how his responsibilities could be distinguished from those of the Secretary of a certain Department, he said, that was easy; unlike the Secretary, he was interested only in policy, not in administration. What, insisted a reporter, was the difference? Well, replied the industrialist, take my company; our board of directors leaves administration to the president; we are interested only in high policy like—well, for example, like the design of a soap wrapper.

This story, of course, is worth cherishing not for its accuracy (not guaranteed) but for its moral. The obvious part of the moral is that men in business often spend their energies on issues less important than those they would deal with in government—which may suggest that the nation could afford to transfer some of their talents to more important public purposes. The less obvious part of the moral is that in government, as in business, high officials may take great satisfaction in dealing efficiently with trivial problems, while the big issues are settled by subordinates, or by accident, or by factional politics, or by default.

For a good many years now we have been informed as to the first of these points. When the Commission on National Goals recently reported to the then President Eisenhower that "the vastly increased demands upon the federal government require at the higher levels more public servants equal in competence and imagination to those in private business and the professions," and suggested that "this involves a drastic increase in their compensation," it was doing little more than repeating what the second Hoover Commission had said soon after Eisenhower took office. But in between, a great many things had happened to change our national attitudes; an administration whose backers at the beginning had looked to it mainly to get government out of competition with business ended by proposing to accept responsibility for inducing economic growth at home and abroad, for producing more physics Ph.D.'s than the Russians did, and for exploring the solar system. It may well be that we are now ready to admit that our government cannot do what we expect of it unless it can claim a larger share of the best administrative ability in the nation. "A great empire and little minds go ill together."

If we come to accept this idea, it will not be merely because the government has grown in size. Even more important are two changes in the kind of things it does, and the way it does them. The first is a change in the degree of specialized competence required to deal with public affairs. This is true of the economic and social as well as the technological aspects of government; in the latter it is only the more obvious. With this change, the technological and scientific corps (in and out of uniform) have begun to exert a more powerful influence on policy. (Who would have dreamed a decade or so ago, when we were holding our annual budget down to thirteen billion, that we would so soon take their word for the need to spend more than twice that much to put a man on the moon!) As a result, the politician may now see in the general administrator, not a bureaucrat who threatens to usurp his policy-making function, but an ally without whose professional help he can never comprehend and control the new social forces.

Second, in the most dynamic sectors of our economy and educational system, we are beginning to change the relation between government and private institutions in much the same way that we changed the relation between the federal government and the states about a quarter of a century earlier. In place of the grants-in-aid that tied the states to Washington in fields like soil conservation and social security, we now have contracts and grants that link Washington with DuPont in atomic energy, with General Dynamics in the missile program and with the Massachusetts Institute of Technology and the California Institute of Technology in fields ranging from physics to international affairs. We therefore have no longer a system in which all private institutions look apprehensively at the higher bureaucracy as the motive power for immoral government spending, and try to suppress such spending. Indeed, it may now be clear, even to extreme conservatives, that it will require very great authority and administrative strength at the center of our government either to enforce economy against private demands for government spending or to direct that spending in the national interest.

These two changes call on us not merely to get more capable men into government, so as to manage efficiently the policies that politicians have prefabricated. That could be done quite simply by raising salaries and providing other incentives. But there is no point in merely transferring to government the avarice of the private sector without its enterprise, by giving high salaries to men who will not rise to the challenge of big problems. This brings us to the second half of our moral. For our traditional prejudices have not merely made it difficult to get for government a fair share of the top administrative talent, but they have forced the able men now in government careers to concentrate their talents on the interests of particular bureaus or services. And so we have made it almost impossible for the career service to do its main job—which is to look ahead at the great problems that confront the nation, to devise and recommend policies to meet them, and to see that the various departments are effectively coordinated in carrying the decisions of responsible political authorities.

Some of the best career men in government know this quite well, and know what should be done about it. But it is hard for them to do their main job well when our system was set up on the assumption that it ought not to be done at all. We are comparatively good at politics, but then we were born free. At the other end of the spectrum, we are very good indeed at technology and detailed management; no nation is better at getting specific things invented or managed. But the connection between these two aspects of government is weak, and sometimes it is not there at all. This is the crucial blind spot in our political vision.

We hardly notice the gap, perhaps because we have no word for the function that is missing. We have taken the word "administration" from British usage, and it will have to do, but its connotations in Whitehall and in Washington are quite different. The British administrative class hardly manages anything: its job is (under general political control) to make policy and see that the departments are effectively coordinated. Its purpose is to be the corporate custodian of a great tradition, and to adjust it to new political needs.

If we are tempted to comfort ourselves by saying that such a career in civil service simply will not fit the American tradition, we ought to forget about the British and look at the career systems we ourselves have created. For, with all their defects—some of which our civil service ought to avoid with the greatest care—the military services and the Foreign Service suggest that, once we decide a career system is worth the cost, we know how to develop it and to train it for the higher functions of policy-making.

We have given up *laissez faire* in any economic issue that we consider of national importance. We are beginning to give it up in education; how many people should be attracted by fellowships into the study of Urdu or microbiology is now acknowledged as a proper matter for Congressional concern. The one field in which we most stubbornly continue our faith in the free play of the market is in the provision of personnel for high administrative positions in government, and this at a time when that type of excellence in government is the key to the success of all our other efforts.

It may be too kind to suggest that this neglect comes from a blind faith in tradition or from absentmindedness. On the face of the matter, it would seem that the system is rigged so that a capable young man, having risen rapidly in government to a position of responsibility for policy, will have to take a private job to protect his family's future.

The main point here is not a very abstruse one. If you talk to a college senior about going into the civil service, you cannot tell him that he will be promoted on the basis of his usefulness to the government as a whole. You are tempted to warn him that, to get ahead, he may have to plan his career in terms of the specialized interest of a single bureau. Happily, there are still men who ignore this counsel of caution, and whose government careers show real dedication to the public service and a breadth of interest that transcends any specialized field in the natural or social sciences or in management. But this is like asking our army to rely on individual heroism or on election by the troops, rather than a system of training and promotion, to develop officers for general staff work.

That, of course, is just what we did do until we saw the importance of the problem. We came to see this only gradually. Today the young man who becomes a military officer knows that the people who decide on his next assignment are instructed to think of it as a step in the purposeful development of his career, in which his rewards for developing as a general officer will be greater than those of any specialty.

There are many important differences between military and civilian administration, but in a rough sense the work of the staff planners

174

and the top command in a military service is like that of central administration in the civil service. Today, in our recognition of the importance of this civilian function, we are not far ahead of where we were in military affairs when President Wilson indignantly ordered the General Staff to stop preparing war plans: we are afraid that such work will usurp the proper function of political leadership.

A half-century ago we had just begun to organize our Army General Staff, in the face of dire predictions that it would lead to a military caste or a dictatorship. Today it is evident that it is possible to develop a professional system for military officers without destroying democratic responsibility: the officer corps of the several services are drawn from a wide variety of civilian universities as well as from the service academies, and the Congressional committees (as well as the President) still maintain a control over military policy that has no counterpart in any other major political system. But the main point is that we recognized in time that we not only needed to have a career system for the officer corps, but that it needed to be headed up in a corporate staff concerned, not with the command of particular divisions or the direction of particular technical services, but with the general policies and strategy of the forces.

It is hard to imagine how we should have survived if we had not developed something like the general staff function in all our military services. The nature of warfare, with its growing complexity, velocity, and lethality, made this function necessary: the new military technology, and the new weapons systems, added immeasurably to the intricacy of military affairs, and to the speed of innovation, and above all to the utterly fatal results of falling behind. If you read the administrative history of the Civil War or the Spanish-American War and compare it with that of the Second World War or the Korean War, the contrast gives a faint idea of the need for general staff work.

Or if your imagination boggles at this comparison, you can try to imagine what the Pentagon would be like if all the staff officers were removed, and their functions were left entirely to part-time consultants from industry, Congressional committee staff members, and political coordinating committees, with a few columnists and commentators taking part occasionally to keep the mixture from being too bureaucratic. This is unthinkable, because everyone understands that the changes in the complexity, velocity, and lethality of our military developments have made a fundamental change in the way in which we must try to keep military matters under democratic control. Political authorities can make decisions on immediate issues only if professional staff officers have worked out acceptable alternative solutions for them, and the most effective use of top political authority may well be to set the professionals to work on issues that have to be faced five or ten years hence—or to develop a system to improve the professional corps so that it can do so.

Political responsibility, in short, depends on having a responsive and well-trained professional corps, and cannot be achieved by keeping it in a state of fragmentation and anarchy. We as a sovereign people are quick to criticize the lack of integration of our military services and their strategic plans, but we would never know of such conflicts if the professional staffs had not prepared the plans and been forced to bring their discrepancies into the open by our civilian political controls. Like any other testy and temperamental sovereign, we resent having our experts bring us hard problems. Perhaps it would be better if they solved them without bothering us. But it would be much worse if they failed to recognize them.

If we are not very worried about the lack of unification of the civilian departments, perhaps it is because they have not been very good about bringing up the issues that we ought not to duck. In the light of the probable developments over the next decade or two, are our agricultural policies as closely coordinated with our plans for industrial development, as our Navy's strategy is with that of our Air Force? I doubt it. Does our planning for the use of radio and television wave lengths take into account our future educational needs? Is someone worrying about the way in which our programs of water conservation relate to the future distribution of our population as it will be affected by our transportation and industrial development and housing policies?

I am not proposing that career administrators have any more authority—but only an opportunity to help bring up the issues that political authority must resolve. Nor am I advocating additional governmental controls—I am only asking whether the extensive controls we already have are being used in a rationally related manner. For if their interrelations are ignored, the waste in our civilian economy will be far greater than could be caused by poor business methods. This is the scale of waste involved not in the mismanagement of logistics, but in civil war. I do not think the metaphor is too strong. President after President has seen the fight between the Army Corps of Engineers and the Reclamation Bureau over the development of water resources; advisory committee after advisory committee has

pointed to the waste involved in this competition; but the strife between these two agencies, and their supporters throughout the country representing two sets of interests and two conceptions of policy,
has not only kept the President and the Congress from putting a
rational single policy into effect, but has destroyed a Presidential staff
agency which tried to deal with the question, prevented the development of another, and restricted the staff which the Secretary of the
Interior could build up to work on the problem.

Similarly, the political battles of the affected interests have kept
our transportation policies mainly in the hands of independent com-
missions, with little relation to each other or to the President or Congress. Here, too, all recent Presidents have seen the issue; I doubt
that any would have been permitted by the Congress even to set up
a staff to work on the problem. And without some staff work to bring
out the issues clearly, there is no grist for the mills of democracy; as
a sovereign people, we do not even effectively know the issues exist,
though we may blindly, by governmental action, be determining the
economic and social fate of whole industries or regions or metropolitan areas.

If this kind of waste were all that was involved, we could stand
it. But there is a graver problem. The basic nature of the relation of
military to civilian affairs has changed since World War II. Then,
we could still get along with a small peace-time army; then, the term
"mobilization" meant that we could wait till after the war began to
draft the soldiers and manufacture the munitions. But now, with the
possibility of instant long-range destruction, the military cannot be
set off in a corner until the shooting starts, when the rest of us can
then volunteer for the duration. It has to be interwoven with every
aspect of our society, and our future plans. Especially our future
plans.

And if the civil government has no future plans of its own, the military will make them. It cannot wait around while civilians squabble
about the nature of the regulatory process and government-business
relations, when it sees the air space over our major cities cluttered
up in a traffic jam of civilian planes that would be fatal in a crisis;
it has to become one of the major political stockholders, so to speak,
of a new Federal Aviation Agency to replace a Civil Aeronautics
Administration. It cannot wait for civilians to settle their arguments
about federal control of education or the relation of a potential National Science Foundation to the President; it has to go ahead
through military grants to support nine tenths of the physics research

177

in the major universities in the country. It cannot wait for Congressman Rooney to ease up on the diplomatic allowances or the training funds or any of the other costs of a high-quality career Foreign Service; it can give the military attaché of an embassy or the head of a Military Assistance Advisory Group much more entertainment money than to the ambassador, and the only American official airplanes available in the country, so that the ambassador may entertain and travel by courtesy of his military colleagues.

Any civilian with even a dim sense of our political tradition, when he hears of such cases, is tempted to draw on the mantle of Hampden or Jefferson and wave the banner of civilian supremacy. But this is an irrational reaction. The problem is not caused by any desire of the military to encroach on civilian functions, but by their expansion to fill a vacuum. The vacuum is the absence, on the civilian side, of anything like an adequate career corps to deal with general policies and government-wide interests. In the army, the function of the general staff is to take care of the big general questions; the special staffs and the technical services take care of the specialized and subsidiary and housekeeping problems. On the civilian side, the typical Department head is permitted to have only some special staff units; the real centers of continuing power are in the bureaus, which are the civilian equivalents of the technical services. A civilian general staff would be considered dangerous.

The results are what you would expect. The real old pros are the men who run the bureaus, and a good pro can usually outclass a good amateur. Consequently, the development of civilian policy rather resembles the way I suppose a war would be run if it were left to the technical services and the politicians.

We are still bemused in the United States by the notion that we tolerate the inefficiency of a spoils system because it makes it easier for a new President to come in with a gallant band of amateurs and, at some cost to efficiency, take over the direction of the bureaus. This is wrong on all counts; we do not change many of the real power centers—the leadership of the bureaus—and it would not do any good if we did. The career head of a bureau symbolizes the professional opportunities, and controls the guiding incentives, of his subordinates. Above his post, advancement is possible but risky; there is no system for it, and no chief of a service with a professional interest in developing his men. It is no wonder that the able career people are likely to keep their interests focused on the problems of their own bureaus, and their loyalties engaged in advancing them. This is

178

a sure recipe for seeing to it that the career administrators are interested in the second rather than in the first rank of national problems, or even that they are emotionally engaged in furthering specialized interests at the expense of national interests.

The great failure in our political vision is our not seeing that the main function of the top career administrators is to help develop policy. If the career administrators above the level of the specialized bureaus do not provide strong support for their political superiors in the development of policy, our system of political responsibility suffers. Then the Secretary of a Department can do little but preside over a group of quasi-independent bureaus, while the important potential issues within the Department and between it and the rest of the government will never be brought up for consideration by the President and the Congress. The big issues—at any rate, the biggest —are rarely brought out in the policies which a bureau and its clientele and the related Congressional committees like to put forward for consideration. In particular, in the wide range of problems in which both military and civilian considerations are involved, the advantage in initiative and staff work will rest with the bigger staff battalions of the Pentagon.

If we are to cure this blind spot, we have to give up three prejudices that have come to be accepted as American traditions. The first is the traditional prejudice against hierarchy. We like to think we are against ranks and titles. This works mainly, we may note, with respect to the ranks and titles of other people or in fields we consider unimportant; it does not hold down the number of vice presidents in any metropolitan bank, or the importance of professorial rank in any university, or the number of general and flag officers; but it does keep us from giving much in the way of rank or status to civilian administrators with broad interests in policy.

We began, during the Federalist period with a rudimentary but respectable corps of career administrators, but the Jacksonian revolution abolished all that. A half-century later, as we began to build up a civil service that would serve the nation rather than the warring parties, we built it from the bottom up, rather than from the top down, as the British had done; we put large numbers in the lower ranks under the merit system in order to deny mass patronage to the bosses, rather than reforming the higher ranks in order to create an effective and responsible system of authority for the President and Congress. Then the organized sciences and some of the professions began to demand that their specialties be exempted from patronage.

The dogmas of frontier democracy found it impossible to admit that general administration required any talent that the average citizen could not supply, but such ideas yielded to the special mysteries of the professions and sciences. In an effort to protect their standards against corrupt or ignorant politics, the engineers and doctors and scientists pushed their men up the hierarchy into the jobs at the heads of their bureaus.

The dogmas of frontier democracy would not accept the pretension of general administrative superiority; if anyone was to be given a government job, he ought to be asked to prove his superior fitness for the specific duties of that job. This was not too troublesome at the lower grades; but at the higher, it had two unhappy effects. The first was that administrators, in order to justify a professional and career status for themselves, were forced to develop various aspects of management into specialized techniques. Personnel administration and budgeting, for example, are normal parts of the functions of an administrator, and he may need some people who specialize in them to help him. But we went far beyond that and made them into technical specialties, emphasizing their peculiar mysteries rather than their utility to the central purpose of administration: the development and execution of policy. And then the top political executives, having hardly any other career administrators at hand, had to put too much reliance on the budget officers for the control of policy.

The second bad effect grew out of the first: those who wanted to strengthen the career service emphasized the management specialties because they could be defended as semiscientific and hence nonpolicy-forming and nonpolitical. Administration became the victim of its own defense mechanism. In the end, this defense was not really persuasive, for the management specialists cannot stay out of policy any more than the admirals or ambassadors can; what is more political than the argument over veterans' preference in personnel administration or over the influence of the budget on military spending? By adopting this defense they perpetuated the dangerous myth that administration is not concerned with policy.

The purpose of a hierarchical pyramid, of course, is to raise to the top the difficult issues that the specialists cannot settle, so that these may be decided by legitimate political authority—in the United States, by the President and the Congress. We still like to think of a President's decision as a lonely act of will at a dramatic instant, just as we like to think of a general's commands as being delivered on horseback, with a wave of the sword. But a decision always requires

staff help, to make it and to carry it out, and for that the President
cannot rely entirely on any one specialty. On any complex and difficult issue—for example, disarmament—it is impossible for a political
executive to make a rational decision merely by taking the well-
organized and strongly conflicting positions and programs of different specialized groups and deciding instantaneously among them. If
a President, for example, receives staff papers prepared separately by
groups of generals, diplomats, and scientists, he probably cannot
take immediate action one way or another; all he can do is to determine some guiding principles, and they will be meaningless unless
he organizes a system of staff work, involving or controlling all three
groups, to work those principles into a program and see that it is
carried out. This requires the help of a career service in which the
top ranks are the rewards of ability to deal imaginatively with major
policy issues in their broadest context—not one of fixed allegiance to
the position of a particular bureau or professional service, and not
one of devotion to a particular management specialty.

The second prejudice we need to modify is the prejudice against
admitting the corporate nature of an administrative service. That
prejudice has a sound core: we should not tolerate a closed bureaucracy; we should do all we can to keep the career service flexible in
its policy attitudes by a certain amount of interchange at all levels
with private careers. But that does not mean that we should not have
a system for the policy level of administration that gives some corporate protection to individual careers. We have been improvising a
system, but the structure of our institutions is still against it. As the
second Hoover Commission said in the best of its reports, "The Civil
Service System emphasizes positions, not people. Jobs are classified,
ranked, rated, and their compensation determined on the bland assumption that they can always be filled like so many jugs, merely by
turning the tap." In short, at a time when the major business corporations and virtually all other major institutions in society (including
universities) have come to put great stress on the planned recruitment and training of top talent and on effective long-term tenure, we
force the civil service (though not the military services or the Foreign Service) to ignore the elements of continuity and corporate
spirit that are essential in order to retain most of the best men it gets.

This tradition that resists the development of a corporate service
above the bureau-chief level misleads us most conspicuously in our
efforts to coordinate policy. You can bring an outsider in to analyze
a scientific problem for you, or a problem in managerial procedure;

both can be defined as separate problems, to be solved by a known form of expertise. But the coordination of policy is fundamentally different. It requires not only some understanding of the main substantive aspects of the policy, but also an appreciation of the subtle interconnections of various parts of the government that can come only from years of experience. More than that, it calls for a professional sympathy, a bond of mutual trust based on a common corporate loyalty, between those working in the several departments concerned. This is why we often make no progress toward coordination either by giving additional authority to a political executive or by legislating elaborate structures of interdepartmental coordination. Structure and procedures do not make an organization. After World War II, when we set up a structure of interdepartmental policy committees (such as the NSC), we were imitating the skeleton of British administration without appreciating the function of its central nervous system.

The myth of the Minute Man dies hard. Those of us who are interested in government like to be called to Washington as consultants, or for brief adventurous periods in emergency administration. We cherish the notion that the real ability is outside the career service. We must simply find better ways of bringing it in for one or two years at a time—perhaps by some scheme for supplementing federal salaries for those who are not willing to sacrifice their private incomes temporarily.

But this will not do the main job (however useful it may be as a supplement), again for the reason that we cannot wait for the outbreak of an emergency to call for volunteers as general staff officers. We are already in the middle of the emergency, in one sense; in the other and more awesome sense, if the emergency comes, everything will be too late that has not been started five or ten years before. And the military problem is only the most easily understandable aspect of the many problems that technology has forced on our society.

This brings us to our third traditional prejudice: that government work must not be made as attractive in material rewards as private careers. This might have seemed plausible at one stage of our history: government was not very important in the production of material goods, and government salaries, like relief payments, had to be kept low so as not to reduce the incentive to go into more productive work. But this way of thinking is obsolete, whether you judge the importance of government in terms of sheer military security, or of the hope of building a more humane civilization. Such rational considerations might not prevail against traditional prejudice. But if our logic is weak, our sense of humor is fairly strong, and surely we will soon appreciate the absurdity of holding down the salary of an administrator who runs a government program while at the same time he runs it by contracting with corporations who use government funds to pay higher salaries for less important work. No better incentive could be devised to get administrators to avoid the careers in which they would be responsible for promoting the general interest, and to take jobs which require them to lobby for special interests.

Nevertheless, we cannot solve this problem by higher salaries alone, any more than we can make our affluent society more civilized merely by shifting funds to the public sector. We have invented too many ways in recent years to use public funds for private purposes, for such measures to suffice. A great deal will depend on whether the career administrators who spend those funds are made into a disciplined corps responsive to the public interest, or whether they continue to shape national policy according to their various *déformations professionelles*.

Our foreign-aid and technical-assistance missions, realizing that many underdeveloped countries fail to progress in specialized fields because they have not learned the arts of administration, complain of the slowness of traditional societies to adapt their governments to modern needs. When we have taught the Asians and Africans how to abandon their traditional prejudices, perhaps we shall be ready to reconsider our own. After all, the British built up their civil service on the principles they had first tried out in the East India Company. It may not be too late for us to learn from the British example and to improve a system whose shortcomings we did not see until we tried to export it.

If we do so, we must surely do the job differently. We should not try to provide the same kind of educational basis for a top civil service, for all our sentimental admiration for the Permanent Secretary who can write Greek verse. The effective theory of the British service was based not on a reverence for the classics but on a determination to get the most capable men by taking them from any field in which they might be studying. "If astrology were taught at our universities," said Macaulay, "the young man who cast nativities best would generally turn out a superior man." This pragmatic approach would lead us in the direction our Civil Service Commision has generally been going, slowly and within the limits of political tolerance, for the past two decades, in recruiting college graduates for government careers on the basis of a solid general education, as well as from the sciences and professions.

When he is recruited, the administrator's training has only begun. From the outset of his career, he will have to learn a twofold job. Its first phase is to deal with the substance of policy. The sciences have swept away the oversimplified notion of the administrator as a complete generalist who needs to know nothing about the content and substance of the policies he administers. More and more we shall be adding men with training in science to our administrative ranks, and those of us who lack it will have to make desperate and belated efforts to comprehend the nature of the impact of science on government and society. That impact is now so great, and science in turn has come to rely so heavily on government policy, that the scientist turned administrator, like the management specialist, will have to acquire an understanding of the complexities of our constitutional system and of the way in which it must bring all techniques into a responsible relation with our basic political values.

The administrator of the future, for all his concern for policy, can never forget the other aspect of his job, which is to organize and coordinate a complex and dynamic system to carry out policy decisions that are made by others. We are in no danger of establishing an irresponsible bureaucracy, so long as the administrator is kept under the direction of responsible executives, and called to account by an independent Congress. For we do not really want administrative leadership: we want political leadership, which requires a strong administrative underpinning in order to be effective. The professional administrator must try to bridge the great gap between the way the scientists think and work and that of the politicians. He can never enjoy the luxury of the intellectual pride of the former, or the power of the latter. Through his professional skills, he must try to reconcile our technology with our democratic values. In this effort, the purpose of his profession is to carry, with a higher degree of concentrated responsibility, the moral burden that in a free society must be shared by all citizens.

ROBERT S. MORISON

The Need for New Types of Excellence

THE TROUBLE WITH WRITING about "the need for new types of excellence" is the obvious fact that it requires a new type of excellence even to begin. In the quiet words of the editors of *Daedalus* who assigned the topic: "As you can see, this is a subject on which the existing literature is negligible, but on which thought ought to be expended." As a start on filling the gap in the existing literature and in order to stimulate the expenditure of thought, I drew a highly biased sample of my friends and wrote each of them a brief note announcing the need. Interestingly enough, although they are all very busy pursuing and promoting currently identifiable forms of excellence, they almost all promptly found time to formulate thoughtful analyses of future needs. This fact alone serves to document an awareness among intellectual leaders for something different and, one hopes, a good deal better than we have now.

The second point of interest is that all seemed reasonably well satisfied with the progress we are already making in expanding knowledge of the physical world and in applying that knowledge to the reduction of poverty and suffering. Although the natural scientists in the sample outnumber the social ones by four to three, only one person (Warren Weaver) mentioned natural science as in need of new forms of excellence. But even Weaver's plea for more attention to what he calls problems of *organized complexity* transcends in large measure what most of us are accustomed to think of as natural science and comes close to the preoccupation with organization, interdisciplinary cooperation, decision making, and value problems which characterizes the rest of the group. His earlier essay on the topic[1] provides a delightfully readable account of the way in which the natural sciences have succeeded by dissecting big problems into little ones which could be dealt with individually and exclusively in order to reveal their shape and function. But now science is increasingly confronted with large problems whose parts are so interdependent that they cannot be dissected without spoiling them for future study. The closing paragraphs of his recent letter may be quoted to show how the scientific problems of the future merge without perceptible transition into the classical problems of the humane arts.

I have a very strong conviction that the "new forms of excellence" required by science over the next half-century will in considerable part consist of techniques for dealing with broader problems, *larger* problems, problems which arise when a moderate number (three to one hundred, just as a shot) of small problems are organically interrelated.

One can start with very obvious and oversimplified examples. The day is past, I would claim, when science can properly treat food supply as an isolated problem, birth rates as another, public health as another. The whole body of servo mechanism and feedback theory; many of the techniques of operations research; the emerging knowledge concerning information and communication theory—these are all groping toward the capacity to deal with problems of organized complexity. . . .

We have been great at producing bits of information, fragments of knowledge. We now need to devote more attention to the fitting together of these bits, to the broader interrelations, and hence to broader utilization.

. . . We have to humanize science, and give more general meaning and structure—and even value—to it.

Most of the other correspondents came directly to the need for synthesizing, interdisciplinary research, better organization, and better decision-making, without bothering to analyze how science has proceeded with its limited task of piling one shining pebble on another. But all recognize that it is the extraordinary dimensions of this pile which shape the demand for new forms of excellence.

For it is science which has: (1) given us so much information that no man can master more than a small portion of it; (2) given reality to the concept of one world; (3) given the populations of some parts of that world so many material possessions and so much power over their own destinies that for the first time the paramount question is not, "How do I get enough to stay alive?" but "What do we do with a life that is more or less guaranteed?"

Each one of these gifts calls for its own sort of expertise, and all of them taken together require a new form of human activity so new that we scarcely can find a word to describe it. The rapid accumulation of raw information and digested knowledge places unprecedented burdens on the minds and characters of those who follow the learned professions. The fact that knowledge of the natural world has been doubling every ten years means, among other things, that the death rate of babies under one year of age has been reduced to perhaps one tenth of what it was in the sixteenth century. It is a good deal less cheering to remember that it also means that this year's entering class of medical students are confronted by four times as much to learn as their teachers encountered a short twenty years ago. Not only this, but, by the time these same boys finish their residencies eight or ten years from now, they really ought to return immediately to the basic sciences they studied as freshmen. After all there will be just as much that is new to them now as there was when they studied the basic sciences the first time. The Red Queen method of dealing with the problem ran itself out long ago. Unable to keep up with new information even in his own field, the scientist must progressively restrict the size of the field he is running in.

It is, of course, not only the possession of specialized bits of knowledge that sets a specialist off from his fellows. His different way of looking at things may erect even more serious barriers. Most specialties in medicine and natural science arose from the need for special skills in observation or manipulation. The ophthalmologist is marked for his use of the ophthalmoscope, gynecology developed hand in hand with the Sims's speculum, the genito-urinary surgeon acquired his special status with his cystoscope, and so on. Whole schemes of thought and discourse have developed to deal appropriately with the findings provided by such separate skills, until ultimately the specialties are divided from one another not only by the possession of special information and manipulative skills but also by wholly different ways of thinking and talking. Nowhere perhaps is this more clear than in the field of psychology. Here we have psychoanalysts, learning theorists, conditioned-reflex addicts, physiological psychologists, and ethologists, all looking at the same set of phenomena in such wholly different ways that they can hardly hold sensible conversations with one another.

The unsatisfactory nature of the foregoing state of affairs is widely recognized and, of course, lies behind the persistent cries for

187

ROBERT S. MORISON

more "interdisciplinary" research, and better "generalists," which fill
the academic atmosphere. All the contributors to my informal correspondence symposium on new forms of excellence mentioned it in
one way or another. But how does one set about becoming excellent
in a general way? If there is some substance to the view that specialization arises from the invention of special methods of observation
and is perpetuated by human incapacity to store and recall more
than a small fraction of our exponentially increasing pile of data, it
seems reasonable to give primary attention to simplifying these
functions or transferring them to other hands. Our best minds might
then become freer to deal with the conceptual and communication
problems which worry us so much.

As a matter of fact, there seems to be some reason to hope that
many of the basic scientific specialties are less separated by technique than they used to be. The electron microscope, a highly specialized instrument, was invented by physicists; but methods for its
use have been worked out by chemists, cytologists, histologists, mi-
crobiologists, and an occasional physiologist. Best of all, it is beginning to give us a view of the biological world which is clearly more
unified than anything that has gone before. Thirty years ago, for
example, the phenomenon of muscle contraction was studied by
anatomists, who described the size and shape of gross muscle bundles, by histologists, who could show that these bundles consisted of
small fibers with rather meaningless cross striations on them, by
physiologists, who traced the speed and strength of contractions on
smoked drums, and by biochemists, who ground up bits of muscle to
find out how they burn carbohydrate. The level or scale at which
each party made his observations differed so greatly that muscle
men had little of consequence to say to one another when they got
together at some rare symposium. Now that instruments exist for
analyzing events at what is essentially the molecular level, the attention of all the specialties is beginning to focus at the same point.
As a result, the histologists, biochemists, and physiologists are now
holding livelier conversations with one another than at any time
since Oliver Wendell Holmes talked to himself on what he called
the settee of anatomy, histology, and physiology at Harvard. Indeed,
it is increasingly difficult to differentiate the basic science departments on the basis of the instrumentation employed within them.
Basic biochemical apparatus, electron and light microscopes, cath-
ode-ray oscillographs, and radiation counters may well be found in
any of them.

188

Part of the increasing homogeneity is due to the recognition that all biological events can be traced to biochemical ones. This means in turn that all biologists must learn to speak the lingua franca of biochemistry—and ultimately of atomic physics at least in so far as the nature of the chemical bond between atoms is concerned.

This tendency of the specialties to come full circle and join hands with one another after a long journey through foreign lands was beautifully illustrated in a recent address[2] by Frank Horsfall, the director of the Sloan Kettering Institute. Dr. Horsfall is a virologist, and it may help those who have little contact with any part of the scientific culture to understand the point of the story if we digress for a moment to explain. Only a short time ago a virologist was a person who studied the little man who wasn't there. All that was known about viruses was that they seemed to be related to disease, were so small nobody could see them, and that they could not "live" outside of living cells. They could only be studied by observing what they did to living animals and by a few test-tube reactions, the nature of which no one understood. In this state of the art, there was very little the virologist could say that interested his friends in other fields, or vice versa. But by the year 1960 it had become possible for Dr. Horsfall to throw a single slide of a single crystal of poliomyelitis virus on the screen and tell us in brief detail what the X-ray crystallographer, the physical and organic chemist, the virologist, the geneticist, the immunologist, and the epidemiologist have had to say about this single elegant object.

Each of these people has approached his subject from his own unique point of view, using the tools of his esoteric trade. At first glance Dr. Horsfall's audience was merely being treated to a replay of the old legend of the elephant and the scholars from different nations; but the punch line was different. Instead of "Les éléphants et ses amours," we found ourselves captivated by the sudden realization that one man—a mere virologist, albeit a very good one—had become quite capable of summarizing the really significant findings of several apparently unrelated disciplines. The splitting of our scientific culture into language blocs does not doom us to the splendid isolation of the Tower of Babel. The separate ways if pursued long enough can lead to an even more splendid and imperial synthesis of crystal clarity. Because of my own background I have chosen scientific examples of what I have in mind, but it is no less possible for a single individual to select and give a meaningful synthesis to the most significant facts and concepts of economics, sociology, history,

ROBERT S. MORISON

business management, and political science—*vide* W. W. Rostow, *The United States in the World Arena.* The point of all this is that as knowledge expands beyond a certain point, the burden on the individual can become less. For it is much easier to grasp and to remember interrelated schemes in which a set of observations developed in one language can be interpreted in terms of another than it is to hold on to a squirming mass of unrelated items. It is also a lot more fun.

It also seems probable that the pursuit of excellence in the technology of data gathering and processing will help to free us from the burdens of specialization. As pointed out above, in the early stages of any natural science the great advances come from devising new ways of observing. Generally speaking, these new methods develop as highly individual and esoteric arts, to be mastered only by a lifetime of devotion. The great histologists of the past were people of infinite patience and inspired good fortune who mastered just the right ways of staining tissues with naturally occurring or synthetic dyes to reveal the detailed structure of cells and tissues. Possibly no more than ten men ever became really expert at using colloidal silver and gold to reveal the delicate processes of nerve cells. The neurophysiologist of twenty years ago spent more time keeping his electrical apparatus in shape than he did in using it to observe the behavior of the nervous system. But recent technical advances have reduced many of the essential manipulative skills to semi-automatic mechanical processes. To mention but one example, there is now a machine which will automatically analyze a complex protein for all its constituent amino acids in a matter of hours. Only a few years ago whole teams of skilled chemists were trying to find out how the job could be done at all. In those cases in which machines have not yet been developed to take over the entire job, much progress has been made in breaking up the data-gathering task into bits which can be appropriately handled by specially trained technicians, leaving the investigator more time to devote to more general, conceptual, or interdisciplinary problems.

The second problem—how to handle the data after they are accumulated—is more difficult. To quote Mr. Weaver again, "We have items of hardware which are capable of doing practically anything we can decide is worth doing" in this field. In other words, we can store nearly any sort of information in any amount we wish and get any part or parts back that we want in a few moments. But what do we want? If we knew the answer, we would not need to go to school

190

at all. Clearly, what we want from any information system is that packet of information which is relevant to the problem at hand. But how are we going to describe the packet when the reason we want to see it is that we do not know what it contains? And unless we can describe it with reasonable precision we are all too likely to get back from our computer a pile of photostats which would take literally years to read.

It remains for the future to devise an excellence which will make the most of the speed and accuracy with which mechanical computers handle large volumes of data, while at the same time it maximizes the associative capacities and instinct for relevance contained within our own skulls. Enough progress has been made so far to suggest that computer techniques will be useful not only in storing and recalling existing information, i.e., in improving the library function. There are great possibilities for the development of machines which will analyze and correlate data as they occur. For example, neurophysiologists and psychologists are now greatly excited by the possibility of correlating electrical events in the nervous system with functions such as perception, learning, and memory. It is technically possible to record electrical activity from several hundred spots at once, but few people have tried it because of the staggering problem of looking at thousands of feet of oscillograph tracings and picking out the relevant from the irrelevant events. Part of the difficulty lies in the fact that the nervous system is necessarily doing a great many things at one time; relatively few cells may be engaged in carrying out the particular perception or memory which we wish to correlate. It would be inappropriate to explain in these restricted pages how this problem of selecting the significant events and correlating them with one another is going to be solved, but it can be confidently asserted that it is already well toward solution.

New forms of excellence are required for developing these new technologies for the accumulation and analysis of data. More interesting perhaps is the challenge the new techniques offer for the development of even newer excellences. It will not be easy for most of us to relinquish to the machine the arts and techniques which have taken us decades to master, and to concentrate on the even more demanding tasks of generalization, synthesis, and judgment which only man can carry out. Perhaps the greatest demands for ingenuity will fall upon the field of education, once it is decided to hand over to other means the mere memorization of information, the computing of sums, and such other routine intellectual tasks as may be found appropriate. It will be an excellent teacher indeed who shows us how to program our school and college experience so as to maximize the capacity to grasp general principles, detect relevance where none was seen before, and create new conceptual schemes. When that day comes, all education will in a sense be general education, since the technical problems which now divide the specialties will in large part have been handed over to the computers, and we will have taught ourselves a language we can all use in common.

We must now attack a set of problems of somewhat greater complexity, which demand forms of excellence that can be far less clearly foreseen. It was said earlier in this essay that science has given reality to the "one world" concept. Clearly, the concept itself is as much poetic and perhaps religious as it is scientific, but science has made its implications inescapable. John Donne's bell was only very vaguely and intermittently audible outside his parish, but now Big Ben can be heard in actuality every night in the remotest corners of the world. The sound and sight of the shots which overthrow an African government are brought right into our living rooms, to be acknowledged by electronic pictures from Baton Rouge which show the world how the mature democracies deal with the same problem. Still other shots are heard around the world, and when the smoke clears away, invisible radiations filter down for months to cause mutational mutilation on a magnificently random sample of the just and the unjust. That we have no very accurate way of estimating the size of the sample at the present time provides no satisfactory answer to the question of principle involved. The point is that we are now living in a world in which almost every one of our actions has in some way an effect on almost everyone else in that world. Perhaps this has always been true in some theoretical sense but two recent developments serve to give practical reality to the situation. The power at our command makes the effect much greater, and the advance of scientific method, especially statistical analyses, makes it possible to give some measure to our awareness of the effects.

C. H. Waddington[3] and more recently Warren Weaver[4] have called attention to the concept of "stochastic" or "statistical morality" and called for what is in effect a new kind of excellence that must be invented to deal with this new state of affairs.[5] As everyone knows, the human race still has difficulty observing moral commands derived from such immediately observable cause-and-effect relationships as jabbing a knife into one's brother, stealing other men's wives, or coveting one's neighbor's Buick. How much more difficult it will be to convince people that it is statistically just as sinful to drive one's own Buick around without an expensive device for eliminating the toxic hydrocarbons which currently poison the free air over Los Angeles! To bring the point even closer to home, let us remember that there are now very good figures to show that boys kill many more people than girls do while driving automobiles. How do we weigh this fact in our moral balances when deciding whether our teen-age son or our twenty-year old daughter will have the family car for the upcoming football weekend? But the problem is very much greater than a few thousands of people doomed to death by automobiles. The whole future of the race is at stake in such matters as the uncontrolled expansion of its numbers in the "population explosion" or the decline in its quality brought about by the genetic effects of advances in modern medicine in combination with our currently casual breeding patterns.[6]

There is a school of thought, particularly well exemplified at the moment perhaps by the tobacco industry, which attempts to shrug off the evidence for all such dangers as "only statistical." The trouble with this is that the evidence for any proposition one wants to name is "only statistical." As David Hume pointed out sometime ago, the only reason we expect the sun to rise tomorrow is that it has done so a large number of times in the past. The calculated probability of such events is said to be one, and we tend to put them in a special class. But there are other cases in which the probability is much less than one and we nevertheless hold people responsible for recognizing a "cause and effect" relationship. For example, Raymond Pearl showed many years ago that any randomly selected act of human sexual intercourse has a chance of only about 1 in 351 of resulting in pregnancy. Nevertheless, a large part of our social and legal structure is built on our belief in a close cause-and-effect relationship.

Each new case that comes along demonstrates how hard it is for most of us to grasp the meaning of probabilities when the odds are fairly long against any particular event and especially in those cases in which the predicted occurrence will not take place for some time. At the present, for example, the best evidence available suggests very strongly that men who smoke a package or more of cigarettes a day die several years earlier than men who do not smoke at all. All sorts of ingenuity is being devoted to explaining these figures on grounds other than the obvious one, that smoking per se reduces human vitality. No other alternative has yet been shown to be as likely as the obvious one, yet so far as one can see smoking habits have changed very little. The explanation seems to lie in the fact that men still find it very difficult to pay serious attention to contingencies that lie more than a very few years in the future and are coupled to present events with a probability of less than one.

Always there have been a few who could do a little bit better than the generality of mankind at foretelling the future and sensing important statistical relationships. By and large they have risen to the top and controlled other men, a fact which led to the celebrated aphorism: "To foresee is to govern."

During the long period in which the world community was made up of many separate entities, the results of lack of foresight could be catastrophic only in a parochial sense. When one culture failed, another was ordinarily preparing itself to take its place, so that broadly speaking the over-all course of human culture has been upward in most measurable senses. Furthermore, the power and size of the human race were not such as to have important effects on the biosphere which it inhabited. The growing interdependence of all cultures is now putting us all together into one world, with the interesting result that the failure of a part may bring disaster to the whole. Power and numbers both have reached such a point that human activity has measurable effects on the physical world in which we live. The physicists tell us that carbon dioxide is accumulating in the atmosphere and could shortly reach levels which would seriously impede the escape of heat from the earth's surface. Conservationists have worried for years over the disappearance of topsoil and forests. Rivers carry sewage and industrial wastes instead of fish. The wonderful productivity of modern agriculture with its pseudo promise of solving the population problem is actually based on a constant expenditure of capital in the form of the fossil fuels used to drive farm machinery and to produce fertilizers, chemical weeders, and insecticides. The human race is no longer in balance with its environment, and nobody but a few farsighted conservationists seems to care.

If we are to continue to rely on democracy as the most promising government for the future (nobody seems to have come up with any satisfactory alternatives), we clearly stand in need of new methods for enabling the innumerable governing class to extend the range of its awareness. The Average Citizen must in some way be brought to realize that what he does here and now affects many other people in other places and in generations yet unborn.

The cognitive problem involved in the foregoing is serious enough; but it goes hand in hand with an equally serious moral problem. People in general must not only *know* that what they do affects everyone everywhere and at all times in the future, but they must *care* about it also. Here indeed is a situation that calls for a new sort of excellence—an educational system in the broadest sense that will acquaint people in general with the reality of action at a distance and a concern for that reality.

Any suggestions of how to begin are bound to sound trivial when measured by the magnitude of the problem. Nevertheless, one might timidly suggest that a good course in statistics and probability makes more sense in the twentieth century than an equally good course in Euclidean geometry. Biology, which would be a required course if we followed the Greek injunction to know thyself, should emphasize the complex interrelations of living things and their environment and the growing power of man to destroy the age-old balances. The study of genetics provides a concrete way of demonstrating how each of us holds in trust a bit of the common code which will later be translated into the future of man. However effective science may be at demonstrating objectively the oneness of the world, it has so far proven incapable of arousing the subjective warmth which seems essential for the functioning of moral and ethical systems. Statistical morality is likely to remain a statistical abstraction unless some way can be found to infuse it with moral fervor. But historically moral fervor has too often been associated with the drawing of fine distinctions between the righteous and the unrighteous, the elect and the damned, to serve a universal purpose. The international geophysical year much more deserves the appellation "ecumenical" than any religious or philosophical movement the world has so far produced.

Even though we cannot at the moment describe how it might operate, may we not at least look for a "new form of excellence" which will combine the clear intellectual demonstration of man's biological unity with an emotional concern for its preservation. The primary requisite for this new excellence is that we pay more attention to what we know than to what we do not know. We do not know the nature of God—perhaps we never can. Why not leave this matter where it should be, in the realm of personal opinion, and stop trying to derive universal solutions from assumptions on which there is certain to be profound disagreement? We do know, however, that no man is an island but part of the main in the thoroughly demonstrable sense that he derives his basic structure and function from a common pool of genes and the rest of the stuff of life from a common biosphere. The integrity of both now stands at the mercy of each and every one of us. Is there a better reason for being merciful?

However much man's survival and in a sense his moral integrity are bound up with our view of him as part of a whole, each one of us does as a matter of fact experience life as an individual. We in the United States, as in the Western democracies generally, are particularly and properly proud of the regard for individual rights which has been built into our political and social systems. Indeed, the very pith and point of the democratic state is to create an environment in which the individual can develop his personal salvation in his own way.

Now that the industrial and scientific revolutions have removed from the great majority the daily concern for food and shelter, more and more individuals find themselves casting about for other objects to which to tie their motivational systems. Personal affluence is not enough, as Galbraith and many others have recently shown, and as the figures for suicide, alcoholism, and divorce in the advanced countries have long documented.

What shall *I* do to be saved is in some ways a more insistent question today than at any time in the past. The more the possibilities which lie before us and the more power we have to alter the natural course of our lives, the less we seem to know what we want to do with them. Edwin Land, in speaking of the present situation in the United States, says, "It is prudent to note that the great mass of men are not quite sure of what to do with their freedom, and that the small mass of scholars are not quite sure of where to apply their excellence."[7]

Ours is not the first generation to ask "What is the point of it all?" nor is it likely to be the last. The only new thing is our discovery that the question becomes more and more insistent as the mere maintenance of existence becomes easier. It seems most unlikely that any foreseeable excellence will provide a single answer to this problem. For some time to come we will probably have to content ourselves with putting up limited objectives of one sort or another. Edwin Land has made a persuasive attempt to fire future engineers with the prospect of taking part in "the majestic stage of the American Revolution" which "involves not the increase of material holdings, or the amount of food and clothing, but the conversion of the everyday working life into one which developed all the talents of the worker, making him into artist, artisan, student, and producer. It seemed to me the time had come in industry for a planned relationship between machines and people in which the machines would work for people, instead of the unplanned and accidental relationship that exists today. . . . The way to avoid having one great planned society, one national planned society, which I think we Americans recognize intuitively is dangerous and foreign to our nature, is to have thousands of small planned societies, each being a cultural variant from the others; each being its own kind of experiment in such questions as: What is worth making? How should it be made? How should people gather together to make it? How do we relate people to one another in each of these separate little gatherings?"

The foregoing concept may be a new form of excellence or an attempt to revive some of the medieval excellences contained in the guild system, but it at least has the virtue of attempting to combine the business structure to which our society is committed with a conscious concern for the spiritual as well as the material welfare of those who man it.

But it is not only big industry that threatens the personal integrity and well being of the individual. Elting E. Morison listed high in his list of new forms of excellence, "A new scheme of morality to deal with the rapidly developing sense of determinism produced by work in psychology and biology." Defective and incomplete though they still are, both sciences have progressed far enough to show that human behavior is indeed the determined result of a complex interplay among genetic and environmental variables. The puzzling old metaphysical question of "free will" now presses upon us in modern mechanical dress, asking questions of much practical consequence. How is each one of us to feel a healthy sense of personal responsibility and purpose when we know that what we are and do is largely a matter of the genes we have inherited and the degree of anxiety with which our mothers handled our toilet training? The law has long recognized that certain forms of insanity can absolve the criminal from his responsibilities, but the famous M'Naghten rules become harder and harder to apply as we come to recognize that everyone is at least a little bit neurotic, and that discontinuities between normal and abnormal give place to points on a Gaussian distribution curve.

The tiresome question of free will has always had more than its share of paradox. Our increasing knowledge of the determinants of human behavior only increases the difficulty of resolution. For, in so far as we come to recognize causes, we increase our capacity to influence results. As Alan Gregg has pointed out, the day has long passed when a parent can absolve himself from the guilt of a child's death by piously referring to God's inscrutable wish to take little so and so from us. The neighbors are sure to ask why you did not take the baby to the children's hospital in time so that he could have received the proper antibiotic. As knowledge or some reasonable facsimile of knowledge of child training accumulates, more and more parents blame themselves when their offspring turn out badly. But the potential devastation of the guilt which arises from an increasing sense of determining events transcends the merely personal. As a young and extraordinarily successful society, America has always been prone to believe that nothing is really impossible, an attitude that led an intelligent European to observe that in America there are no tragedies, only mistakes.

The implied promise of ultimate success carries with it a reciprocal promise of despair. For at any given moment mistakes are bound to occur. The necessary knowledge for their avoidance may be less certain than supposed or a basically sound doctrine may be ill applied. In any case, the mistake occurs and those who are unaccustomed to accepting sordid evil or magnificent tragedy as part of the structure of life are poorly prepared to bear the consequences. The national tragedies that can occur in this way are illustrated by the immature clamor for scapegoats which attended the "failure" of a China policy which, however inept it may have been, was the best that men of the highest ability and good will could work out at the time. If we are to become mature in both our personal and our collective national lives, we will have to probe much more deeply into Thucydides' famous maxim, "Men do what they can and suffer what they must." Since the Greeks had a word for it, this form of excellence may not be exactly new but it would be new for us.

To follow the trail of paradox one step further, it may be observed that an increasing sense of control of some determinants of one's own life is curiously coupled with a growing awareness that much of what used to be called character is determined by factors quite beyond one's influence. The first increases responsibility, the second decreases it almost at the same time. As the paradox sharpens, the need for individual moral excellence becomes ever more obvious. What is not obvious is how to meet it.

Another and rather clearer consequence of our increasing knowledge of the determinants of behavior is the load placed upon individuals and groups with responsibility and authority over the welfare of others. Medical men, for example, are beginning to be uncomfortably aware of the power modern medicine gives them to prolong life far beyond the normal limits of desirability.[8] Such questions as who should bear children, how many, and of what kind, which used to be comfortably relegated to an all-wise providence, are now uncomfortably turning up as potential matters for human choice.

At another level the classical rhetoric of persuasion is haltingly but apparently steadily giving way to the engineering of consent. Even though opinion polling and deeper studies of buyer and voter motivation still lack precision and B. F. Skinner's learning machine has not yet been adapted to teaching us all to believe in one God, the applied sciences of propaganda and public enlightenment provide sufficiently frightening examples of what may lie ahead.

The good thing about the classical forms of tyranny was (and is) that their implements of consent could be all too clearly seen and keenly felt. Constitutional guarantees could be worked out to restrain the excesses of the secret police and nullify the evidence of the rack. Even where official propaganda is unrestrained by a free press, its ravages have until now been tempered by the tendency of all living tissue to build protective calluses or more subtle antibodies against recognized invaders.

But what happens when persuasion becomes so skillful that the chains that confine or the reins that guide the mind remain invisible, or, if visible, are not regarded as unwelcome? It seems unlikely that constitutional guarantees can be written to protect the individual against such encroachments.

It is admittedly difficult to cite unexceptionable evidence for the power of an existing persuasive apparatus which is not contaminated with more overt methods of control. There seems little real doubt, however, that Stalin did better than Peter the Great at westernizing Russia because he controlled a much better system of propaganda and education. It also seems not unlikely that one of the reasons intelligent Americans spend a larger proportion of their incomes on automobiles, household appliances, and cosmetics and less on books, theatres, and concerts than do Europeans is the tremendous public-relations effort that has gone into persuading Americans that the former are to be equated in some way with the "good things of life."

More serious at the present time perhaps than the conscious use of organized persuasion by the few to influence the many are the malfunctions of the complicated set of feedback systems which we think of as our free press, radio, and TV. The very fact that they are as free as we can make them may render them more rather than less dangerous to the public welfare than are the recognizably controlled systems of dictatorial propaganda. For we lack the protection against credulity which is built into every news service which is known to be controlled by interested minorities. The difficulty with our public news media is not, as some would have us believe, that they are controlled by big business. The real problem is that they are controlled to such a large degree by ourselves. Basically, all of us would like to believe that life is simpler than it really is, and we therefore tend to patronize those media which give us an appropriately simplified view of our position. The results are as evident in the low estate of the artistic productions on the TV screen as they are in the reassuring nature of much "straight reporting" and editorial comment. In the classical TV western, the problem of good and evil reduces itself to a problem of good guys and bad guys, and disappears down the barrel of a revolver. In principle, the situation is little different when the commentator on the adjoining channel attempts to reduce the complex economic and socio-political struggle of the emerging nations to a whodunit based on the question of whether or not the current riots are communist inspired. The temptation to oversimplify is not limited merely to the technical levels of communication media but reaches up to the very highest stages of the news sources themselves. Here again feedback from the public reinforces in particularly poignant form the natural desires of government officials to present a simple and palatable picture of their own doings. For it must have occurred to those who vetoed "Operation Candor" and classified the Gaither Report that the voters might prefer someone else if "the gap" became officially confirmed.

To summarize the rather broad spectrum of human activity, which has necessarily been rather sketchily analyzed—the doctor advising his patient whether or not to have children and in special cases whether or not to resort to artificial insemination; the scientist placing the facts about radiation, food additives, or tobacco before the general public; the artist who holds a mirror up to life in general; the newspaperman reporting a press conference; or the government official giving a fireside chat about the missile gap—all have the following things in common. Each, in one way or another, has access to a special body of information, the exact meaning and relevance of which is beyond the capacity of his hearers to grasp on their own. The message which must be conveyed is critically important for reaching a sound decision on actions which have important potential effects on each individual hearer and equally important but perhaps somewhat different effects on society at large. What he selects to say from the large body of information and concepts at his command will in large measure determine the resulting decision. This is a situation that calls for a combination of the highest sort of intellectual and moral attainments. In the first place, it should be unnecessary in a democracy to point out that the speaker has no business to try to make the final decision for his hearers. This would in fact be the simple way out and is the common procedure in dictatorships, theocracies, and other controlled societies. Democracy rests, however, on the assumption that people in general will reach the right decision if they are given the truth. But the truth is impossible to define in abstract terms, and even in concrete matters like the effect of radiation on genetic anomalies is not much more than a fluctuating area of agreement.

The telling of this kind of truth cannot be guaranteed by constitutional articles or perjury laws. But as more and more features of our life fall under the control of those who wield a specialized body of knowledge over it, we must seek some protection against misuse. This, it seems to me, can be found only in the individual moral and intellectual excellence of those who develop, hold, and disseminate knowledge.

REFERENCES

1. Warren Weaver, "Science and Complexity," *American Scientist*, 1948, *36*: 536-544.

2. Frank L. Horsfall, Jr., "On the Unity of the Sciences," *Science*, 1961, *133*: 1059-1060.

3. C. H. Waddington, *The Scientific Attitude*. Harmondsworth, Middlesex: Penguin Books, 1941.

4. Warren Weaver, "Statistical Morality," in *Christianity and Crisis* (to be published).

5. As early as 1907, E. A. Rose in *Sin and Society*, Boston: Houghton Mifflin, wrote in an eloquent, muck-raking style of the sins that are "largely impersonal" and are committed by "the man who picks pockets with a railway

rebate, murders with an adulterant instead of a bludgeon . . . or cheats with a company prospectus instead of a deck of cards." The contemporary preoccupation with malefactors of great wealth apparently kept him from extending the idea to the level of generality implied by Waddington and Weaver.

6. Hoagland and Burhoe, *Evolution and Man's Progress,* New York: Columbia University Press, 1962, deals with this problem in more detail.

7. Edwin H. Land, "On Entering the Majestic Stage of the American Revolution." Address delivered at the Massachusetts Institute of Technology Commencement, 10 June 1960 (mimeographed).

8. Joseph Francis Fletcher, "The Patient's Right To Die," *Harper's Magazine,* October 1960, pp. 138-143; also, Sir George Pickering *et al.,* at the Dartmouth Convocation on the Great Issues of Conscience in Modern Medicine, 8-10 September 1960.

STEPHEN R. GRAUBARD

Democracy and Its Critics

THERE IS NO idea more congenial to the twentieth century than the one which suggests that it is an epoch unique in world history. No previous generation experienced comparable dilemmas; statesmen were never more sorely tried; hazards were never more imminently lethal; the burdens of office were never so onerous or of such transcendent importance. The age insists on its uniqueness. It will abide no comparisons. This is the badge of its inordinate pride—also, perhaps, the symbol of its ignorance. It is the source of its most primitive myths. These derive their credibility from certain incontrovertible facts: technological progress has never been more rapid; social revolution is proceeding at an unprecedented pace; the rise of new nations is rendering obsolescent more than just the work of yesterday's cartographers; all this is happening against a stark atomic background which makes uncertain the survival of the human race.

In these circumstances, the Apocalypse and the Heavenly City (to be achieved in this life on earth) vie for public attention. Reason tells us that the force of the atom may lead men unwittingly to destruction; a residual will to survive makes us wish to believe in Utopia. That such an age encourages a love of grandiloquence and a taste for hyperbole is in no way surprising. Posterity must be relied upon to view these excesses with charity, recalling the unusual circumstances which produced them. It is difficult enough to cope with present problems, in the belief that they are unique; to be denied the solace of that belief, to be required to see that earlier generations experienced comparable trials, is to ask a great deal. As is becoming increasingly evident, it is not easy to live in a world which believes total destruction to be an imminent possibility.

This, then, is a time made for exaggeration. The past is ignored or distorted; the present is made to appear incomparably important; the future is a blank sheet of paper on which total catastrophe or exceptional good fortune waits to put its mark. Such a pattern mocks man's reason even as it appeals to his emotions. It makes history seem a chronicle of successive "golden ages" alternating with "times of trouble." That such peaks and valleys exist only in the imagination does not prevent us from wishing to believe in an idyllic world where all are secure in their persons and property, confident about the future, and concerned only that the present afford opportunities for happiness. While these utopian formulations provide a standard by which existing things may be judged, and a goal no less real for being unrealizable, they do not describe the past as man has ever lived it. Leadership has never been easy; security is famous for its impermanence; progress is almost always halting— these are commonplaces of history.

Not the least of the distinctions of the twentieth century is its refusal to admit this fact, together with its preference for ideas and images that dwell on the extraordinary and unique dangers to which modern man is exposed. In the West today there is a deep (and legitimate) concern about the security of democratic institutions. Some see the threat principally in the malevolent intentions of an energetic and hostile state, whose rockets, aimed in this direction, may at any moment bring about our ruin. Mr. Khrushchev's words, less dangerous if taken only as metaphor, imply the early demise of Western democracy at history's impatient hands; there is small comfort to be derived from them. The idea that the struggle is fundamentally ideological, and that democracy will stand or fall depending on its capacity to convince the "new nations" that its model is superior to any yet invented by Marxist ideologues has a certain appeal. Both as an avenue to virtue and as a road to improvement (material, of course), democracy is said to be undergoing a severe test. Something called "world opinion" (the twentieth century's version of the "impartial spectator" of the eighteenth century) is supposed to be observing, waiting to award the palm to one side or the other. Finally, there are those who gaze out on long rows of nearly identical suburban detached houses, each with its carport, television antenna, plot of grass, and picture window (fronting, of course, on a road) and ask whether all history has led simply to this, and whether it is not a mockery of man's epic striving that this should be the end to which he has been led.

204

Each of these situations, rendered in an idiom grave and forbidding, is intended to make us feel a sense of awe before the magnitude of the chasm which threatens us. Extinction—physical, political, or spiritual—is not a welcome prospect at any time. Since a denial of the hazard offers no protection against it, the temptation to join the chorus crying "crisis, crisis" is almost overwhelming. Only our natural modesty (sensitive always to feelings of self-importance and self-pity) warns us to go slowly. Otherwise, we romp with the rest, scarcely aware that we are being taken in. At times we talk only of the hazards of the day. When we tire of this, we wax eloquent about the glories of the "space age," forgetting that half of it is real, rather like the ocean which beckoned Columbus, but that the other half is an abstraction—a huge joke perpetrated by men who understand the arts of propaganda in the contemporary world. To land a man on the moon is obviously important. The engineering skill that such a feat requires will reveal conclusively what we already know: man's intellect is formidable, and his purposes, if supported by sufficient human and material resources, are often attained. Is there anyone who seriously doubts that this particular objective, great though it is, will be achieved? That we do not know whether the space ship will bear American or Soviet markings is what makes the "race" militarily, politically, and diplomatically important. This, however, does not affect the general assumption that one or the other of the contestants will succeed.

To put the matter as simply as this is to risk giving offense. If the imagination is not stimulated by the prospect of a man sitting on the moon, the fault, quite obviously, is with the mind so closed to modern heroic achievement that it fails to respond to the really significant events of the day. The only possible defense against such a charge is to suggest that there have been too many "significant" events in the twentieth century, too many "crises," "challenges," "opportunities," and "unique happenings." The words have been cheapened by their frequent use. Gresham's Law is relevant even to so common a commodity as mass-produced language.

Democracy is said to be on trial. History suggests that this is its normal situation. The idea that, in some pre-Soviet, pre-Marxist, pre-industrial age, men agreed about the superior virtues of democracy and waited anxiously for its universal establishment in the quiet confidence that this would bring about the eradication of poverty, the increase of knowledge, the end of war, and all sorts of other benefits, runs counter to a historic record that cannot be

205

altered to conform with contemporary needs. A few men, certainly, entertained such expectations. The greater number, however, whether partial or hostile to the democratic idea, never believed it would introduce the millennium. The question of whether democracy would encourage excellence and produce leaders capable of managing the intricate affairs of government did not originate when a Soviet projectile hurtled through space and went into orbit around the earth. If democracy insists on regarding its present predicament as in some way exceptional, it risks mistaking an asset for a liability, thus confusing the whole account. It is well to be reminded in this connection that the term democracy did not enter into common usage until the end of the eighteenth century and that, when it was employed then, its meaning was generally pejorative, signifying Jacobinism or mob rule.[1]

Democracy—the child of the American and the French Revolutions—entered the scene to something other than universal applause. Americans take pride, very properly, in the extraordinary achievements of their eighteenth-century forebears.[2] There is no hazard in that commendation, so long as the accomplishment it praises is not made to appear so utterly beyond our present competence that the eighteenth-century American emerges as a giant and his twentieth-century heir a dwarf. The eighteenth-century example, while necessary for our instruction, ought not to be inhibiting. More than that, its significance on the world scene ought not to be exaggerated. Democracy's victories in the eighteenth century were in no sense conclusive. Benjamin Franklin, arriving at Versailles for his audience with the King, bespectacled and without wig or sword, in a suit of brown velvet—the incarnation of all the virtue that men accustomed to splendor associated with nature—offered an almost too beguiling portrait. What more charming pose could any man have adopted before a court whose queen sought the simple pleasures of rural life in playing milkmaid on a miniature dairy farm? There was no duplicity in Franklin's behavior; he was simply exaggerating those aspects of his personality which the French for one reason or another valued. Such behavior, however, did little to convert the court to "democratic" beliefs and had even less effect on the ordinary French citizen. Europe was not led to democracy by its esteem for America's success in winning its war against the British. Men like Franklin and Jefferson built a reservoir of good feeling for the young Republic, and thought this a quite sufficient achievement. They did not bring a new gospel to Europe. The

206

American Revolution gave no verdict for or against democracy. This was reserved for another time and place.

In July 1789, France, the most powerful state in Europe, experienced the beginning of a Revolution which was destined to obliterate her traditional institutions and inaugurate a period of massive war and disorder. Little of this was anticipated in the days of July and August, when a Paris mob took the Bastille, and the Estates-General, meeting as the National Assembly, revoked feudal rights and privileges which had existed from time immemorial. In the first months of revolution, many believed that France was simply "reforming" herself, becoming a "limited monarchy" in the way that Montesquieu and others had imagined England to be. The disorder was expected to end with the proclamation of a new constitution which would ratify what violence (and the threat of violence) had already accomplished.

It was in November, 1790, not in Paris, but in London, that these sanguine hopes received their most chilling denial. In that month, booksellers in the British capital began to exhibit a work by Edmund Burke, Member of Parliament, who had achieved a great reputation by his defense of the American colonial claims against the mother country. Burke's *Reflections on the Revolution in France* developed a thesis previously unheard, in language so insistent and passionate that it could not fail to command a hearing. Burke took issue with those who imagined that the Revolution in France concerned only those who had suffered it. On the contrary, he said, it involved all Europeans and all men interested in the maintenance of civilized values. The idea propagated by the French revolutionaries and by their friends and allies in other countries (including England) threatened all existing forms of authority. If these ideas became dominant, religion would fall, and liberty as Europe had known it would be extinguished. Burke showed disdain for the new men who had come forward in France, seeking to govern that great kingdom. They were small men, he said, recently come from the provinces, who hoped to profit personally from the disorder they had helped to create. They had no idea of the difficulties of government. They had no experience which could prepare them for it. Burke thought their philosophy false, their actions cruel, and their purposes base. If Europe did not gather its strength to defeat these men and the theories they propagated, a new tyranny would establish itself, more terrible than any Europe had ever known.[3]

207

These words fell with a force suggesting that the ground had been prepared for their coming. Latent suspicions about what the French experience might imply for the future seemed to be confirmed by this passionate outburst. Burke was summoning traditional Europe to take up arms against a "novel doctrine" which promised nothing but disaster. He was asking that men realize the gravity of the moment and spare no effort in the task which lay at hand. Burke's *Reflections* passed through eleven editions within a year of publication; in six years some 30,000 copies were sold. Many who read the work were instructed by it; others were shocked, appalled, and angered. The latter hurried to answer him, determined that the last word in the controversy should not be his. Burke had condemned what they regarded as the greatest event of the century; the one which gave greatest hope for the future. They thought his book wicked and wrong, the work of a man who could not understand that the days of privilege were numbered and that democracy was destined to sweep Europe as it had already done in America and France. Thomas Paine was one of many who hastened to reply. In language no less passionate than Burke's, he proclaimed that "every age and generation must be free to act for itself in all cases as the ages and generations which preceded it. The vanity and presumption of governing beyond the grave is the most ridiculous and insolent of all tyrannies."[4] Paine, in common with other democrats, resented Burke's suggestion that the people had no right to choose their own governors. This, on the contrary, he thought to be their most fundamental privilege. He refused to believe that any government was good which did not represent popular choice, and which did not allow the people to dismiss those they had chosen when their services were no longer desired. The people were sovereign. This, Paine thought, was the message proclaimed by the American and the French Revolutions.

The debate that opened so violently in 1790 continued unabated in the forty years that followed. Both sides were guilty of excess; the stakes were so large as to legitimate almost every argument. Louis XVI's execution on the guillotine, the expropriation of Church property, the growth of the terror in France following on the outbreak of war—all these events seemed to fulfill Burke's dire prophecies. Patriotism, as much as any other emotion, caused men outside France to believe themselves endangered. In these circumstances, "democrat" became a word of obloquy; its synonym, "Jacobin," a word of hate. There was no longer any incentive to scrutinize carefully the accompishments of "popular" government, whether in France or in America. One took one's position either for or against the phenomenon. The French Revolution frightened men in a way that the American Revolution had never done. If the reaction was one of scorn and contempt, it was often only a flimsy cover for a deeply felt fear.

Those who persisted in believing that the people were qualified to govern and that democracy would bring in its train a new and better civilization were everywhere in Europe an embattled minority. The "democrats" paid a price for their beliefs; even in England, where constitutional guarantees protected them in the expression of their opinions, it was dangerous after 1793 to express sympathy for "democratic" principles. Napoleon's arrival only exacerbated the ideological conflict. The French example was thought to provide all the evidence that any rational individual could demand about what happened when men sought to replace hereditary institutions with others of their own invention.

Napoleon's defeat at Waterloo opened the prospect that these emotional responses might at last be set aside and that a more generous and dispassionate criticism might again develop. Those who expected a rapid return to the inquiring spirit of the eighteenth century were certainly disappointed. Aristocratic values and institutions had come too close to disaster for the men restored to places of authority to forgive the persons they held responsible for all that had happened. In the two decades after 1815, feelings about popular government were not very different from what they had been in the preceding twenty years. Those in positions of power tended to disparage democratic forms and to create defenses against them. In Europe, at least, only those who were unafraid of being tarred with the "radical" brush spoke enthusiastically for popular sovereignty. In these circumstances, the incentives to study the American or any other democratic experiment were limited. Men knew how they stood on the question and did not imagine that they needed to inform themselves about it. It is for this reason that the year 1835 becomes important, coinciding as it does with the possibility of a new sort of criticism. Just as the period of impassioned argument about the merits of democracy began with the publication of a book, so the new era opened also with the printing of a significant volume. This time the author was French, an aristocrat by birth, just past his thirtieth year. The work was Alexis de Tocqueville's *Democracy in America*.[5]

STEPHEN R. GRAUBARD

The book was based largely on experiences and observations which the author owed to a visit he made to the United States in 1831. In that year, in the company of a fellow magistrate, Gustave de Beaumont, he crossed the Atlantic, ostensibly to study American prisons. His real purpose, however, as he explained in a letter, was considerably more ambitious: "We are leaving with the intention of examining, in detail and as scientifically as possible, all the mechanism of that vast American society which everyone talks of and no one knows. And if events leave us the time, we are counting on bringing back the elements of a fine work or, at the very least, of a new work; for there is nothing on this subject."[6]

De Tocqueville's first volume was something more than a detailed description of an exotic foreign society in which the French had long interested themselves. The work had a moral—a new one for Europe. In effect, de Tocqueville suggested that he had seen in the New World the face of Europe's own future. If it seemed strange that old Europe should be prefigured in this new and still largely uninhabited country, it was because Europe did not know the irresistible forces at work in the world. These showed above the surface in the United States; they would soon emerge also in the Old World. De Tocqueville believed that his age was moving inevitably and inexorably towards equality. There was no resisting the movement, and no defeating the popular passion which lay behind it. Privilege, on which aristocratic Europe had based its institutions, was destined to disappear. A new sort of society, which de Tocqueville called "democracy," was certain to take its place. De Tocqueville had seen this new society in the United States. While not unimpressed by much that he had observed, he was aware also of defects, even more, of hazards. Men concerned with the preservation of liberty had reason to be worried, de Tocqueville wrote, for it was by no means certain that, in the new democratic age, liberty as Europe had known it would survive.

The meaning of de Tocqueville's message was unmistakable. Democracy was coming; nothing could impede its progress. The words of Burke and the weapons of armies were nothing against the rising tide which based itself on a popular demand for equality. Privilege was doomed. The only question remaining was whether liberty would remain intact when equality became established. De Tocqueville asumed, as Burke had, that Europe had known liberty under its traditional aristocratic institutions. The Jacobins had argued that democracy—sometimes called the "general will" or popu-

210

lar sovereignty—was the precondition of liberty. De Tocqueville denied this. To accept the Jacobin interpretation was to make Europe's past appear as a bleak narrative of autocratic and despotic rule. De Tocqueville, like Burke, thought this a caricature of Europe's historical experience. So long as there had been independent powers in the society—Church, guilds, towns, universities, each with its inherited rights and privileges—the authority of the monarch was limited. So long as a society boasted powerful men (bishops, dukes, lords) with whom the monarch was obliged to treat, and whose consent and cooperation he had to win for the implementation of his policies, liberty was secure. The idea of an omnicompetent state, caring for all and treating all men as equals, was inconceivable in a society of privilege. Certain forms of authority and certain types of tyranny were not possible in a hierarchical society.[7]

The French Revolution, in inscribing Liberty, Equality and Fraternity on its banners, implied that the three were joined and interdependent. The Jacobins argued in effect that the consequence of their success would be a diminishing of control by *every* authority over *every* individual. Each man would see his freedom increased as that of the traditional authorities (king, Church, and noble) declined. De Tocqueville asked whether this would in fact prove to be the case. Would the power of the state decline, or would it grow to unparalleled proportions? Might there not soon develop a tyranny of the majority, infinitely more galling and oppressive than any ever exercised by a monarch? The new "tyranny," if it did indeed come to pass, would take new forms, quite unknown to history. The "democratic" despot—the state acting in the name of the majority—would be mild, de Tocqueville wrote, degrading men but not tormenting them. Its purpose would be to watch over the citizens, helping them to gratify their pleasures, but demeaning them in the process. According to de Tocqueville, this power would be "absolute, minute, regular, provident and mild." The authority would be rather like that of a parent, except that a parent's aim was to prepare the child for manhood, whereas the state would seek to keep men perpetually children. It would provide for their security, give them their necessities, facilitate their pleasures, and direct their industry. What would remain, de Tocqueville asked, "but to spare them all the care of thinking and all the trouble of living?" A democratic people might rapidly come to show the qualities of a "flock of timid and industrious animals," answering to the shepherd, the state.[8]

The prospect alarmed de Tocqueville, and he gave much thought to considering ways of preventing this new sort of tyranny from developing. The problem, he knew, was complicated by the fact that a democratic society would inevitably show a certain homogeneity of character. As men came to be increasingly alike, the possibilities of independent thought and action would diminish. Nothing different from the norm would be held out for the young to emulate; there would be no real conflict between differing opinions or different schemes of living. Values would tend to be the same throughout the society. Implicit in this was the idea that, in a privileged world, the monk and the courtier represented different principles of existence. Both were separated from the merchant, and never thought of competing with him. In such a society, tolerance was automatic. It was the one absolutely necessary condition for existence. Were the priest to denounce the values of the knight or seek to upset them, he would meet resistance. The defense of his own values required him to respect those of others. To live in such a society was to be constantly aware of difference. The individual, confronted with a multiplicity of forms, recognized the value of diversity, and accepted its necessity. In a society of equal men, all essentially alike, such diversity was uncommon. Only the outsider was in a position to instruct a democratic people. Knowing, however, that his criticism would be unwelcome, he would generally choose to remain silent. De Tocqueville feared for those who might seek to correct the democratic majority.[9]

In reflecting on the civilization he expected democracy to produce, he emphasized the impossibility of men enjoying in the new situation the advantages they had previously known. A democratic society, constructed on principles of equality, would necessarily have distinctive values and standards. Only in the most superficial ways would it resemble what had gone before. De Tocqueville felt some misgivings about these developments, but he saw no way of avoiding them. Men would simply need to accustom themselves to the new values and practices. He did not believe it would prove difficult for them to do so.

De Tocqueville's analysis of democratic forms went beyond anything previously attempted. This was not the work of an aristocrat, seeking to hold back the tide, warning that there was still time to avoid a catastrophe. On many issues the die was cast. Democratic civilization would simply not duplicate what had already been achieved; its objectives would be of a quite different order. John Stuart Mill, whose democratic sympathies were ardent and who had learned much from de Tocqueville's work, accepted the inevitability of the new order of things. Writing about the cultural aspects of democratic society, he said: "There is a greatly augmented number of moderate successes, fewer great literary and scientific reputations. Elementary and popular treatises are immensely multiplied; superficial information far more widely diffused; but there are fewer who devote themselves to thought for its own sake, and pursue in retirement those profounder researches, the results of which can only be appreciated by a few. Literary productions are seldom highly finished; they are got up to be read by many, and to be read but once."[10] These lines might just as easily have come from de Tocqueville's pen; they accepted with equanimity what was felt to be democracy's inevitable effects on civilization.

Mill, however, like de Tocqueville, felt differently about the political consequences. The hazards were obvious, but they were not inevitable. The tyranny of the majority, for example, might be avoided. Mill's essay, *On Liberty*, was an impassioned demand that the right of the dissenter be respected. Without a contrary opinion, the view of the majority would never be capable of correcting itself. All progress depended upon the minority being able to voice its opinion.[11] Mill repeated the plea in his *Representative Government*, in which he spoke of the weight of mediocre minds crushing the views of the minority on any subject. Every effort had to be made to protect and encourage the opinion which did not simply parrot what the majority, at a particular moment, chose to believe. Mill supported the principle of proportional representation because he imagined it a device calculated to prevent the majority from carrying everything before it.[12] De Tocqueville made an enormous impression on his generation, particularly on those sympathetic to democratic government. They felt called on to explore in greater depth the problems he had laid open.

De Tocqueville's influence, however, was not limited to those who could be counted democracy's friends. For those who remained hostile to the democratic idea—and their number was large—the work came as a welcome confirmation of what they had long believed. It confirmed them in their prejudice, and gave them new reason to question whether popular government ever achieved the objectives which its friends insisted were its characteristic results. These critics accepted de Tocqueville's analysis while refusing to admit the accuracy of his prophecy. They saw no reason to believe that democracy's advent was assured. The events of the American Civil War gave them new confidence in their judgment. Nothing is more telling in this connection than the words of Walter Bagehot, the Liberal economist and literary critic who was Editor of the *Economist*. Writing in 1861, after the outbreak of hostilities, he expressed his conviction that the Northern and Southern states would never reunite. A permanent separation was inevitable.

The reason, Bagehot thought, was not hard to find. Although the American Founding Fathers had introduced defenses against "pure democracy" in the Constitution, succeeding generations had abandoned these, preferring to grant the suffrage to all. The "lower orders" profited from these changes, and "common laborers" came to control the state. These men could not be relied on to govern wisely. Europe was "deeply displeased," he said, by the "low vulgarity" of American political life, and would not mourn the end of the miserable experiment. Never before had "the unpleasantness of mob government" been so conspicuously demonstrated; in no previous age had it "been worked upon so large a scene." England, governed by the "respectable higher middle class," enjoyed its age-old liberties. Such men, by their reasonableness, cultivation, and business-like moderation, protected the state. The United States enjoyed no comparable protection. A great man would never seek to be President of the United States, Bagehot wrote, and were he to seek the office, he would never attain it. America for two generations had existed as "a democracy without ideals; at that moment it stood in danger of dying as a democracy without champions." Any government which based itself on the same false principle of the sovereignty of the people would end in a similar way.[13]

These were harsh words. They were not uncharacteristic of middle-class English Victorian opinion at the time. The view persisted that democratic government meant mob rule, and that this would always produce inefficiency and corruption. Worse still, it would be government by men constantly pushed away from moderate courses by the many who insisted on rapid and immediate change. That such methods would never achieve their intended objectives was implicit in the whole of this argument. These were no longer the arguments of aristocrats on the defensive, seeking to maintain traditional privileges against those who would destroy them. These were middle-class views, expressing middle-class values and standards. The order and security which Walter Bagehot and other Victorian contemporaries prized seemed threatened by the advent of democracy. It was to safeguard that security and to assure its continuance that these men took up their pens to write against democracy. They imagined that progress depended on middle-class virtue, with which the working class was still too little familiar, and which it could not be relied on to protect.

Had the middle class been of one mind on this issue, something like ideological class warfare would have followed. Actually, there was no danger of this. Many in the middle class shared with the workers an intense belief in democratic ideas and institutions. E. L. Godkin, the English journalist who settled in the United States in 1856, was one of many who questioned the prevailing pessimism about democracy's future. He believed that de Tocqueville's influence had been too great, and that men had accepted too easily the accuracy of his interpretation. Writing in 1865 in the *North American Review,* he questioned what he called "aristocratic opinions of democracy." Godkin found none of the vulgarity in democracy to which others were so quick to point. On the contrary, the absence of leisure, he believed, encouraged man's industry, one of the surest guarantees of achievement, not only in the field of art but also in politics. Summarizing democracy's achievements, Godkin wrote: "The emancipation of the negroes, Catholic emancipation, Parliamentary reform, law reform, especially the reform in the criminal law, free trade, and in fact, nearly every change which has had for its object the increase of national happiness and prosperity, has been conceived by men of low degree, and discussed and forced on the upper classes by men busy about many other things."[14]

Godkin's defense of democracy was not limited to an enthusiasm for its political accomplishment. He saw no reason to denigrate the civilization which democracy had brought in its wake. Explicit in his reservations about the argument de Tocqueville had done so much to make popular, Godkin wrote: "M. de Tocqueville and all his followers take it for granted that the great incentive to excellence, in all countries in which excellence is found, is the patronage and encouragement of an aristocracy; that democracy is generally content with mediocrity. But where is the proof of this? The incentive to exertion which is widest, most constant, and most powerful in its operation in all civilized countries, is the desire of distinction; and this may be composed either of love of fame or love of wealth, or of both."[15] Godkin saw no reason to apologize for democracy. For him it was clearly the equal, possibly the superior, of all other political forms.

The American Civil War constituted a sort of watershed in the history of democratic criticism. Before 1860, "radicals" tended to espouse democratic aims, and "conservatives" were inclined to raise questions of an embarrassing sort. In the latter part of the nineteenth century the situation became more complicated. It was in this period that men on the Left, generally partial to democracy, and enthusiastic about its over-all purposes, began to ask whether democracy had in fact triumphed in any country. These men believed in popular government, but refused to admit that universal suffrage had produced the good originally expected. The work of Henry George, the "prophet of San Francisco," was enormously influential in causing new questions to be raised. *Progress and Poverty*, published in 1879, made Europeans aware of what Americans had long known: political democracy did not produce universal well-being. The consequences of the Industrial Revolution in America were not significantly different from what they were in Europe. Democratic procedures did little to alleviate the condition of the ordinary man. George saw that there was no fundamental contradiction between material progress and proletarian poverty. In monopolistic practices he detected the cause of much that was inequitable in his time.[16] By the end of the century an increasing number of "socialists," "radicals," and "populists" were arguing that democracy's triumph was still to come. The idea that the people had been cheated out of their heritage, either by cunning aristocrats, grasping industrialists, or legally trained adventurers, appeared in a hundred forms and permutations. If democracy had not brought all the good that had been expected, it was simply because it had not yet had its day.

The idea was a romantic one, suited to an age that wished to believe that history was a tale of successive corruptions and aggressions, in which the many (the weak) lost to the few (the strong). There was a new and powerful incentive for political organization to take back from those who were entitled to nothing what they had seized illegally and would abandon only under the most intense pressure. Politics in the two decades before the First World War assumed a pattern which reflected this interpretation of the social struggle. Everywhere, "socialists," "progressives," "laborites"—the name varied with time and place—assumed the offensive, prepared to do battle with those already occupying the places of power. The

216

"new democracy" and the "new freedom" seemed appropriate slogans for such a campaign, and in one form or another figured on the banners of every "radical" and reformist movement.

World War I did a great deal to cause men to think in other terms. As the casualties mounted and as the full horror of the destruction sank into the public consciousness, there was a growing incentive to make men believe that this sort of thing need never happen again. In the new age which was to dawn with victory, soldiers would return to "a country fit for heroes to live in"; and men would enjoy abundance and peace forever. Woodrow Wilson helped to develop and perpetuate the myth. In sending American boys to Europe "to make the world safe for democracy," he encouraged all who believed that wars were made by militarists, that diplomats in their closed conferences abetted this evil work, and that both might be defeated by the firm resolve of nations to take nothing to which they were not entitled, and to give up all thought of threatening their neighbors. The Fourteen Points was a noble document, cruel only because it made men believe what they wished to be true, but what the state of the world (and the character of the men who inhabited it) guaranteed would not happen.

The disillusion which followed the Armistice was intense. Nowhere did men gain the objects they imagined were their due. Europe, abandoned by the United States, tried to make peace as best it could. National rivalries seemed scarcely attenuated. The "spirit of Locarno," which hovered over Europe for half a decade, disappeared as rapidly as it had come. Prosperity seemed an increasingly evanescent goal. The twenties took on a certain luster only because the thirties by comparison were even darker. In these circumstances, democracy's friends were as unsure of their beliefs as they had ever been. The barbarous doctrines which issued from Germany were not calculated to impress them, but the message which emanated from Moscow had a greater appeal. Many who visited the Soviet Union saw in full employment, the extension of public power, the construction of schools and nurseries, the development of natural resources, the only utopia they expected to find in their generation. The stories of slave camps and treason trials were dismissed as untrue or irrelevant. Men wanted to believe, and this seemed as credible a social experiment as any other. Life in the democracies was exceedingly hard (psychologically even more than economically) in the decade before Hitler sent his armies crashing into the Polish defenses.

World War II, rather like the first, confounded the prophets. It began in a way few had anticipated, and proceeded along lines which no one had been prescient enough to foresee. After the German attack on Soviet Russia, there was a renewal of the propaganda imagery the men of 1914-1918 had done so much to develop. The "democracies" were again fighting for their existence. Few cared to inquire too closely into why or how the Soviet Union figured as a democracy. What the Allies would have been unwilling to accept in time of peace, necessity made them more than grateful for in time of war. Embarrassing questions were not put. The task was hard enough without them. Hitler's defeat, followed by the dropping of atom bombs and the collapse of Japan, caused men to speak again of a new age. This time, they were more reluctant to prophesy what it would be.

While it is certainly too early to offer any but the most tentative judgments on what the last years have meant or on how they will be regarded when time makes some perspective possible, it is clear that they have been filled with uncertainty. The development of weapons with unparalleled possibilities of destruction have made men in every corner of the globe feel insecure. In the democracies—particularly in the United States, but to some extent everywhere—there have been soul-searching and self-inspection, as much perhaps as ever has taken place. The awesome possibilities invite introspection. What is most remarkable, however, about this frenetic intellectual activity is that it has led to so little new thought. Again and again, though in vastly inflated language, the ideas of the eighteenth and nineteenth centuries have been repeated. It is as if the new generation, unwilling to read the past and pretending always that its problems are fundamentally different, finds itself constantly led back to what was said before. The diagnosis is classic, and even the remedies seem old-fashioned.

Occasionally the analysis is embarrassing, in part because certain misgivings about democracy are not supposed to be aired. Thus, for example, when Walter Lippmann in *The Public Philosophy* suggests that the people are not equipped to make decisions in complex fields (e.g., foreign policy), and that their intervention has only proved the incapacity of democracies "to wage war for rational ends and to make a peace which would be observed or could be enforced,"[17] his friends wish secretly that he would keep silent. Reservations of this sort about the people are felt to be impolitic in the middle of the twentieth century. Even if one believes what Lippmann has blurted out—and many do—discretion is supposed to recommend that one say nothing about it. Neither de Tocqueville nor Mill would have understood this attitude. In 1955 Lippmann expressed doubts about democracy which were fully explored in the nineteenth century. Whether his remedies are superior to those suggested earlier is a matter for his contemporaries to judge, but there is no advantage in making his criticism seem novel.

If Lippmann's analysis offends public taste, there are others which express perfectly what contemporary democratic society wishes to hear. These are contained in books whose titles are familiar to all who are accosted by modern advertising: *The Lonely Crowd, The Organization Man, The Affluent Society.* Each of these, and a dozen others which closely resemble them, describe American civilization in terms which would have given no surprise to a French citizen who had just put down de Tocqueville in 1831. This is not to suggest that these works simply follow de Tocqueville or that they fail to take account of recent changes in American society; it is only to say that they have not gone sufficiently beyond the earlier work to support the idea that a fundamental revolution has taken place in the twentieth century. The situations they describe and the criticism they imply are all very familiar.

Why should this matter? The answer quite simply is that, if the twentieth century is in fact an age of hyperbole, then its fundamental drive is to exaggerate and dramatize whatever it experiences. In this situation, it is disinclined to admit how many of its problems are only versions of other problems on which there is already an abundant store of experience and criticism. The idea that America is experiencing today, perhaps in an acute form, what democratic societies have had to contend with from the beginning is startling only because it repudiates what is generally said. Were this opinion to take hold, however, it might prove to be a really beneficial palliative. If understood correctly, it would lead to a more searching inquiry into what is novel in the contemporary world. The temptation to repeat old shibboleths, dressed to appear new, is hazardous because it confuses us about what we do in fact know and what it is necessary to learn. Excellence and leadership in a democracy are old themes—the Russians did not create them, even if they helped to remind us of their significance. The challenge is to think about each of them in ways which take account of the reality we presently live with. If solemnity can be avoided in these inquiries, thus reducing the value of a currency with which the age is surfeited, another even more important purpose will be served, which is to make the small voice of reason again audible in a room filled with noise.

REFERENCES

1. Raymond Williams, *Culture and Society, 1780-1950*. New York: Columbia University Press, 1958, p. xiv.

2. See above, Henry Steele Commager, "Leadership in Eighteenth-Century America and Today," pp. 25-46.

3. Edmund Burke, *Reflections on the Revolution in France*. New York: Rinehart and Co., 1959.

4. Thomas Paine, *The Rights of Man*. New York: E. P. Dutton, 1930, Everyman edition.

5. Alexis de Tocqueville, *Democracy in America*, 2 vols. New York: Alfred A. Knopf, 1945.

6. George W. Pierson, *Tocqueville and Beaumont in America*. New York: Oxford University Press, 1938, p. 32.

7. De Tocqueville, *op. cit.*, vol. 2, book 4, ch. 5, pp. 303-315.

8. *Ibid.*, vol. 2, book 4, ch. 6, pp. 316-321.

9. *Ibid.*, vol. 2, book 3, ch. 21, pp. 251-263.

10. John Stuart Mill, *Dissertations and Discussions*. New York: Henry Holt, 1874, vol. 2, pp. 146-147.

11. Mill, *On Liberty, Representative Government, The Subjection of Women*. London: Oxford University Press, 1946, pp. 5-141.

12. *Ibid.*, pp. 145-423.

13. *The Works and Life of Walter Bagehot*, edited by Mrs. Russell Barrington. London: Longmans, Green & Co., 1915, vol. 3, pp. 365-384.

14. Edwin L. Godkin, *Problems of Modern Democracy*. New York: Charles Scribner's Sons, 1898, pp. 65-66.

15. *Ibid.*, pp. 56-57.

16. Henry George, *Progress and Poverty*. New York: Robert Schalkenbach Foundation, 1955, 75th anniversary edition.

17. Walter Lippmann, *Essays in the Public Philosophy*. Boston: Little, Brown and Company, 1955, pp. 8-27.

Notes on the Authors

D. WILFRED ABSE, born in Cardiff, Wales, in 1915, is professor of psychiatry at the School of Medicine, University of North Carolina. Trained at the Welsh National School of Medicine, the University of London, and the University of Wales, he came to the United States in 1952 as clinical director of the Dorothea Dix Hospital in Raleigh, North Carolina. Besides numerous medical papers, he has published *The Diagnosis of Hysteria*.

JAMES MACGREGOR BURNS, born in Melrose, Massachusetts, in 1918, is professor of political science at Williams College. In 1948 he served on the Hoover Commission, and he has often taken an active part in Massachusetts politics. Among his books are: *Congress on Trial; Government by the People* (with Jack W. Peltason); *Roosevelt: The Lion and the Fox;* and *John Kennedy: A Political Profile*.

HENRY STEELE COMMAGER, born in Pittsburgh in 1902, is professor of history and American studies at Amherst College and adjunct professor at Columbia University. He has taught widely, both in this country and abroad, and has edited many studies, including a forty-volume work, *The Rise of the American Nation* (in process). His own books among others are: *The American Mind; Europe and America Since 1492; Living Ideas in America;* and *The Spirit of Seventy-Six*.

JOHN CONWAY, born in Toronto in 1916, is lecturer in history and master of Leverett House at Harvard University. His special concern is freedom and authority in the modern world, and he conducts a course that surveys the equation between these two principles in European governments from 1700 until today. He is the author of a study, "On the Round Table," that examines the group of imperialist thinkers originating in Lord Milner's "kindergarten," the talented young men who assisted him in working out plans for South African federation after the Boer War.

STEPHEN RICHARDS GRAUBARD, born in New York City in 1924, is editor of *Dædalus* and lecturer on history and general education at Harvard University, where he has taught since 1950. His publications include: *British Labour and the Russian Revolution;* and *Burke, Disraeli, and Churchill: The Politics of Perseverance*. He is currently engaged on a study of World War I, particularly as it affected England and France.

GERALD HOLTON, born in 1922 in Berlin of Austrian parents, is professor of physics at Harvard University; since 1957 he has been Editor of the American Academy of Arts and Sciences and, until 1961, editor of *Dædalus*. His research interests are in the physical properties of materials under high pressure and in the history and philosophy of science. Among his publications are: *Introduction to Concepts and Theories in Physical Science; Experimental Physics; Foundations of Modern Physical Science* (with D. H. D. Roller); *Science and the Modern Mind* (as editor).

LUCIE NEY JESSNER, born in Frankfurt, Germany, in 1896, is professor of psychiatry at the School of Medicine of the University of North Carolina, and a teaching and training analyst at the Washington Psychoanalytic Institute. She received her early training at the universities of Koenigsberg and Berlin, and since 1939 has practiced in the United States. She has contributed to professional journals and is the author of *Dynamic Psychopathology in Childhood*.

DAVID C. McCLELLAND, born in Mount Vernon, New York, in 1917, is professor of psychology and chairman of the Center for Research in Personality at Harvard University. He has served in various administrative capacities on governmental and foundation projects studying the motivation for achievement and the early identification of talent. His most recent publications are: *Talent and Society* (with others); three chapters in *Motives in Fantasy, Action, and Society* (edited by John W. Atkinson); and *The Achieving Society*.

HELEN HILL MILLER, born in Highland Park, Illinois in 1899, is a contributing editor of the *New Republic*. She has had a long career as a writer and lecturer in the field of economics and political science. In 1955-1956 she was president of the Women's National Press Association. Besides her numerous contributions to periodicals, she is the author of *George Mason, Constitutionalist; Yours for Tomorrow: A Personal Testament of Freedom;* and *Greek Horizons*.

ROBERT S. MORISON, born in Milwaukee in 1906, is director of medical and natural sciences at the Rockefeller Foundation, to which he has been attached since 1944. His special interests are neurophysiology (specifically, the electrical activity of the central nervous system), on which he has written extensively, and the advancement of scientific education and research, particularly in underdeveloped countries.

HENRI PEYRE, born in Paris in 1901, is professor and chairman of the Department of Romance Languages at Yale University. His reputation as a critic of contemporary culture is international, and his numerous publications deal not only with modern French literature but also with the field of politics and international relations. His most recent book is *The Contemporary French Novel*.

DON K. PRICE, born in Middleboro, Kentucky, in 1910, is dean of the Harvard Graduate School of Public Administration. He has held a number of administrative posts in federal government and from 1954 to 1958 was vice president of the Ford Foundation. His books include: *The Political Economy of American Foreign Policy; Government and Science; City Manager Government in the United States* (with others); and *United States Foreign Policy, Its Organization and Control* (with others).

ADAM YARMOLINSKY, born in New York City in 1922, is a Washington lawyer, now Special Assistant to the Secretary and the Deputy Secretary of Defense. He has served as consultant to various philanthropic foundations and has compiled a report on the reliability of intelligence tests for the Edgar Stern Family Fund. Besides his contributions to periodicals, he has published *Case Studies in Personnel Security* and *The Recognition of Excellence*.